Get the eBook FREE!
(PDF, ePub, Kindle, and liveBook all included)

We believe that once you buy a book from us, you should be able to read it in any format we have available. To get electronic versions of this book at no additional cost to you, purchase and then register this book at the Manning website.

Go to https://www.manning.com/freebook and follow the instructions to complete your pBook registration.

That's it!
Thanks from Manning!

Practices of the Python Pro

Practices of the Python Pro

DANE HILLARD

MANNING
SHELTER ISLAND

For online information and ordering of this and other Manning books, please visit
www.manning.com. The publisher offers discounts on this book when ordered in quantity.
For more information, please contact

    Special Sales Department
    Manning Publications Co.
    20 Baldwin Road
    PO Box 761
    Shelter Island, NY 11964
    Email: orders@manning.com

Manning Publications Co.
20 Baldwin Road
PO Box 761
Shelter Island, NY 11964

Development editor:	Toni Arritola
Technical development editor:	Nick Watts
Review editor:	Aleks Dragosavljević
Production editor:	Lori Weidert
Copy editor:	Andy Carroll
Proofreader:	Carl Quesnel
Technical proofreader:	Jens Christian Bredahl Madson
Typesetter:	Gordan Salinovic
Cover designer:	Marija Tudor

ISBN 9781617296086
Printed in the United States of America

brief contents

contents

preface

Python, like me, was born in December of 1989. Although I've accomplished a great deal in the subsequent three decades, Python's success is prolific. More people than ever before are picking it up to accomplish fascinating things in data science, machine learning, and more. Since I learned Python, this "second-best language for everything" has in reality been my first choice for many endeavors.

I had a rather traditional path into programming through the Electrical Engineering and Computer Science Department at the University of Michigan. At that time, the coursework focused mainly on C++ and MATLAB—languages I continued to use in my first job out of school. I developed some shell scripting and SQL chops in my next position, processing big data for bioinformatics. I also started using PHP to work on a personal WordPress site from scratch.

Although I was getting results (and cool ones, in some cases), none of the languages I was using *resonated* with me. But I was oblivious. I assumed that programming languages were purely means to an end, and they had little chance of being *fun* to work with. Around this time, a friend invited me to join him in a hackathon project to build a Ruby library.

The world exploded with color, fruits tasted sweeter, and all that. The ease of using an interpreted language and the human-friendly syntax of Ruby really made me think about the tools I'd been using. Although I didn't stick with Ruby for too long, I decided to give Python and the Django web framework a try for the next iteration of my personal site. It gave me the same joy and shallow learning curve I'd seen with Ruby, and I haven't looked back since!

Now that Python is recognized widely as a language of choice for many tasks, folks coming into software development don't need to go through the trial and error process I did. New and interesting pathways into a career in software are opening up all around too. Despite these differences, I hope we can all share in the common experience of finding joy in programming with Python. I also hope this book can contribute to that joy.

Come along on the wonderful Python journey I fell into somewhat haphazardly. I want to see you build a website, a data pipeline, or an automated plant-watering system. Whatever you fancy. Python's got your back. Send photos and code samples of your projects to python-pro-projects@danehillard.com.

acknowledgments

I didn't write this book alone. My appreciation runs deep for everyone who helped me along the way, at every stage and in every capacity. You are loved.

Most anyone who's been involved in the production of a book can tell you that it's always more work than you think. I heard this many times throughout the process, and it certainly was a lot of work. What's not always clear is that the real struggle is balancing all that extra work with your existing life.

To my partner, Stefanie: your support, encouragement, and tolerance of my ranting and raving were paramount in making this book a reality. Thank you for judging my neglect lightly and extricating me from this project during the roughest times. I could not have done this without you.

Thank you to my parents, Kim and Donna, for always funneling my energy toward curiosity, creativity, and compassion.

Thanks to my dear friend Vincent Zhang for spending countless nights at the coffee shop coding by my side. You were there when the concept for this book was born, and your validation helped spur me to take on this endeavor.

Thank you to James Nguyen for persevering as you changed paths to become a developer. You embody the audience for this book, and your input has been invaluable. I'm proud of your accomplishments.

My gratitude goes to all my colleagues at ITHAKA and beyond for your input and support. I thank you for enduring what has undoubtedly been a flighty period for me.

To Toni Arritola, my editor: thank you for your determination in pushing me ever toward higher-quality teaching. The writing process is fraught with many unexpected snags, but you provided me consistency and stability. Thank you.

To Nick Watts, my technical editor: your feedback has pushed the content of this book from frantic ramblings to plausible software teachings. Your candor and insight are much appreciated.

Thank you to Mike Stephens and Marjan Bace at Manning for believing in this idea and trusting me as its shepherd. Thank you to everyone at Manning for working tirelessly to bring authors' ideas to life.

To all the reviewers—Al Krinker, Bonnie Bailey, Burkhard Nestmann, Chris Wayman, David Kerns, Davide Cadamuro, Eriks Zelenka, Graham Wheeler, Gregory Matuszek, Jean-François Morin, Jens Christian Bredahl Madsen, Joseph Perenia, Mark Thomas, Markus Maucher, Mike Stevens, Patrick Regan, Phil Sorensen, Rafael Cassemiro Freire, Richard Fieldsend, Robert Walsh, Steven Parr, Sven Stumpf, and Willis Hampton—your suggestions helped make this a better book.

A final thank you to anyone and everyone else who has had a positive influence—directly, intentionally, or otherwise—on my journey in programming and this book. I cannot hope to produce an exhaustive list; names not appearing here are due expressly to the limitations of my own mind. Thank you to Mark Brehob, Dr. Andrew DeOrio, Jesse Sielaff, Trek Glowacki, everyone at SAIC (in our little Ann Arbor office), everyone at Compendia Bioscience (and friends), Brandon Rhodes, Kenneth Love, Trey Hunner, Jeff Triplett, Mariatta Wijaya, Ali Spittel, Chris Coyier, Sarah Drasner, David Beazley, Dror Ayalon, Tim Allen, Sandi Metz, and Martin Fowler.

about this book

Practices of the Python Pro introduces several concepts that software developers in almost any language can use to improve their work. This would be a great book to read after learning the fundamentals of the Python language.

Who should read this book

Practices of the Python Pro is for anyone in the early stages of their programming journey. In fact, people outside the software industry altogether who use software to supplement their work can find value in this book. The concepts contained in these pages will help readers build software that's more maintainable, which in turn makes their software easier to collaborate on.

In the sciences, reproducibility and provenance are important aspects of the research process. As more research comes to rely on software, code that people can understand, update, and improve is a major consideration. But college curricula are still catching up to this intersection of software with other disciplines. For those with limited experience in formal software development, this book provides a set of principles for producing shareable, reusable software.

If you're seasoned in object-oriented programming and domain-driven design, you may find this book too introductory for your benefit. On the other hand, if you're relatively new to Python, software, or software design, give this book a try. There's something in here for you.

How this book is organized: A roadmap

Practices of the Python Pro consists of 11 chapters in 4 parts. Parts 1 and 2 provide discussion along with short examples and an occasional exercise. Part 3 builds on what you've learned in earlier chapters and contains a variety of exercises. Part 4 provides strategies for learning more, along with recommendations about what to try after reading this book.

Part 1, "Why it all matters," sets the stage for Python's rise to fame and why software design is valuable.

- Chapter 1 covers some recent history of Python and why I enjoy developing Python programs. It goes on to explain software design, why it's important, and how it manifests in your day-to-day work.

Part 2, "Foundations of design," covers the high-level concepts that underpin software design and development.

- Chapter 2 covers separation of concerns, a fundamental activity that provides a basis for several others in the book.
- Chapter 3 explains abstraction and encapsulation, showing you how hiding information and providing simpler interfaces to more complex logic helps you keep a handle on your code.
- Chapter 4 prompts you to think about performance, covering different data structures, approaches, and tools to help you build speedy programs.
- Chapter 5 teaches you about testing your software, using a variety of approaches, from unit testing to end-to-end testing.

Part 3, "Nailing down large systems," walks you through building a real application using the principles you've learned.

- Chapter 6 introduces the application you'll build in the book and provides exercises for creating a program's foundation.
- Chapter 7 covers the concepts of extensibility and flexibility and includes exercises that add extensibility to the application.
- Chapter 8 helps you understand class inheritance, providing recommendations about where and when it should be used. It continues on with exercises that examine inheritance in the application you're building.
- Chapter 9 steps back a bit, introducing tools and an approach for keeping code from growing too large as you go along.
- Chapter 10 explains loose coupling, providing some final exercises to reduce the coupling in the application you're building.

Part 4, "What's next?" gives you some recommendations for how and what to learn next.

- Chapter 11 shows you how I map out new learning material and gives you a few areas of study to try if you're interested in going deeper into software development.

I recommend reading *Practices of the Python Pro* from cover to cover, though you may choose to skip chapters in parts 1 and 2 if you're familiar with the material. Part 3 is best read in order so you can go through the exercises in a linear fashion.

There's an appendix that will help you install Python, should you need it:

- The appendix covers which version of Python you should install, along with the most common approaches folks use to install it on their systems.

About the code

You can get the full source code for the book's examples and exercises in the book's repository on GitHub (https://github.com/daneah/practices-of-the-python-pro). Alternatively, you can visit the book's homepage (www.manning.com/books/practices-of-the-python-pro) and click Source Code to download the code.

This book contains many examples of source code, both in numbered listings and in line with normal text. In both cases, source code is formatted in a `fixed-width font like this` to separate it from ordinary text.

In many cases, the original source code has been reformatted; we've added line breaks and reworked indentation to accommodate the available page space in the book. In rare cases, even this was not enough, and listings include line-continuation markers (➥). Additionally, comments in the source code have often been removed from the listings when the code is described in the text. Code annotations accompany many of the listings, highlighting important concepts.

For each chapter, the code is organized into Python modules that are referenced in the text. In general, you're expected to write your own version of the code and use the provided source only to check your work. In part 3, the projects in each chapter build on the code from previous chapters, but each chapter provides a full working copy of the source.

All code in this book is written in Python 3, and more specifically is intended to work with Python 3.7+. Most of the code could be made to work on earlier versions without much fuss, but consider installing a relatively new version of Python for use with this book.

liveBook discussion forum

Purchase of *Practices of the Python Pro* includes free access to a private web forum run by Manning Publications where you can make comments about the book, ask technical questions, and receive help from the author and from other users. To access the forum, go to https://livebook.manning.com/#!/book/practices-of-the-python-pro/discussion. You can also learn more about Manning's forums and the rules of conduct at https://livebook.manning.com/#!/discussion.

Manning's commitment to our readers is to provide a venue where a meaningful dialogue between individual readers and between readers and the author can take place. It is not a commitment to any specific amount of participation on the part of the author, whose contribution to the forum remains voluntary (and unpaid). We suggest you try asking the author some challenging questions lest his interest stray! The forum and the archives of previous discussions will be accessible from the publisher's website as long as the book is in print.

about the author

Dane Hillard is currently a lead web application developer at ITHAKA, a nonprofit in higher education. His prior experience includes building inference engines for telemetry data and ETL pipelines for bioinformatics applications.

Dane's first forays into programming included creating custom styling for his MySpace page, scripting for the Rhinoceros 3D modeling application, and making custom skins and weapons for the MS-DOS game Liero. He enjoys creative coding and is actively seeking ways to combine his loves of music, photography, food, and software.

Dane has spoken at Python and Django conferences internationally and plans to continue until someone asks him to stop.

about the cover illustration

Saint-Sauver

The figure on the cover of *Practices of the Python Pro* is captioned "Homme Finnois," or "Finnish Man." The illustration is taken from a collection of dress costumes from various countries by Jacques Grasset de Saint-Sauveur (1757–1810), titled *Costumes de Différents Pays,* published in France in 1797. Each illustration is finely drawn and colored by hand. The rich variety of Grasset de Saint-Sauveur's collection reminds us vividly of how culturally apart the world's towns and regions were just 200 years ago. Isolated from each other, people spoke different dialects and languages. In the streets or in the countryside, it was easy to identify where they lived and what their trade or station in life was just by their dress.

The way we dress has changed since then and the diversity by region, so rich at the time, has faded away. It is now hard to tell apart the inhabitants of different continents, let alone different towns, regions, or countries. Perhaps we have traded cultural diversity for a more varied personal life—certainly for a more varied and fast-paced technological life.

At a time when it is hard to tell one computer book from another, Manning celebrates the inventiveness and initiative of the computer business with book covers based on the rich diversity of regional life of two centuries ago, brought back to life by Grasset de Saint-Sauveur's pictures.

Part 1

Why it all matters

When you set out to learn new topics, it's important to consider the big picture, to frame and focus your thinking. The first part of this book will familiarize you with Python's importance in modern software development, and it will provide a framework for understanding the value of software design principles and practices in furthering your career in programming.

Whether you're new to programming, looking for the next language you'd like to learn, or trying to advance your skills to tackle bigger projects, this part of the book should convince you that Python is a great choice.

The bigger picture

This chapter covers
- Using Python in complex software projects
- Getting familiar with the high-level process of software design
- Recognizing when you should invest in design

I'm glad you picked up this book; it means you'd like to take the next step with software development. Maybe you're looking to enter the software industry, or maybe you're looking to use software to supplement your work. Maybe you've even been paid to write software before. Congratulations—you're already a pro! Coding like a pro just means learning the concepts and strategies that will help you build and maintain big software for the long term.

By reading on, you're committing yourself to learning how Python can help you think big and go from writing utility scripts to writing complex software. I'll help you lay a foundation on which you can construct your software development skills.

Throughout your career, you will likely be exposed to ever-increasing software complexity. That software could be something you build over time, or it could very well be an existing heap of code thrust upon you at the most inopportune moment.

Whatever the case, you'll want to have a suite of utilities at your disposal so you can be prepared to make sense of it.

By reading this book, you'll gain experience and familiarity with how complex software systems work so that you can use that expertise to improve upon them. You'll be learning how to envision these kinds of systems before building them to minimize surprises and risks. Once you're through with this book, you should be able to dive headlong into things that you're confused or anxious about now with a newfound enthusiasm.

You'll learn about putting the complexities of your code into easy-to-understand, reusable wrappers. You'll make sure your code is neatly organized by its purpose so you can remember what's what. These tools will help you help yourself and become more productive in your projects, both new and old!

I'm going to use Python as the vehicle for the examples in this book. Python has been my favorite programming language for some time now, and I hope it's one of yours too. If you haven't had a chance to get to know Python much yet, take the time to do that first. *The Quick Python Book*, third edition, by Naomi Ceder (Manning, 2018), is a great place to get started.

All examples in this book are written with a recent version of Python 3 in mind. I strongly recommend you install Python 3 before proceeding. See the appendix if you need some guidance on the installation process.

The great divide

Are you using Python 2 or Python 3? A sizable number of people are still using Python 2, even though Python 3 came onto the scene a while ago—*quite* a while ago, in 2008. To put that in perspective, Flo Rida's "Low" and Alicia Keys' "No One" were at the top of the charts that year.

Python 3 brought with it several backward-incompatible changes whose effects are still being felt today. Many of these changes have been backported to later versions of Python 2 to ease the transition. Developers on large projects using Python 2 have some hurdles to overcome, but some people seem to be taking their Python 2 software to the grave with them.

If you need a bit of convincing about why Python is a good choice of language, read on a bit further.

1.1   *Python is an enterprise language*

The Python programming language has been treated historically as a scripting language. Developers perceived its performance and applicability negatively, choosing other languages for their enterprise software needs. Python was used for small data-processing jobs or personal tools, but enterprise software was still a job for languages like Java, C, or SAS.

1.1.1 The times they are a-changin'

Over the last few years, the notion that Python couldn't stand up to enterprise use has shifted dramatically. Python is now being applied to nearly every discipline out there, from robotics to machine learning to chemistry. Python has powered some of the most successful internet companies of the last decade and doesn't show any signs of slowing.

1.1.2 What I like about Python

Python is a breath of fresh air. Like many of my friends and colleagues, I learned a great deal of C++ in school, along with a bit of MATLAB, Perl, and PHP. I built my first website in PHP and even tried a Java Spring version at one point. PHP and Java are, as many successful companies will attest, perfectly capable languages in this arena, but they didn't click with me for some reason.

I found that Python excelled in its syntax; this is often cited as one reason for its accelerating popularity. The syntax comes closer to written English than other languages, and as a result it can be more approachable for those new to programming, as well as for people who don't like the verbosity of other languages. I've seen people light up with joy when asking Python to `print('Hello world!')` and seeing it do exactly that. Even now I will occasionally have one of those moments when I uncover a standard library module I didn't know about before.

Python is readable. This translates to faster development even for fairly seasoned developers. Hui Ding, an engineer at Instagram, astutely points out that "Performance speed is no longer the primary worry. Time to market speed is."[1] Python enables rapid prototyping and, as you'll see later on, the ability to solidify software into a robust, maintainable codebase. This is what I like about Python.

1.2 Python is a teaching language

In 2017, Stack Overflow revealed that, in high-income countries, questions related to Python made up more than 10% of all questions on the platform, surpassing all other major programming languages.[2] Python is the fastest growing programming language today, which is why it's a handy teaching tool. The thriving developer community and wealth of information available online mean that it will be a safe choice for the next several years.

Throughout this book, I'll assume you have a foundational knowledge of Python syntax, data types, and classes. You've seen it and played with it, but you don't need to have won awards with it. (Do they have those?). Anyone with a bit of programming under their belt and a few hours of learning and using Python on their own should have no problem with the code in this book. You're going to go through this book with Python as the conduit for designing bigger, better software. That being said, what you learn here will, with any luck, be applicable to any language you choose to use. You'll find that many software design concepts transcend any particular technology.

---

[1] Michelle Gienow, "Instagram Makes a Smooth Move to Python 3," *The New Stack*, http://mng.bz/Ze0j. This is a great write-up on Instagram's transition from Python 2 to Python 3.

[2] See David Robinson, "The Incredible Growth of Python," *Stack Overflow Blog*, http://mng.bz/m48n.

1.3   *Design is a process*

Although the word *design* often describes a tangible outcome, the value of design is in the *process* of arriving at that outcome. Consider fashion designers. Their goal is ultimately to create pieces that will end up in the hands of the people wearing them. For the designer to reach customers with the next great trend, though, a lot of steps—and people—are involved (see figure 1.1).

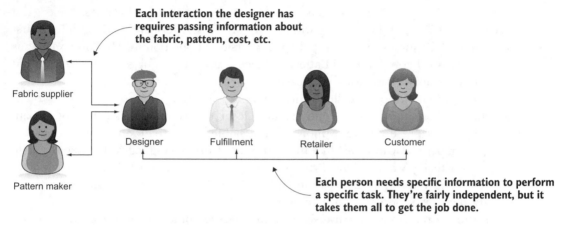

Figure 1.1   The workflow for a fashion designer. The designer works with a number of other people to get the job done.

Designers usually work with a fabric supplier to source the right materials for the look, fit, and texture they want. Once they've designed a piece, they work with a patterer to get different sizes made. Once they produce the pieces, they're sent through fulfillment to retail stores where customers can finally buy the clothing. This can take months!

As in fashion, art, and architecture, design in software is the process of sketching out the plans for a system so that it can be executed for maximum effect. In software, these plans help us understand the flow of data and the pieces of the system operating on that data. Figure 1.2 shows a high-level diagram of an e-commerce workflow, outlining how a user would progress through the steps.

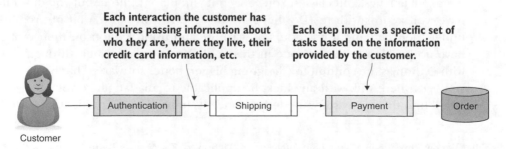

Figure 1.2   The workflow for an e-commerce website. The system performs a number of activities to get the job done.

A customer looking to buy something online usually logs in, enters their shipping information, and pays for the item. This creates an order for the company to process and ship. Workflows like these require a great deal of design to nail down. The software that runs these systems tackles complex rules, error-state checking, and more. And it has to do it all without missing a beat, because users are sensitive to errors. They might abandon or even actively speak out against a product that isn't working well for them.

1.3.1 The user experience

Workflows that appear concise and clear often take a *lot* of work to create. Creating software that works smoothly for all use cases requires market research, user testing, and robust design. Some products work well for the *intended* use case, but companies may find after release that users are doing something totally unexpected with the product. The software may work for that use case, but it wasn't *optimized* for it. There may be gaps in the design that need to be considered.

When software works well, we hardly notice. People using software products like to have a *frictionless* experience, and developers working on software like it too. Working with code that hasn't been maintained can lead to frustration, and not knowing how to fix it can lead to anger! Take a deep breath.

Friction

Imagine ice skating at the local hockey rink. When you get on the ice right after the Zamboni finishes smoothing it out, skating requires little effort. You can lean into each step just a little, letting the skate do the work. After some time, everyone's skates start to cut up the ice. It gets more difficult to glide; you have to push hard into each step.

Friction in a user experience is a lot like the rough ice. The user may still be able to accomplish what they're trying to do, but that doesn't mean it's fun. A frictionless experience is one that guides users along lightly, to the point that they hardly notice they're doing work.

Say you've been tasked with updating the reporting software at your company. It's currently using comma-separated values (CSV) in its export files, but users have been talking about how much they like *tab*-separated values (TSV). You think, "I'll just go update the delimiter in the output function to a tab instead of a comma!" Now imagine opening up the code to find that the lines of output are all being built up like so:

```
print(col1_name + ',' + col2_name + ',' + col3_name + ',' + col4_name)
print(first_val + ',' + second_val + ',' + third_val + ',' + fourth_val)
```

To change the output from CSV to TSV, you'd have to make sure you changed the comma to a tab in *six* places. This leaves some room for human error; maybe you saw the first line printing the header but missed the line printing the data rows. To make this more friendly to the next developer who uses the code, you can store the delimiter value in a constant and make use of it where needed. You could also use a Python function to make building the string easier on yourself. Then, when users decide they like the commas better after all, the change could be made in just one place:

```
DELIMITER = '\t'
print(DELIMITER.join([col1_name, col2_name, col3_name, col4_name]))
print(DELIMITER.join([first_val, second_val, third_val, fourth_val]))
```

By sitting down and thinking through the system at a high level, you'll start to notice rough areas you didn't see before, or realize that certain assumptions you had aren't accurate. You'll surprise yourself more than once, and this kind of enlightenment can motivate you to keep at it. Once you start seeing repeated patterns and common mistakes, you can start recognizing which thorns can be pulled out. It can be quite therapeutic.

1.3.2   *You've been here before*

Whether you realize it or not, you've almost certainly gone through a design process in the past. Think of a time when you stopped writing code for a moment to revisit the goal you were trying to achieve. Did you notice something that made you change direction? Did you see a more efficient way of doing things?

These little moments are design processes in themselves. You take stock of the goal and current state of your software and use them together to inform what you do next. Generating these moments intentionally and early on in your software process will have both short- and long-term benefits.

1.4   *Design enables better software*

I'll level with you: good design requires time and effort. It's not something you get for free. Although embedding design thinking into the development work you do everyday is ideal, an independent design step before writing (or rewriting) your code is crucial.

Planning out a software system will help you uncover areas that present risk. You can identify where sensitive user information might be exposed to a vulnerability. You can also see which pieces of the system might be performance bottlenecks or single points of failure.

You can save time and money by simplifying, combining, or splitting up pieces of the system. Gains like this are difficult to identify when looking at a component in isolation because it isn't clear whether other components are doing similar jobs. Viewing the system as a whole allows you to regroup and make informed decisions about the path forward.

1.4.1 Considerations in software design

We often think about writing software for "the user," but software can often serve multiple audiences. Sometimes "the user" is a person using the product the software is a part of, whereas other times "the user" is a person trying to develop additional features of the software. Often, you're the only user of your software! By looking at software from these different points of view, you can better identify the qualities of the software you want to build.

The following are some common aspects consumers use to assess software for their use cases:

- *Speed*—The software does its job as quickly as it can.
- *Integrity*—Data used or created by the software is protected from corruption.
- *Resources*—The software uses disk space and network bandwidth efficiently.
- *Security*—Users of the software can read and write only data for which they're authorized.

In addition, these are some common outcomes you as a developer might want:

- *Loose coupling*—Components of the software are not intricately dependent on one another.
- *Intuitability*—Developers can discover the nature of the software and how it works by reading it.
- *Flexibility*—Developers can adapt the software to related or similar tasks.
- *Extensibility*—Developers can add or change one aspect of the software without affecting other aspects.

The pursuit of these outcomes often involves real-world costs. As an example, committing to increasing security in your software likely means you'll have to spend more time in development. Because that development time may increase your expenses, you may choose to sell your software at a higher price. Effective planning and an understanding of the trade-offs between these outcomes will help you minimize the costs to you and your consumers.

Programming languages don't typically address most of these considerations head on; they simply provide tools that will enable developers to cater to them. For example, *high-level languages* like Python, which allow developers to write in something similar to human language instead of machine language, provide some protections in terms of memory corruption. Python also encourages the use of efficient data types through its syntax; you'll learn more about this in chapter 4.

That being said, there's still a lot of work we can do on our own, because even Python can't predict all the ways developers might screw things up. This is where careful design and thinking about the system as a whole will help.

1.4.2   *Organically grown software*

Unlike the produce at your local farmers' market, organically grown software is not good for your health. In the context of software, a system that has grown organically over time is likely a system ripe for *refactoring*. Refactoring code is the process of updating code so it's better designed and reflects your latest best practices. It might involve improving the performance, maintainability, or readability of code.

As the term suggests, organically grown software has become an organism, complete with a nervous system and a mind of its own. Bits of other software may have been plastered onto it (usually more than once), methods that haven't been used in years are in there somewhere, rotting, and maybe there's one function that does about 150% of the work. Choosing when to refactor a system like this can be difficult, but it's sometime before the moment that makes you yell, "It's alive!"

An example of this phenomenon is shown in figure 1.3, which depicts the checkout process for an e-commerce site. It involves several important steps:

1 Determine that the product is available in the inventory.
2 Based on the price of the product, calculate the subtotal.
3 Based on the region of purchase, calculate:
  a Tax
  b Shipping and handling
4 Based on the current promotions, calculate any discounts.
5 Calculate the final total.
6 Process the payment.
7 Fulfill the order.

In this system, some of the steps are separated clearly. Not bad! But there is a rough patch in the middle. It looks like all of the price-related logic happens in one big chunk. If there's a bug in that process, it might be difficult to understand exactly *which* step contains the bug. You may see that the price is wrong, but there will be a lot of code to sift through to figure out why. The payment processing and fulfillment are also lumped

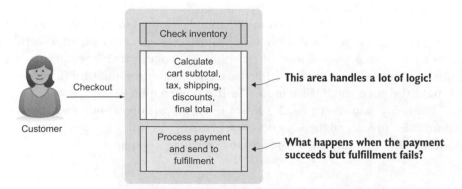

Figure 1.3   An e-commerce system that grew organically

together, so with an ill-timed error it's possible you could process the payment success-fully but never fulfill the order. That would make for a disgruntled customer.

A good start on the path to making this workflow more robust is to split its logical steps up (figure 1.4). If each step is handled by its own service, the service for a partic-ular step only needs to concern itself with one job. The inventory service keeps track of how many items are in stock. The pricing service knows the cost and tax for each item. This isolates each step from the others, making each one less likely to suffer from bugs.

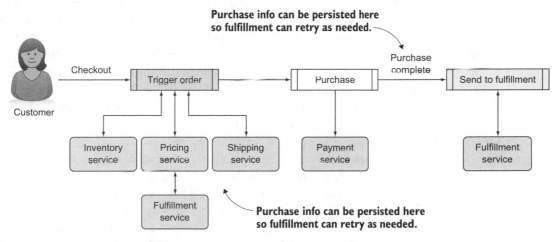

Figure 1.4   What a thoughtfully planned e-commerce system might look like

Design often allows you to see where a system's existing pieces can be broken down into simpler ones. This idea of *decomposition* is just one of the tools we'll explore more thoroughly in the chapters to come. Keep in mind that this work is almost never done; refactoring and redesigning code will happen constantly. By internalizing some of the techniques you'll learn in this book, though, you'll find these tasks get easier and quicker in a given project over time. Stay sharp and recognize opportunities for improving your existing code!

1.5   *When to invest in design*

We tend to focus our efforts on creating new software to complete tasks. But as proj-ects grow, we forget about the implementation of working code until it gets in our way. Some code gets in the way so often that it creates more trouble than value. At this point the project incurs technical debt, because additional work must be done to remain productive.

The more frequently a gnarly piece of code gets in the way, and the more difficult it is to deal with it *when* it gets in the way, the more time you should allot to getting in there and sweeping up the mess. This is often based on a gut feeling after a system is already built, but sometimes you can catch things early.

Intentional software design up front can save time and headaches down the road. When software is flexible enough to be extended to new use cases, it can be a pleasure to work with, so putting thought into the system before writing a line of code is a good way to keep productivity up. I like to think of this as a technical *investment* because it's putting work in up front for a later return.

One place you may have encountered this is in a *framework*. Frameworks are large libraries of code that act as guides to some goal. A framework might help you make your website look wonderful, or it may help you build a neural network for detecting faces in video. Regardless of its function, a framework seeks to provide the building blocks that you can use to make something all your own. For a framework to be useful, it must be flexible enough to handle a variety of use cases and extensible enough that you can write new functionality that the original developers didn't think of. Python developers have created numerous frameworks: Requests, for making HTTP calls; Flask and Django, for web development; and Pandas, for data analysis, to name a few. In a way, much of the code you write is a framework. It provides some useful functionality that you may need to use again and again or for different purposes along the way. Writing your code with these facts in mind will keep you from putting hurdles in your own way.

The process of designing software, whether revisiting a project or starting a new one, is an investment. The hope is that the return on this investment will be code that adapts to the needs of developers and consumers without incurring a great deal of overhead or frustration. There will be times when some code is in poor shape but may not warrant the time and effort good design can require. How often the code is used or updated is an important consideration, because spending weeks improving a script that's used once or twice in its lifetime isn't economical.

1.6   *New beginnings*

When you set out to be more mindful of design, the opportunities for improvement can become overwhelming. There is so much to learn and do that trying to manage it all at once won't be fun. Taking on design concepts little by little, until they become a part of your mindset, is a more sustainable approach to success. In this book, I'll introduce small sets of concepts in each chapter, and you can revisit particular chapters at any time to reinforce what you learned there.

1.7   *Design is democratic*

Up to now, it's quite possible that you've worked on projects mostly by yourself. If you did any coding as part of a class, you may have been *required* to write all the code yourself. In the real world, this doesn't happen often for large projects. In companies writing software for business uses, there may be tens of developers working on a single product. Each developer has a unique set of experiences that can affect how they choose to work. This diversity of viewpoints can lead to a more robust system because experiences with previous bugs, failures, and successes all inform directions to take in upcoming work.

It's to your benefit to get input from other developers, especially at the early stages. There's rarely one way of doing something, so learning many approaches, along with their pros and cons, will empower you to make educated choices, or at least to choose what feels best if all other things are equal. Some approaches will make sense for one use case but not for another, so knowing several will increase your productivity.

If you don't have the privilege of working with an active team of developers, examining some open source projects is another way to get some exposure to the collaborative nature of software. Look for discussions where developers disagreed (constructively!) about how to achieve some task, and see what kinds of considerations came into play on the way to a resolution. The thought process that leads to a solution is often more important than the specific solution the developers choose. This kind of reasoning and discussion capability will get you through more difficulties than knowing a specific algorithm.

1.7.1 Presence of mind

It's easy to get carried away when writing software. Think about a time when you were excited to get something done. You were probably anxious to see your code work, and it's often difficult in that situation to sit still and be deliberate about writing perfect code.

When working with a small script or doing some exploratory work, a quick feedback cycle can be valuable in staying productive. I often do this kind of work in Python's *read-eval-print loop* (REPL).

The REPL

The REPL—pronounced REH-pull—is what's hiding behind the >>> when you type `python` at the terminal. It *reads* what you type, *evaluates* it, *prints* the result, and waits for it all to happen again (the *loop*). Many languages provide a REPL so developers can interactively test a few lines of code.

But beware: at some point, the back and forth of writing a quick line of code and seeing how it changes the program's output becomes tedious. You'll want to write lengthier or longer-lived code in a file and run it with the interpreter. Each person has a different threshold; I usually hit mine when I want to reuse a line of code I previously wrote, and it's 15 lines back in my history.

The example in listing 1.1 shows how you might work through transforming a dictionary of data. Given a dictionary that maps states in the United States to their capital cities, you want to produce a list of all capital cities in alphabetical order. The approach is something like this:

1 Get the city values from the dictionary.
2 Sort the city values.

Listing 1.1   Getting the United States capitals in alphabetical order

```
>>> us_capitals_by_state = {          ◁——    A dictionary that maps state
    'Alabama': 'Montgomery',                  names to capital names
    'Alaska': 'Juneau',
    ...
}
>>> capitals = us_capitals_by_state.values()   ◁——  Only the capital names
dict_values(['Montgomery', 'Juneau'])
>>> capitals.sort()                    ◁——     Whoops! This isn't a "list", so
Traceback (most recent call last):             no "sort" method is available.
  File "<stdin>", line 1, in <module>
AttributeError: 'dict_values' object has no attribute 'sort'
>>> sorted(capitals)                   ◁——
['Albany', 'Annapolis', ...]                   New (sorted) list using "sorted",
                                               which accepts any iterable
```

This task wasn't too bad; there was only one fumble along the way. But as a project grows and the scope of the change you're making increases, taking a step back and planning your actions in advance is helpful.

Some thoughtful planning will often save you time in the long run because you won't be going two steps forward and one step back as you develop. If you do this up front, you can also get into a good habit of recognizing opportunities to refactor as they happen, rather than when you're further down the road. When I'm in this mode, I typically shift to writing my code in a real Python module, even if I'm still writing a pretty short script. This encourages me to slow down a bit and keep the bigger goal in mind during development.

In the case of the state capitals code, imagine you'll need the list of state capitals in many contexts. You might need it on a registration form, a shipping form, or a billing form. To avoid doing the same calculation over and over, you could wrap that calculation in a function and call it whenever you need it, as shown in the following listing.

Listing 1.2   Wrapping the state capital logic in a function

```
def get_united_states_capitals():        ◁——    Same code as listing
    us_capitals_by_state = {'Alabama': ...}      1.1, in a function
    capitals = us_capitals_by_state.values()
    return sorted(capitals)
```

Now you have a reusable function. But looking at this function, you can see that it operates on constant data but does a bit of calculation each time it's called. If this function is called frequently in the program, it can be refactored further to improve its performance.

In fact, it turns out a function isn't necessary at all. You can achieve the reusability while still making only one set of calculations by storing the result in a constant for later use, as shown in the following listing.

Listing 1.3   Refactored code reveals a more concise solution

```
US_CAPITALS_BY_STATE = {'Alabama': 'Montgomery', ...}          Constant data,
US_CAPITALS = sorted(US_CAPITALS_BY_STATE.values())           defined once

                 Also constant, no need for a function;
                 just reference "US_CAPITALS".
```

This has the added benefit of cutting the number of lines of code in half without sacrificing readability.

The process we just went through from initial problem statement to a final solution is a design process. As you progress, you may find that you can identify areas for improvement earlier and earlier. Eventually, you may even decide to start drawing high-level diagrams that represent several complex pieces of software, using your diagrams to assess opportunities and risk before writing any code. Not everyone works this way, of course, so you'll need to use what you learn in this book where it gives you the most value.

You might be feeling the urge to scrap everything and start your project anew at this point, but hold on! As you go through this book, you'll see that the processes of designing and refactoring software are not only interrelated, but in fact are two sides of the same coin. Doing one often means doing the other, and they're both continuous processes throughout the life of a project. Nothing and no one is perfect either, so it's valuable to revisit code early and often, especially when you start to feel friction.

With that in mind, take a deep breath and relax. There's plenty more to cover.

1.8   How to use this book

Generally speaking, this book is best experienced from cover to cover. I've laid out the parts of the book so they build on one another; later parts use concepts from earlier parts. In part 3, each chapter builds upon a software project you'll start in chapter 6. But feel free to skim or skip chapters that cover things you already know, with the caveat that you may need to thumb back to an earlier chapter from time to time.

Most chapters will leave you in a good place to incorporate a new concept or practice into your software development routine. If there's a chapter whose concepts you find particularly valuable, you might want to work on applying those concepts to your projects until you've got the hang of them. Once you feel comfortable, you can come back and read the next chapter.

Remember that the code for the examples and exercises is in this book's GitHub repository (https://github.com/daneah/practices-of-the-python-pro), and also remember that most of the source code is meant as a way to check your own work after completing an exercise. Use the provided code if you're stuck or you want to compare solutions, but give each exercise your own effort first.

Happy coding!

Summary

- Python pulls as much weight in complex, enterprise projects as other major programming languages.
- Python has one of the fastest growing user bases of any programming language.
- Design isn't only a thing you draw on paper; it's the process you follow to get there.
- Design up front is an *investment* that will reward you with clean and flexible code later on.
- You need to build software with a diverse audience in mind.

Part 2

Foundations of design

The basis for effective software is intentional design, and in the process of designing software, you'll find that the same few concepts pop up again and again. Part 2 of this book will prepare you for the intricacies of large software projects by covering these fundamentals of software design. You'll learn how to organize code, make it more efficient, and test that it works as you expect.

As you read the rest of this book, you'll see these concepts explicitly reiterated from time to time. See if you can also tie the new things you learn back to these concepts on your own. Frequent repetition of software design fundamentals will help you make them part of your day-to-day work, where they'll be most effective.

Separation of concerns

This chapter covers

- Using Python's features for code organization and separation
- Choosing how and when to separate code into distinct pieces
- The levels of granularity in separating code

A cornerstone of *clear code* is the division of its various behaviors into small, manageable pieces. Clear code requires you to keep less knowledge in your head at any given time, making the code simpler to reason about. Short segments of code with clear intent are a big step in this direction, but bits of code should not be broken up along arbitrary boundaries. Separating them by *concern* is an effective approach.

> **DEFINITION** A *concern* is a distinct behavior or piece of knowledge your software deals with. Concerns can range in granularity from how to calculate a square root to how payments are managed in an e-commerce system.

In this chapter, I'll discuss the tools built into Python for separating the concerns in your code, as well as the philosophy that goes into deciding how and when to use them.

NOTE If you haven't yet, you'll want to set up Python on your computer so you can follow along with the code in this book. The installation and best practices are all covered in the appendix, so before you go too much further, you should head there and get set up. I'll be right here when you're ready. Remember that you can get the full source code for the book's examples and exercises in the book's repository on GitHub (https://github.com/daneah/practices-of-the-python-pro).

2.1 Namespacing

Like many programming languages, Python isolates code through the concept of *namespaces*. As a program runs, it keeps track of all the known namespaces and the information available in those namespaces.

Namespaces are helpful in a few ways:

- As software grows, multiple concepts will need similar or identical names. Namespaces help minimize collisions so it remains clear to which concept a name refers.
- As software grows, it becomes exponentially more difficult to know what code is already present in the codebase. Namespaces help you make educated guesses about where code might live, if it does exist.
- When adding new code to a large codebase, the existing namespaces can guide where the new code should live. If no obvious choice exists, a new namespace might be appropriate.

Namespaces are so important, in fact, that they are included as the last statement in "The Zen of Python" (if you're unfamiliar with "The Zen of Python," try firing up the Python interpreter and typing `import this`).

> *Namespaces are one honking great idea—let's do more of those!*
>
> —The Zen of Python

The names for all the variables, functions, and classes you've ever used in Python were names in one namespace or another. Names, like `x` or `total` or `EssentialBusinessDomainObject`, are references to something. When your Python code says `x = 3`, it means "assign the value 3 to the name x," and you can then refer to `x` in your code. A "variable" is a name that refers to a value, though names can refer to functions, classes, and more in Python.

2.1.1 Namespaces and the import statement

When you first open the Python interpreter, the *built-in* namespace is populated with all the stuff built into Python. This namespace contains built-in functions like `print()` and `open()`. These built-ins have no prefix, and you don't need to do anything special to use them. Python makes them available to you anywhere in your code. That's why the famously easy `print('Hello world!')` Just Works™ in Python.

Unlike in some languages, you won't *explicitly* create namespaces in your Python code, but your code structure will affect what namespaces are created and how they interact. As an example, creating a Python *module* automatically creates an additional namespace for that module. At its simplest, a Python module is a .py file that contains some code. A file named sales_tax.py, for example, is "the sales_tax module":

```
# sales_tax.py

def add_sales_tax(total, tax_rate):
    return total * tax_rate
```

Each module has a *global* namespace, which code in the module can access freely. Functions, classes, and variables that aren't nested inside anything are in the module's global namespace:

```
# sales_tax.py

TAX_RATES_BY_STATE = {          TAX_RATES_BY_STATE is in the
    'MI': 1.06,                 module's global namespace.
    # ...
}

def add_sales_tax(total, state):         Code in the module can
    return total * TAX_RATES_BY_STATE[state]    use TAX_RATES_BY_STATE
                                         without any fuss.
```

Functions and classes in a module also have a *local* namespace that only they can access:

```
# sales_tax.py

TAX_RATES_BY_STATE = {
    'MI': 1.06,                 tax_rate is only in the local
    ...                         scope for add_sales_tax().
}

def add_sales_tax(total, state):         Code in add_sales_tax()
    tax_rate = TAX_RATES_BY_STATE[state]    can use tax_rate without
    return total * tax_rate              any fuss.
```

A module that wants to use a variable, function, or class from another module must *import* it into its global namespace. Importing is a way of pulling a name from somewhere else into the desired namespace.

```
# receipt.py                    The add_sales_tax function is
                                added to the receipt global
from sales_tax import add_sales_tax    namespace.


def print_receipt():
    total = ...
```

```
state = ...
print(f'TOTAL: {total}')
print(f'AFTER TAX: {add_sales_tax(total, state)}')
```

add_sales_tax still knows about TAX_RATES_BY_STATE and tax_rate from its own namespace.

So, to refer to a variable, function, or class in Python, one of the following must be true:

- The name is in the Python built-in namespace.
- The name is the current module's global namespace.
- The name is in the current line of code's local namespace.

The precedence for conflicting names works in the opposite order: a local name will override a global name, which will override a built-in name. You can remember this because generally the definition most specific to the current code is the one that gets used. This is shown in figure 2.1.

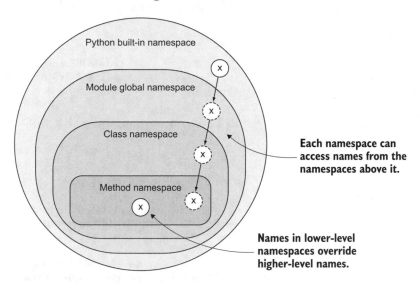

Figure 2.1   The specificity of namespaces

You might have seen a `NameError: name 'my_var' is not defined` error sometime in your adventures with Python. That means the name `my_var` wasn't found in any of the namespaces known to that code. This usually means you never assigned `my_var` a value, or you assigned it somewhere else and need to import it.

Modules are a great way to begin splitting up code. If you have one long script.py file with a bunch of unrelated functions in it, consider breaking those functions out into modules.

2.1.2 *The many masks of importing*

The syntax for importing in Python seems straightforward at first, but there are a few ways to go about it, and each results in subtle differences in the information brought into the namespace. Earlier, you imported the `add_sales_tax()` function from the sales_tax module into the receipt module:

```
# receipt.py

from sales_tax import add_sales_tax
```

This adds the `add_sales_tax()` function to the global namespace of the receipt module. That's all well and good, but suppose you add ten more functions to the sales_tax module and want to use them all in receipt. If you continue down the same path, you'll end up with something like this:

```
# receipt.py

from sales_tax import add_sales_tax, add_state_tax, add_city_tax,
➥ add_local_millage_tax, ...
```

There's an alternative syntax that improves on this a bit:

```
# receipt.py

from sales_tax import (
    add_sales_tax,
    add_state_tax,
    add_city_tax,
    add_local_millage_tax,
    ...
)
```

Still not great. When you need a host of functionality from another module, you can import that module in full instead:

```
# receipt.py

import sales_tax
```

This adds the whole sales_tax module to the current namespace, and its functions can be referenced with a `sales_tax.` prefix:

```
# receipt.py

import sales_tax


def print_receipt():
    total = ...
    locale = ...
    ...
    print(f'AFTER MILLAGE: {sales_tax.add_local_millage_tax(total, locale)}')
```

This has the benefit of avoiding long `import` statements, and, as you'll see in the next section, the prefix helps avoid namespace collisions.

> **WARNING** Python allows you to import all the names from a module in short-hand using `from themodule import *`. It's tempting to use this form instead of prefixing those names with `themodule.` throughout your code, but *please don't!* These wildcard imports can cause name collisions and make problems hard to debug because you can't see the specific names being imported. Stick to explicit imports!

2.1.3 *Namespaces prevent collisions*

If you want to get the current time in a Python program, you can do so by importing the `time()` function from the time module:

```
from time import time
print(time())
```

You should see output like this:

```
1546021709.3412101
```

`time()` returns the current Unix time.[1] The datetime module also contains something with the name `time`, but it does something different:

```
from datetime import time
print(time())
```

This time you should see this output:

```
00:00:00
```

This `time` is actually a class, and calling it returns a `datetime.time` instance that defaults to midnight (0 hours, 0 minutes, and so on). What happens when you import them both?

```
from time import time
from datetime import time
print(time())                    ◁────  Which time is this?
```

In cases of ambiguity, Python uses the most recent definition it knows about. If you import `time` from one place and then import another `time` from another place, it will only know about the latter. If you don't make use of namespaces, it will be difficult to tell which `time()` is being referenced in the code, and you might use the wrong one by mistake. This is a compelling reason to import modules as a whole; it forces you to prefix names from the module so that it's clear where the names come from.

---

[1] See the Wikipedia article for an explanation of Unix time: https://en.wikipedia.org/wiki/Unix_time.

```
import time
import datetime
now = time.time()
midnight = datetime.time()
```

**It's clear which
time this means.**

**This time is referenced
uniquely as well.**

Sometimes name collisions are difficult to avoid, even with the tools you've seen so far. If you create a module with the same name as a module built into Python or from a third-party library, and you need them both in one module, you'll need more fire-power. Fortunately, it's one Python keyword away. You can alias a name to another name when you import it, using the as keyword:

```
import datetime
from mycoollibrary import datetime as cooldatetime
```

Now datetime is available as expected, and the third-party datetime is available as cooldatetime.

You shouldn't override Python's built-in functionality unless you have a compelling reason to, so it's best to avoid using the same names as built-ins unless you intend to replace them. But if you don't know the whole standard library (I sure don't!) it might still happen by accident on occasion. You could alias your module to a new name wherever you import it on other modules, but I recommend renaming the module and updating any references to it throughout your code so your imports stay consistent with the module's filename.

> **NOTE** Most integrated development environments (IDEs) will give you a warning when you override the name of a Python built-in so you don't go too far down that road by accident.

With these importing practices, you should be able to import everything you need without issue. Remember that module name prefixes (like time. and datetime.) are helpful in the long run because namespace collisions can and do happen. When you run into a collision, take a deep breath and confidently rework your import statements or create an alias and be on your way!

2.2 *The hierarchy of separation in Python*

One way to distinguish separate concerns is to follow the Unix philosophy of "do one thing and do it well."[2] When a particular function or class in your code is concerned with a single behavior, you can improve it independent of the code that uses it. In contrast, if behaviors are duplicated and mixed together throughout your code, it may be difficult to update a particular behavior without thinking about—and in the worst case, breaking—several other behaviors. Many functions on a website, for example, might rely on information from the currently authenticated user.

---

[2]See the Wikipedia article on Unix philosophy: https://en.wikipedia.org/wiki/Unix_philosophy.

If they all check authentication and fetch information about that user themselves, they'll all need to be updated when the details about authentication change. That's a lot of work, and if one function is missed, it may start doing unexpected things or stop working altogether.

Just as namespacing has a hierarchy of granularity in Python, so too does the wider approach to separation of concerns. There are no steadfast rules about how deep or shallow to make this hierarchy; sometimes it makes sense to call a function that calls a function that calls a function. Remember that the goal of separating concerns is to group like activities together and keep dissimilar activities isolated.

The next sections cover the structural tools Python programs use to organize and keep concerns separate. If you feel good about functions and classes, you can skip ahead to section 2.2.3.

2.2.1 *Functions*

If you're not too comfortable with *functions*, think back to math class. Mathematical functions are formulas, notated (in non-Python syntax) like $f(x) = x^2 + 3$, that map inputs to outputs. Inputting $x = 5$ returns $f(5) = 5^2 + 3 = 25 + 3 = 28$. In software, functions play the same role. Given a set of input variables, a function performs some calculation or transformation and returns a result.

This way of thinking about functions leads naturally to the idea that functions in software should generally be short. If a function becomes too long or does too many things, it can be difficult to characterize and therefore difficult to name. $f(x) = x^2 + 3$ is a quadratic function of x, whereas $f(x) = x^5 + 17x ^ 9 - 2x + 7$ is more difficult to name. In software, mixing too many concepts leads to a nebulous mass of code that can't be named easily.

Small functions are one of the first tools to reach for when trying to break up your code. A function wraps a few lines of code and gives them a clear name for later reference. Creating a function not only makes it clearer what's happening, but lets you reuse the code as needed. Python itself does this: if you've used `open()` to read a file or `len()` to get the length of a list, you've made use of functionality Python deemed important enough to wrap and give a name.

The process of breaking a problem into small, manageable pieces is called *decomposition*. Imagine a mushroom breaking down a fallen tree. It turns the wood, made of complex molecules, into more fundamental materials like nitrogen and carbon dioxide. These then get recycled back into the ecosystem. Your code can be decomposed into functions that get recycled back into your software's ecosystem, as shown in figure 2.2.

Suppose you're creating a fan site for the Three Stooges (an American comedy troupe[3]). To build the home page, you need to introduce the stooges: Larry, Curly, and Moe. Given the list of names and the title of the act, the code should produce the

---

[3] https://en.wikipedia.org/wiki/The_Three_Stooges

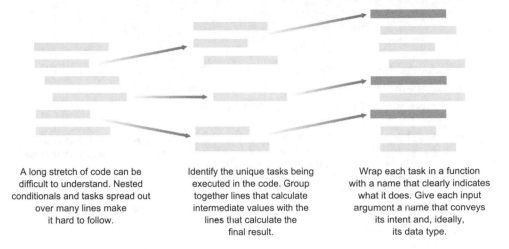

A long stretch of code can be difficult to understand. Nested conditionals and tasks spread out over many lines make it hard to follow.

Identify the unique tasks being executed in the code. Group together lines that calculate intermediate values with the lines that calculate the final result.

Wrap each task in a function with a name that clearly indicates what it does. Give each input argument a name that conveys its intent and, ideally, its data type.

Figure 2.2 The value of decomposition

string `'The Three Stooges: Larry, Curly, and Moe'`. An initial implementation could look like this:

```
names = ['Larry', 'Curly', 'Moe']
message = 'The Three Stooges: '
for index, name in enumerate(names):
    if index > 0:
        message += ', '
    if index == len(names) - 1:
        message += 'and '
    message += name
print(message)
```

After doing some research, you realize the original lineup of the stooges was different, and you want an accurate page for each lineup. Your initial temptation is to add code to do the same work for the original lineup:

```
names = ['Moe', 'Larry', 'Shemp']
message = 'The Three Stooges: '
for index, name in enumerate(names):
    if index > 0:
        message += ', '
    if index == len(names) - 1:
        message += 'and '
    message += name
print(message)

names = ['Larry', 'Curly', 'Moe']
message = 'The Three Stooges: '
for index, name in enumerate(names):
    if index > 0:
        message += ', '
    if index == len(names) - 1:
```

```
        message += 'and '
    message += name
print(message)
```

This works, but the original code wasn't terribly clear to begin with, and now there are *two* of them! Extracting the introduction logic into a function reduces the duplication and gives the code a name to clarify what it does:

```
def introduce_stooges(names):                    ◁——————  The extracted function takes
    message = 'The Three Stooges: '                        character names as a parameter.
    for index, name in enumerate(names):
        if index > 0:
            message += ', '
        if index == len(names) - 1:
            message += 'and '
        message += name
    print(message)


introduce_stooges(['Moe', 'Larry', 'Shemp'])    ◁——  Multiple sets of names can be
introduce_stooges(['Larry', 'Curly', 'Moe'])         used with the same function.
```

Now the behavior has a clear name, and if you want to spend some time making the code even clearer, you can focus on the `introduce_stooges` function body alone. As long as the function continues accepting a list of names and continues printing the introduction you want, you can be confident your code still works.[4]

Pleased with your Three Stooges fan page, you decide to expand to other famous groups. As you start working on the Teenage Mutant Ninja Turtles,[5] though, you notice an issue: the `introduce_stooges` function only introduces stooges (as you might guess). As it turns out, the function has two concerns:

- Knowing the introduction is for the Three Stooges
- Introducing a list of names as the stooges

How do you move past this? You can generalize the function and separate the first concern by extracting the group title ("The Three Stooges", "Teenage Mutant Ninja Turtles", and so on) as another argument to the function.

```
def introduce(title, names):                 ◁——————  _stooges is dropped from the
    message = f'{title}: '                             function name, and title is passed in.
    for index, name in enumerate(names):
        if index > 0:
            message += ', '
        if index == len(names) - 1:
            message += 'and '
```

---

[4]For a detailed discussion on extracting functions (and other valuable exercises), I highly recommend Martin Fowler and Kent Beck, *Refactoring*, second edition (Addison-Wesley Professional, 2018), https://martin-fowler.com/books/refactoring.html.

[5]http://mng.bz/RPan

```
        message += name
    print(message)
```

The group title gets passed in when the function is called.

```
introduce('The Three Stooges', ['Moe', 'Larry', 'Shemp'])
introduce('The Three Stooges', ['Larry', 'Curly', 'Moe'])

introduce( 'Teenage Mutant Ninja Turtles',
    ['Donatello', 'Raphael', 'Michelangelo', 'Leonardo']
)

introduce('The Chipmunks', ['Alvin', 'Simon', 'Theodore'])
```

Different groups can be introduced with one function.

The function accommodates the requirements of your fan site now: it knows only that groups have a title and several named members, and it uses that information to perform the introduction. It can accept new groups easily as you expand your site. If at some point you need to change how you introduce the groups, you'll know to head over to the introduce() function.

After decomposing code into functions, it's likely you'll end up with code that's longer than the original. But if you carefully decompose code by its concerns, drawing out and explicitly naming the different things going on, you should see an improvement in the readability of that code. Overall code length isn't so important; it's the length of individual functions and methods that makes a difference.

To that end, there's still some work to be done on the introduce function. Its duty is to form an introduction string from the group title and names. It shouldn't necessarily know how that list of names should be joined together, using commas and an Oxford comma and so on. We can extract that bit into its own function as well.

```
def join_names(names):
    name_string = ''
```

This function handles only how names are joined.

```
    for index, name in enumerate(names):
        if index > 0:
            name_string += ', '
        if index == len(names) - 1:
            name_string += 'and '
        name_string += name
    return name_string
```

This function now knows only that introductions are titles followed by joined names.

```
def introduce(title, names):
    print(f'{title}: {join_names(names)}')
```

This will look like overkill to some—the introduce function doesn't do much anymore. The value in this kind of decomposition, where each concern is separated into a function, pays dividends later when you're trying to fix bugs, add features, and test your code. If you notice a bug in the way names are joined, it's easier to find the lines to change in join_names than if it were all a single introduce function.

In general, decomposition into functions that separate concerns allows for more *surgical* changes; that is, you can be more precise with a change and have minimal impact on the surrounding code. Over the course of a project, this can save you a significant amount of time.

I've mentioned that design, refactoring, and now decomposition and separation of concerns are practices you should incorporate into a healthy iterative development process. It might start to feel like you're spinning plates instead of shipping code, but as you progress into bigger software, you'll find that you draw on these practices regularly. The longevity and success of many projects is influenced by the quality of the code, which is in turn influenced by the care taken in creating it. Try to sprinkle these approaches into your development process as a seasoning to start with, and eventually you'll find that they become the staple ingredients.

TRY IT OUT

Now that you've got some experience extracting functions, see what functions are hiding within listing 2.1, a (probably shoddy) implementation of Rock, Paper, Scissors. I suggest running the code frequently as you work, to make sure the behavior remains consistent. I've extracted an example set of functions in listing 2.2. As a hint, I decomposed the original code into six functions. Your mileage may vary, but remember that you're shooting for functions that have only one concern.

Listing 2.1   Shoddy procedural code

```python
import random

options = ['rock', 'paper', 'scissors']
print('(1) Rock\n(2) Paper\n(3) Scissors')
human_choice = options[int(input('Enter the number of your choice: ')) - 1]
print(f'You chose {human_choice}')
computer_choice = random.choice(options)
print(f'The computer chose {computer_choice}')
if human_choice == 'rock':
    if computer_choice == 'paper':
        print('Sorry, paper beat rock')
    elif computer_choice == 'scissors':
        print('Yes, rock beat scissors!')
    else:
        print('Draw!')
elif human_choice == 'paper':
    if computer_choice == 'scissors':
        print('Sorry, scissors beat paper')
    elif computer_choice == 'rock':
        print('Yes, paper beat rock!')
    else:
        print('Draw!')
elif human_choice == 'scissors':
    if computer_choice == 'rock':
        print('Sorry, rock beat scissors')
    elif computer_choice == 'paper':
```

```
        print('Yes, scissors beat paper!')
    else:
        print('Draw!')
```

Listing 2.2 Code with extracted functions

```
import random

OPTIONS = ['rock', 'paper', 'scissors']


def get_computer_choice():
    return random.choice(OPTIONS)


def get_human_choice():
    choice_number = int(input('Enter the number of your choice: '))
    return OPTIONS[choice_number - 1]


def print_options():
    print('\n'.join(f'({i}) {option.title()}' for i,
          option in enumerate(OPTIONS)))


def print_choices(human_choice, computer_choice):
    print(f'You chose {human_choice}')
    print(f'The computer chose {computer_choice}')


def print_win_lose(human_choice, computer_choice, human_beats,
                   human_loses_to):
    if computer_choice == human_loses_to:
        print(f'Sorry, {computer_choice} beats {human_choice}')
    elif computer_choice == human_beats:
        print(f'Yes, {human_choice} beats {computer_choice}!')


def print_result(human_choice, computer_choice):
    if human_choice == computer_choice:
        print('Draw!')

    if human_choice == 'rock':
        print_win_lose('rock', computer_choice, 'scissors', 'paper')
    elif human_choice == 'paper':
        print_win_lose('paper', computer_choice, 'rock', 'scissors')
    elif human_choice == 'scissors':
        print_win_lose('scissors', computer_choice, 'paper', 'rock')


print_options()
human_choice = get_human_choice()
computer_choice = get_computer_choice()
print_choices(human_choice, computer_choice)
print_result(human_choice, computer_choice)
```

2.2.2   *Classes*

Code is made up of behaviors and data that accumulate over time. You've seen how to extract behaviors into functions that accept input data and return a result. Over time, you might start to notice that several functions work in tandem frequently. If you're passing the result of one function to another to another often, or if several of your functions require the same input data, it's possible a *class* is waiting to be extracted from your code.

Classes are templates of closely related behaviors and data. You can use classes to create *objects*, or instances of the class that have the data and behaviors defined in the class. The data becomes the *state* of the object; in Python, the data composes the *attributes* of the object because the data is *attributed* to the object in question. The behaviors become *methods*, which are special functions that receive the object instance as an additional argument (ubiquitously named `self` by Python developers). This allows the methods to access or change the instance's state. Together, the attributes and methods are the *members* of a class.

Classes in many languages contain a *constructor*, which is a special method used to create an instance of the class. In Python, the __init__ method (an initializer) is more commonly used. The class instance has already been constructed when __init__ is called, and the method sets up the initial state of the instance. __init__ accepts at least one argument, which most Python developers call `self`, that is a reference to the instance that's been created. The method commonly accepts additional arbitrary arguments that are used to set the initial state. The syntax for creating a class instance in Python looks a lot like using a function: you use the class name instead of the function name, and the arguments are the arguments (excluding `self`) to __init__.

Have another look at the functions you decomposed from Rock, Paper, Scissors (listing 2.3). What do you notice? All of the behavior and data are based on the three options and which one each player chooses. Some of the functions use the same data; these things seem closely related. Maybe a class for playing this game is waiting to be born.

Listing 2.3   Revisiting the Rock, Paper, Scissors code

```python
import random

OPTIONS = ['rock', 'paper', 'scissors']


def get_computer_choice():              ◁——┐  Functions use OPTIONS
    return random.choice(OPTIONS)          │  to determine the choices
                                              of the players.

def get_human_choice():
    choice_number = int(input('Enter the number of your choice: '))
    return OPTIONS[choice_number - 1]


def print_options():
```

```
    print('\n'.join(f'({i}) {option.title()}' for i,
 option in enumerate(OPTIONS)))


def print_choices(human_choice, computer_choice):
    print(f'You chose {human_choice}')
    print(f'The computer chose {computer_choice}')


def print_win_lose(human_choice, computer_choice, human_beats,
 human_loses_to):
    if computer_choice == human_loses_to:
        print(f'Sorry, {computer_choice} beats {human_choice}')
    elif computer_choice == human_beats:
        print(f'Yes, {human_choice} beats {computer_choice}!')


def print_result(human_choice, computer_choice):
    if human_choice == computer_choice:
        print('Draw!')

    if human_choice == 'rock':
        print_win_lose('rock', computer_choice, 'scissors', 'paper')
    elif human_choice == 'paper':
        print_win_lose('paper', computer_choice, 'rock', 'scissors')
    elif human_choice == 'scissors':
        print_win_lose('scissors', computer_choice, 'paper', 'rock')
```

Several functions use the human and computer choices for the simulation.

The human and computer choices get passed around frequently.

Given that the concerns of gathering and printing different pieces of the simulation are nicely separated into functions, you're now free to consider the separation of higher-level concerns. Separating Rock, Paper, Scissors from other areas of your code (maybe you're making a whole arcade!) can be done with a class like the one shown in figure 2.3. Notice the new `simulate()` method, which will hold the code that calls all the other methods.

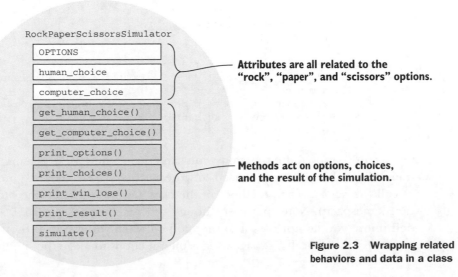

Attributes are all related to the "rock", "paper", and "scissors" options.

Methods act on options, choices, and the result of the simulation.

Figure 2.3 Wrapping related behaviors and data in a class

You can start by creating the class definition and moving the functions into it as methods, as shown in the following listing. Remember that methods take `self` as their first argument.

Listing 2.4   Moving functions into a class as methods

```python
import random

OPTIONS = ['rock', 'paper', 'scissors']


class RockPaperScissorsSimulator:
    def get_computer_choice(self):
        return random.choice(OPTIONS)

    def get_human_choice(self):
        choice_number = int(input('Enter the number of your choice: '))
        return OPTIONS[choice_number - 1]

    def print_options(self):
        print('\n'.join(f'({i}) {option.title()}' for i,
 option in enumerate(OPTIONS)))

    def print_choices(self, human_choice, computer_choice):
        print(f'You chose {human_choice}')
        print(f'The computer chose {computer_choice}')

    def print_win_lose(self, human_choice, computer_choice,
 human_beats, human_loses_to):
        if computer_choice == human_loses_to:
            print(f'Sorry, {computer_choice} beats {human_choice}')
        elif computer_choice == human_beats:
            print(f'Yes, {human_choice} beats {computer_choice}!')

    def print_result(self, human_choice, computer_choice):
        if human_choice == computer_choice:
            print('Draw!')

        if human_choice == 'rock':
            self.print_win_lose('rock', computer_choice, 'scissors', 'paper')
        elif human_choice == 'paper':
            self.print_win_lose('paper', computer_choice, 'rock', 'scissors')
        elif human_choice == 'scissors':
            self.print_win_lose('scissors', computer_choice, 'paper', 'rock')
```

> **Methods need a "self" argument.** (points to `def get_computer_choice(self):`)

> **Methods with existing arguments still need "self".** (points to `def print_choices(self, human_choice, computer_choice):`)

Once you've moved the functions, you can create a new `simulate` method for calling them all. Within a class, you need to write `self.some_method()` to indicate you want to call the `some_method` method on the class (as opposed to some other function in the namespace). Note that even though `some_method` takes a `self` argument in its definition, you do not pass it to the method when you call it. Python passes `self` to methods automatically. `simulate` calls the functions to make the simulation run:

```
...
    def simulate(self):
        self.print_options()
        human_choice = self.get_human_choice()
        computer_choice = self.get_computer_choice()
        self.print_choices(human_choice, computer_choice)
        self.print_result(human_choice, computer_choice)
```

You might have noticed that even though everything's contained in a class now, the data is still being passed all over. But now that things are contained, it's easier to make some additional changes. You can create an initializer that sets up the attributes you need for the class, namely `human_choice` and `computer_choice`, with a default value of `None`:

```
...
    def __init__(self):
        self.computer_choice = None
        self.human_choice = None
```

Now methods can access these attributes using the `self` argument instead of passing them around. As a result, you can update the method bodies to use `self.human_choice` in place of `human_choice` and remove the `human_choice` argument altogether. `computer_choice` gets the same treatment.

The code boils down to what you see in the following listing.

Listing 2.5 Using `self` to access attributes

```
import random

OPTIONS = ['rock', 'paper', 'scissors']


class RockPaperScissorsSimulator:
    def __init__(self):
        self.computer_choice = None
        self.human_choice = None
                                                      Methods can set
                                                      attributes on self.
    def get_computer_choice(self):          ⟵
        self.computer_choice = random.choice(OPTIONS)

    def get_human_choice(self):
        choice_number = int(input('Enter the number of your choice: '))
        self.human_choice = OPTIONS[choice_number - 1]

    def print_options(self):
        print('\n'.join(f'({i}) {option.title()}' for i,
 ↪ option in enumerate(OPTIONS)))
                                                      Methods don't need to take
                                                      attributes as parameters.
    def print_choices(self):                ⟵
```

```
            print(f'You chose {self.human_choice}')
            print(f'The computer chose {self.computer_choice}')

        def print_win_lose(self, human_beats, human_loses_to):
            if self.computer_choice == human_loses_to:
                print(f'Sorry, {self.computer_choice} beats {self.human_choice}')
            elif self.computer_choice == human_beats:
                print(f'Yes, {self.human_choice} beats {self.computer_choice}!')

        def print_result(self):
            if self.human_choice == self.computer_choice:
                print('Draw!')

            if self.human_choice == 'rock':
                self.print_win_lose('scissors', 'paper')
            elif self.human_choice == 'paper':
                self.print_win_lose('rock', 'scissors')
            elif self.human_choice == 'scissors':
                self.print_win_lose('paper', 'rock')

        def simulate(self):
            self.print_options()
            self.get_human_choice()
            self.get_computer_choice()
            self.print_choices()
            self.print_result()
```

> ◁ **Methods can read attributes from self.**

It took some work to add `self.` to the attribute references throughout the class, but much of it is simplified. In particular, the methods take fewer arguments, and the `simulate` method does little more than glue the other methods together. Another great outcome is that the code to simulate a game of Rock, Paper, Scissors now looks like this:

```
RPS = RockPaperScissorsSimulator()
RPS.simulate()
```

Pretty concise, huh? You first decomposed a bunch of code into functions to separate some concerns. You then grouped them into a class to separate a higher-level concern. Now it's easy to call on all the hard behind-the-scenes work with a short expression. This is thanks to carefully selecting and grouping related data and behaviors.

When a class's methods and attributes are closely related, it is said to have high *cohesion*. A class is cohesive if its contents make sense together as a whole. We want our classes to have high cohesion because if everything in a class is closely related, our concerns are likely to be well separated. A class with too many concerns has low cohesion because those concerns muddy the intent of the class. Usually I end up creating a class only when this cohesion is already clear to me; some code already exhibits relatedness through the data and behaviors it contains.

When a class depends on another class, those classes are said to be *coupled*. If a class depends on many details of another class, such that changing one requires changing the other, those classes are *tightly* coupled. Tight coupling is expensive because it can lead to spending more time managing the ripple effects of a change. *Loose* coupling is the desired end state. You'll learn more strategies for achieving loose coupling in chapter 10.

A set of highly cohesive classes serves much the same purpose as a set of clear functions. It clarifies intent, helps us navigate existing code, and guides us in adding new code. This all helps us produce the features we want faster, instead of requiring us to spend time spelunking in the caverns of our software.

2.2.3 Modules

You've already learned the basics of creating modules in Python: a .py file that contains valid Python code is already a module! I touched on the question of when to create one, but let's circle back to that.

You might have started this chapter knowing that most of your code lived in one giant procedural blob in script.py. And if you've got a short attention span like me, you might have gone and extracted a number of functions and classes from it already. Welcome back.

Although your code is now nicely separated into well-named functions, classes, and methods, it all still lives in script.py. Eventually, the minimal structure provided by a single file will be insufficient for holding all your code in a sensible way. You won't remember if the function you're looking for is on line 5 or line 205. Breaking it down into memorable categories of behavior is the path forward.

The concerns you identify will map well to the modules you should create. Be conservative with the effort you spend guessing what these categories should be up front. They'll change frequently at the start anyway, as your mental model of the system evolves and improves. But spend a little time sketching out what you think you'll need, and remain open to the possibility that a different structure will make more sense later. The clearest code is the code you don't write: every line adds additional cognitive load. The next best thing after *no* code is *well-organized* code.

Modules create additional structure around the code in them, exclaiming, "The code contained here is all about statistics!" If you need to do statistics things, you know to `import statistics` and use what's there. If what you need isn't there already, at least you have a good idea where to put it. Can you say the same for a 500-line script.py file? Perhaps, but not for long.

2.2.4 Packages

I've been praising the use of modules for their ability to neatly break code up. Why do we need anything else?

Remember that separation of concerns is a hierarchy and that name collisions can still happen. Suppose your fan site has gotten popular, and now you need a database and a search page to keep track of it all. You've written record.py, a module for creating database records, and query.py, a module for querying the database:

```
.
├── query.py
└── record.py
```

Now you need to write a module for creating search queries. What do you call it? search_query.py might be an okay name, but then it would make sense to rename query.py to database_query.py for clarity:

```
.
├── database_query.py
├── record.py
└── search_query.py
```

When two modules are conflicting in name or concept like this, you've outgrown the structure you have in place. *Packages* add further structure by splitting modules up into related groups. In Python, a package is nothing more than a directory that contains modules (.py files) and a special file that tells Python to treat the directory as a package (__init__.py). This file is often empty, but it can be used for more complex management of imports. Like a sales_tax.py file becomes "the sales_tax module," an ecommerce/ directory becomes "the ecommerce package."

> **WARNING**   The term "packages" also refers to third-party Python libraries you
> can install from the Python Package Index (PyPI). I will do my best to disam-
> biguate where needed in this book, but be warned that some resources won't
> make the distinction.

For the database and search modules, a database package and a search package would make good sense. Then the `database_` and `search_` prefixes for the modules will be redundant and can be removed.

You can expand your code hierarchy into a package, which ultimately creates a nice structure that you can read and navigate. Each package addresses a high-level area of concern, and each module in a package manages a smaller concern. Within each module, classes, methods, and functions further clarify the different pieces of the application.

```
.
├── database
│   ├── __init__.py
│   ├── query.py
│   └── record.py
└── search
    ├── __init__.py
    └── query.py
```

Where you previously would have written `import query` to use the database query *module*, you'll now need to import it from the database *package* instead. You can write `import database.query`, which will require you to prefix names from the module with `database.query.`, or you can write `from database import query`. If you're only using the database code in a particular module, the latter might be fine. But if you need to use the new search query code *and* the database code in a module, you must disambiguate the names, and it helps to maintain the prefixes:

```
import database.query
import search.query
```

You could also use the `from` syntax and alias each module:

```
from database import query as db_query
from search import query as search_query
```

Aliases can be too verbose, though, and sometimes downright confusing if they're poorly named. Use them sparingly to avoid naming collisions.

You can nest packages in a process similar to creating an initial package. Create a directory with an `__init__.py` file, and put modules or packages inside:

```
.
└── math
    ├── __init__.py
    ├── statistics
    │   ├── __init__.py
    │   ├── std.py
    │   └── cdf.py
    ├── calculus
    │   ├── __init__.py
    │   └── integral.py
    └── ...
```

In this example, all the math code is in the math package, and each subfield of mathematics has its own subpackage that contains modules. If you want to look at the code for calculating an integral, you can make a guess that it's in math/calculus/integral.py. This aspect of packages—being able to navigate to where code is likely to live—becomes invaluable as a project grows in size.

Importing the integral module works like before, with additional prefixes to get to the module of interest:

```
from math.calculus import integral
import math.calculus.integral
```

Note that `from math import calculus.integral` won't work; you can only import a full dotted path using `import ...` or a single name using `from ... import ...`.

Summary

- Separation of concerns is a major key to understandable code; many design concepts arise directly from this principle.
- Functions extract named concepts from procedural code. Clarity and separation are the primary objectives of extraction; reuse is a secondary benefit.
- Classes group closely related behaviors and data together into an object.
- Modules group related classes, functions, and data while keeping independent concerns separate. Explicitly importing code from other modules makes it clear what's being used where.
- Packages help create a hierarchy of modules that helps with naming and code discovery.

Abstraction and encapsulation

3

This chapter covers

- Understanding the value of abstraction in large systems
- Encapsulating related code into classes
- Using encapsulation, inheritance, and composition in Python
- Recognizing programming styles in Python

You've already seen that organizing your code into functions, classes, and modules is a great way to separate *concerns*, but you can also use these techniques to separate *complexity* in your code. Because it's difficult to remember every detail about your software at all times, in this chapter you'll learn to use abstraction and encapsulation to create levels of granularity in your code so you can worry about the details only when you need to.

3.1   *What is abstraction?*

When you hear the word *abstract*, what do you think of? Usually a Jackson Pollock painting or a Calder sculpture runs through my mind. Abstract art is marked by a freedom from concrete form, often only suggestive of a specific subject. *Abstraction*, then, would be the process of taking something concrete and stripping it of specifics. When speaking about abstraction in software, this is exactly right!

3.1.1   *The "black box"*

As you develop software, pieces of it will come to represent concepts in full. Once you've finished developing a particular function, for example, it can be used for its intended purpose over and over again without you having to think too hard about how it works. At this point, the function has become a *black box*. A black box is a calculation or behavior that "just works"—it doesn't need to be opened up and examined each time you need it (see figure 3.1).

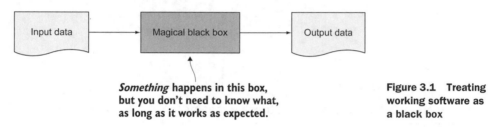

Something happens in this box, but you don't need to know what, as long as it works as expected.

Figure 3.1   Treating working software as a black box

Suppose you're building a natural-language processing system that determines if a product review is positive, negative, or neutral. Such a system has many steps along the way, as shown in figure 3.2:

1 Break up the review into sentences.
2 Break each sentence into words or phrases, generally called *tokens*.
3 Simplify word variations to their root words, called *lemmatization*.
4 Determine the grammatical structure of the sentence.
5 Calculate the polarity of the content by comparing it to manually labeled training data.
6 Calculate the overall magnitude of polarity.
7 Choose a final positive, negative, or neutral determination for the product review.

Each step in the sentiment analysis workflow is composed of many lines of code. By rolling that code up into concepts like "break into sentences" and "determine grammatical structure," the whole workflow becomes easier to follow than if you were trying to comprehend all the code at once. If someone wants to know the specifics of a particular step in the workflow, they can choose to take a deeper look. This idea of abstracting an implementation is useful for human comprehension, but it's also something that can be formalized in code to produce more stable results.

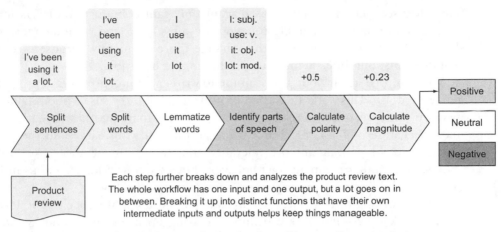

Figure 3.2 **Determining whether a product review is positive, negative, or neutral**

In chapter 2, you learned how to identify the concerns of your code and extract them into functions. Abstracting a behavior into a function allows you to freely change *how* that function calculates a result, as long as the inputs and return data type stay the same. This means if you find a bug or a faster or more accurate way of performing the calculation, you can swap that behavior in without other code needing to change as a result. This gives you flexibility as you iterate on software.

3.1.2 *Abstraction is like an onion*

You saw in figure 3.2 that each step in a workflow generally represents some lower-level code. Some of those steps, though, such as determining the grammatical structure of a sentence, are quite involved. Complex code like this will often benefit from *layers* of abstraction; low-level utilities support small behaviors, which in turn support more involved behaviors. Because of this, writing and reading code in large systems is often like peeling an onion, revealing smaller, more tightly packed pieces of code underneath (figure 3.3).

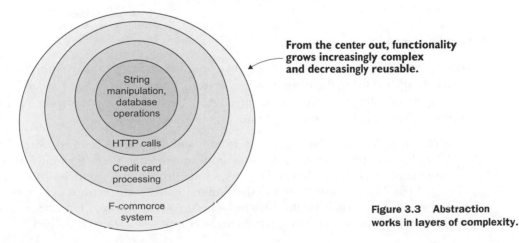

Figure 3.3 **Abstraction works in layers of complexity.**

Small, focused behaviors that get used again and again sit in the lower layers and need to change infrequently. The big concepts, business logic, and complex moving parts show up as you go further out; they change more frequently because of changing requirements, but they still make use of the smaller behaviors.

When you're starting out, it's common to write one long, procedural program that gets a job done. This works fine when prototyping, but it reveals its poor maintainability when someone needs to read all 100 lines of code to figure out where they need to make a change or fix a bug. Introducing abstraction with features of the language makes it easier to pinpoint the relevant code. In Python, features like functions, classes, and modules help abstract behavior. Let's see how using functions in Python helps with the first two steps of the sentiment-analysis workflow.

When working through the code in listing 3.1, you might notice that it does some similar work twice—the work of splitting a string up by sentence and by individual words in each sentence is quite similar. Each step performs the same operation, with different inputs. This is usually an opportunity to factor a behavior into its own function.

Listing 3.1   A procedure for splitting a paragraph into sentences and tokens

The product review as a string

```python
import re

product_review = '''This is a fine milk, but the product
line appears to be limited in available colors. I
could only find white.'''

sentence_pattern = re.compile(r'(.*?\.)(\s|$)', re.DOTALL)
matches = sentence_pattern.findall(product_review)
sentences = [match[0] for match in matches]

word_pattern = re.compile(r"([\w\-']+)([\s,.])?")
for sentence in sentences:
    matches = word_pattern.findall(sentence)
    words = [match[0] for match in matches]
    print(words)
```

Matches full sentences ending with a period

Finds all sentences in the review

findall returns list of (sentence, white space) pairs

For each sentence, gets all the words

Matches single words

You can see that the work to find the `sentences` and `words` is similar, with the pattern to match against being the distinguishing feature. Some logistics also have to be taken care of, like dealing with the output of `findall`, that clutter up the code. At a quick glance, the intent of this code might not be obvious.

> **NOTE** In real natural-language processing, splitting sentences and words is difficult, so difficult, in fact, that the software to parse them generally uses *probabilistic modeling* to determine the result. Probabilistic modeling uses a large body of input testing data to determine the likely correctness of a particular result. The result might not always be the same! Natural languages are complex, and it shows when we try to make computers understand them.

How can abstraction help improve the sentence parsing? With a little help from Python functions, you can simplify this a bit. In the following listing, the pattern-matching is abstracted into a get_matches_for_pattern function.

Listing 3.2 Refactored sentence parsing

```
import re

def get_matches_for_pattern(pattern, string):        ◁──┐ A new function to do
    matches = pattern.findall(string)                     the pattern-matching
    return [match[0] for match in matches]


product_review = '...'

sentence_pattern = re.compile(r'(.*?\.)(\s|$)', re.DOTALL)
sentences = get_matches_for_pattern(            ◁──
    sentence_pattern,                               Now you can ask the function
    product_review,                                 to do the hard work.
)

word_pattern = re.compile(r"([\w\-']+)([\s,.])?")
for sentence in sentences:
    words = get_matches_for_pattern(        ◁──┐ You can reuse the function
        word_pattern,                              whenever you need to.
        sentence
    )
    print(words)
```

In the updated parsing code, it's more clear that the review is being broken into pieces. With well-named variables and a clear, short for loop, the two-stage structure of the process is also clear. Someone looking at this code later will be able to read the main code, only digging into how get_matches_for_pattern works if they're curious or want to change it. Abstraction has introduced clarity and code reuse into this program.

3.1.3   Abstraction is a simplifier

I want to emphasize that abstraction is useful for making code easier to understand; it achieves this by keeping the intricacies of some functionality hidden away until you want to know more. This is a technique used in writing technical documentation as well as designing the interfaces used to interact with code libraries.

Understanding code is much like understanding a passage from a book. A passage has many sentences, which are like the lines of code. In any given sentence, you may find a word with which you're unfamiliar. In software, this might be a line of code that does something new or different than you're used to. When you find such words in books, you might look them up in the dictionary. The only equivalent when dealing with lengthy procedures is diligent code commenting.

One way you can tackle this is by abstracting related bits of your code into functions that clearly state what they do. You saw this in listings 3.1 and 3.2. The function `get_matches_for_pattern` gets the matches for a given pattern from a string. Before it was updated, though, the intent of that code was not so clear.

> **TIP** In Python, you can add additional context to a module, class, method, or function using *docstrings*. Docstrings are special lines near the beginning of these constructs that can tell the reader (as well as some automated software) how the code behaves. You can read more about docstrings on Wikipedia (https://en.wikipedia.org/wiki/Docstring).

Abstraction reduces *cognitive load*, the amount of effort required by your brain to think about or remember something, so that you can spend your time making sure your software does what it needs to do!

3.1.4 *Decomposition enables abstraction*

As I mentioned in chapter 2, decomposition is the separation of something into its constituent components. In software, that means doing the kinds of things you saw earlier: separating sections of code that do a single thing into functions. In fact, it also relates to the discussion on design and workflow from chapter 1. The common theme here is that software written in small parts that work in tandem often leads to more maintainable code than software written in one large blob. You've seen that this can help reduce cognitive load and make code easier to understand. Figure 3.4 shows how a huge system can be decomposed all the way down to achievable tasks.

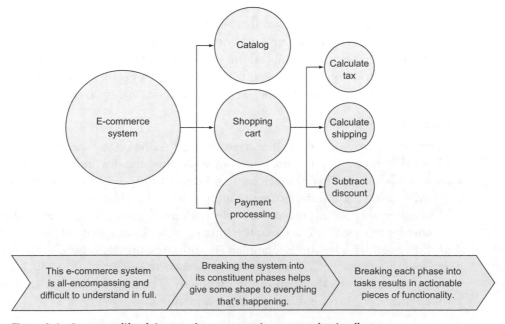

Figure 3.4 Decomposition into granular components eases understanding.

See how the pieces get smaller from left to right? Trying to build something big in one piece like the left side is like packing your whole house in a shipping container. Building things like the right side is like organizing each room of your house into small boxes you can carry. Decomposition helps you handle big ideas in small increments.

3.2 Encapsulation

Encapsulation is the basis for object-oriented programming. It takes decomposition one step further: whereas decomposition groups related code into functions, encapsulation groups related functions and data into a larger construct. This construct acts as a barrier (or capsule) to the outside world. What constructs are available in Python?

3.2.1 Encapsulation constructs in Python

Most often, encapsulation in Python is done with a class. In classes, functions become *methods*; methods are similar to functions, but they are contained in a class and often receive an input that is either an instance of the class or the class itself.

In Python, *modules* are also a form of encapsulation. Modules are even higher-level than classes; they group multiple related classes and functions together. For example, a module dealing with HTTP interactions could contain classes for requests and responses, as well as utility functions for parsing URLs. Most *.py files you encounter would be considered modules.

The largest encapsulation available in Python is a *package*. Packages encapsulate related modules into a directory structure. Packages are often distributed on the Python Package Index (PyPI) for others to install and reuse.

Take a look at figure 3.5 and notice that the pieces of the shopping cart are decomposed into distinct activities. They're also isolated; they don't depend on each other to perform a task. Any cooperation between activities is coordinated at the higher shopping-cart level. The shopping cart itself is isolated inside the e-commerce application; any information it needs will be passed into it. You can think of encapsulated code as having a castle wall around it, where the functions and methods are the drawbridge for getting in or out.

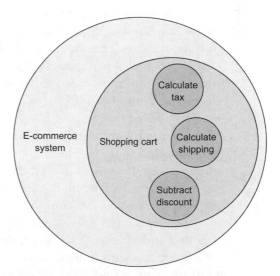

Figure 3.5 By decomposing a system into small parts, you can encapsulate behaviors and data into isolated pieces. Encapsulation encourages you to reduce the responsibilities of any given portion of code, helping you avoid complicated dependencies.

Which of these pieces do you think would be a

- Method?
- Class?
- Module?
- Package?

The three smallest pieces—calculating tax, calculating shipping, and subtracting a discount—would likely be methods inside a class that represents the shopping cart. The e-commerce system seems like it could have enough functionality to be a package because the shopping cart is just one part of that system. Different modules within the package could arise depending on how closely related they are to each other. But how do they work together if they're each surrounded by a castle wall?

3.2.2   *Expectations of privacy in Python*

Many languages formalize the "castle wall" aspect of encapsulation by introducing the concept of *privacy*. Classes can have *private* methods and data that can't be accessed by anyone but instances of the class. This is in contrast to *public* methods and data, which are often referred to as the *interface* of the class because this is how other classes interface with it.

Python has no true support for private methods or data. Instead, it follows a philosophy of trusting developers to do the right thing. A common convention does help in this arena, though. Methods and variables intended for use within a class but not from outside the class are often prefixed with an underscore. This provides a hint to future developers that a particular method or variable isn't intended as part of the public interface of the class. Third-party packages often state loudly in their documentation that such methods are likely to change from version to version and should not be explicitly relied on.

In chapter 2, you learned about coupling between classes, and that loose coupling is the desired state. The more methods and data a particular class depends on from another class, the more coupled they become. This is magnified when a class depends on the *internals* of another class because that means most of the class can't be improved in isolation without the risk of breaking other code.

Abstraction and encapsulation work together by grouping related functionality together and hiding the parts of it that don't matter to anyone else. This is sometimes called "information hiding," and it allows the internals of a class (or system in general) to change rapidly without other code having to change at the same rate.

3.3   *Try it out*

I'd like you to get some practice with encapsulation now. Suppose you're writing code to greet new customers to an online store. The greeting makes customers feel welcome and offers them an incentive to stick around. Write a greeter module that contains a single class, `Greeter`, that has three methods:

1 _day(self)—Returns the current day (Sunday, for example)

2 _part_of_day(self)—Returns "morning" if the current hour is before 12 P.M., "afternoon" if the current hour is 12 P.M. or later but before 5 P.M., and "evening" from 5 P.M. onward

3 greet(self, store)—Given the name of a store, store, and the output of the previous two methods, prints a message of the form

```
Hi, welcome to <store>!
How's your <day> <part of day> going?
Here's a coupon for 20% off!
```

The _day and _part_of_day methods can be signified as private (named with a leading underscore) because the only functionality the Greeter class needs to expose is greet. This helps encapsulate the internals of the Greeter class so that its only public concern is performing the greeting itself.

TIP You can use datetime.datetime.now() to get the current datetime object, using the .hour attribute for the time of day and .strftime('%A') to get the current day of the week.

How did it go? Your solution should look something like the following example.

Listing 3.3 A module to generate greetings for an online store

```
from datetime import datetime


class Greeter:
    def __init__(self, name):
        self.name = name                        Formats the datetime to
                                                 get the current day name
    def _day(self):                        ◁
        return datetime.now().strftime('%A')


    def _part_of_day(self):                      ◁   Determines the part of day
        current_hour = datetime.now().hour            based on the current hour

        if current_hour < 12:
            part_of_day = 'morning'
        elif 12 <= current_hour < 17:
            part_of_day = 'afternoon'
        else:
            part_of_day = 'evening'

        return part_of_day                  Prints the greeting using
                                             all the calculated bits
    def greet(self, store):            ◁
        print(f'Hi, my name is {self.name}, and welcome to {store}!')
        print(f'How\'s your {self._day()} {self._part_of_day()} going?')
        print('Here\'s a coupon for 20% off!')

    ...
```

The `Greeter` prints the desired message, so everything's great, right? If you look carefully, though, the `Greeter` knows how to do too much. The `Greeter` should only greet people; it shouldn't be responsible for determining the day of the week and what part of the day it is! The encapsulation isn't ideal. What are you to do?

3.3.1 *Refactoring*

Encapsulation and abstraction are often iterative processes. As you write more code, constructs that made sense before may seem awkward or forced. I assure you that this is totally natural. The feeling that your code is working against you might mean it's time to *refactor*. Refactoring code means updating how it's structured to serve your needs more effectively. When you refactor, you will often need to change the ways you represent behaviors and concepts. Moving data and implementations around is a necessary part of improving the code. It's kind of like rearranging the living room every few years to fit your current mood.

Refactor your `Greeter` code now by moving the methods for getting information about the day and time out of the `Greeter` class and making them standalone functions within the module.

The functions never used the `self` argument when they were methods, so they'll look pretty much the same but without that argument:

```python
def day():
    return datetime.now().strftime('%A')


def part_of_day():
    current_hour = datetime.now().hour

    if current_hour < 12:
        part_of_day = 'morning'
    elif 12 <= current_hour < 17:
        part_of_day = 'afternoon'
    else:
        part_of_day = 'evening'

    return part_of_day
```

The `Greeter` class can then call these functions by referencing them directly instead of with the `self.` prefix:

```python
class Greeter:
    ...

    def greet(self, store):
        print(f'Hi, my name is {self.name}, and welcome to {store}!')
        print(f'How\'s your {day()} {part_of_day()} going?')
        print('Here\'s a coupon for 20% off!')
```

Now the `Greeter` only knows the information it needs to make a greeting, without worrying about the details of how to get that information. What's also nice is that the `day` and `part_of_day` functions can be used elsewhere if needed, without having to reference the `Greeter` class. That's two benefits in one!

Eventually, you might develop more datetime-related features, at which point it could make sense to refactor all those features into their own module or class. I often wait to do this until several functions or classes present a clear relationship, but some developers like to do this from the start to be strict about keeping things separate.

3.4 *Programming styles are an abstraction too*

A number of programming styles (or *paradigms*) have become popular over the years, often sprouting out of a particular business domain or user base. Python supports several styles, and they are abstractions in their own ways. Remember that abstraction is the act of storing concepts away so they can be digested easily. Each programming style stores information and behavior a bit differently. No one style is "right," but some are better than others at tackling specific problems.

3.4.1 *Procedural programming*

I've discussed and shown some examples of *procedural programming* in this and previous chapters. Procedural software prefers to operate using *procedure calls*, which we tend to call "functions." These functions aren't encapsulated into classes, so they often rely only on their inputs and occasionally on some global state.

```
NAMES = ['Abby', 'Dave', 'Keira']

                              A standalone function that
                              relies only on NAMES
def print_greetings():
    greeting_pattern = 'Say hi to {name}!'
    nice_person_pattern = '{name} is a nice person!'
    for name in NAMES:
        print(greeting_pattern.format(name=name))
        print(nice_person_pattern.format(name=name))
```

If you're fairly new to programming, this style will likely feel familiar because it's a common jumping-off place. Going from one long procedure to a procedure that calls a few functions tends to feel natural, so it's a good approach to teach first. The benefits of procedural programming strongly overlap with those discussed in section 3.1.4 because procedural programming focuses heavily on functions.

3.4.2 *Functional programming*

Functional programming *sounds* like it would be the same as procedural programming—*function* is right there in the name! But although it's true that functional programming relies heavily on functions as the form of abstraction, the mental model is quite different.

Functional languages require you to think about programs as compositions of functions. `for` loops are replaced by functions that operate on lists, for example. In Python, you might write the following:

```
numbers = [1, 2, 3, 4, 5]
for i in numbers:
    print(i * i)
```

In a functional language, you might write it like this:

```
print(map((i) => i * i, [1, 2, 3, 4, 5]))
```

In functional programming, functions sometimes accept other functions as arguments or return them as results. This is seen in the previous snippet; `map` accepts an anonymous function that takes one argument and multiplies it by itself.

Python has a number of functional programming tools; many of these are available using built-in keywords, and others are imported from built-in modules like functools and itertools. Though Python *supports* functional programming, it isn't often a preferred approach. Some common features of functional languages, like the `reduce` function, have been moved to functools.

Many feel that the imperative Python way of performing some of these operations is more clear. Using functional Python features would look like this:

```
from functools import reduce

squares = map(lambda x: x * x, [1, 2, 3, 4, 5])
should = reduce(lambda x, y: x and y, [True, True, False])
evens = filter(lambda x: x % 2 == 0, [1, 2, 3, 4, 5])
```

The preference in Python would be the following:

```
squares = [x * x for x in [1, 2, 3, 4, 5]]
should = all([True, True, False])
evens = [x for x in [1, 2, 3, 4, 5] if x % 2 == 0]
```

Try each approach and print the variables afterward. You'll see that they produce identical results; it's up to you to use the style you find most understandable.

One functional feature of Python I enjoy is `functools.partial`. This function allows you to create a new function from an existing function with some of the original function's arguments set. This is sometimes clearer than writing a new function that calls the original function, especially in cases where a general-use function behaves like a more specifically named function. In the case of raising numbers to a power, x to the power of 2 is commonly called the *square* of x, and x to the power of 3 is commonly called the *cube* of x. You can see how this works in Python with the `partial` helper:

```
from functools import partial
```

```
def pow(x, power=1):
    return x ** power
```

A new function, square, that acts like pow(x, power=2)

```
square = partial(pow, power=2)
cube = partial(pow, power=3)
```

A new function, cube, that acts like pow(x, power=3)

Using familiar names for behaviors can help a great deal for those reading your code later down the line.

Functional programming used carefully can offer a number of performance benefits compared to procedural programming, making it useful in computationally expensive areas like mathematics and data simulation.

3.4.3   Declarative programming

Declarative programming focuses on declaring the parameters of a task without specifying how to accomplish it. The details of accomplishing the task are mostly or fully abstracted from the developer. This is useful when you need to repeat a highly parametric task with only slight variations to the parameters. Often this style of programming is realized via *domain-specific languages* (DSLs). DSLs are languages (or language-like markup) that are highly specialized for a specific set of tasks. HTML is one such example; developers can describe the structure of the page they want to create without saying anything about how a browser should convert a <table> to lines and characters on a screen. Python, on the other hand, is a *general-purpose language* that can be used for many purposes and requires direction from a developer.

Consider exploring declarative programming when your software lets users do something highly repetitive, like translating code to another system (SQL, HTML, and so on) or creating multiple similar objects for repeated use.

A widely used example of declarative programming in Python is the plotly package. Plotly lets you create graphs from data by describing the type of graph you'd like. An example from the plotly documentation (https://plot.ly/python/) looks like this:

Declares the intent to build a scatter plot

Declares the shape of the x-axis data

```
import plotly.graph_objects as go

trace1 = go.Scatter(
    x=[1, 2, 3],
    y=[4, 5, 6],
    marker={'color': 'red', 'symbol': 104},
    mode='markers+lines',
    text=['one', 'two', 'three'],
    name='1st Trace',
)
```

Declares the shape of the y-axis data; easy to compare to x

Declares the line marker appearance

Declares that markers and lines will be used in the plot

Declares the tooltip text for each marker

This sets the data for the plot, as well as the visual characteristics. Each desired outcome is *declared* instead of being added procedurally.

For comparison, imagine a procedural approach. Instead of supplying several pieces of configuration data to a single function or class, you would instead perform each configuration step as an independent line of a longer procedure:

```
trace1 = go.Scatter()
trace1.set_x_data([1, 2, 3])              Each piece of information is
trace1.set_y_data([4, 5, 6])              set explicitly with methods.
trace1.set_marker_config({'color': 'red', 'symbol': 104, 'size': '10'})
trace1.set_mode('markers+lines')
...
```

Declarative style can provide a more succinct interface when a lot of configuration is to be done by the user.

3.5   *Typing, inheritance, and polymorphism*

When I talk about *typing* here, I don't mean typing on a keyboard. A language's typing, or type system, is how it chooses to manage data types of variables. Some languages are compiled and check data types at compilation time. Some check types at runtime. Some languages infer the data type of x = 3 to be an integer, whereas others require int x = 3 explicitly.

Python is a *dynamically typed* language, meaning that it determines its data types at runtime. It also uses a system called *duck typing*, whose name comes from the idiom, "If it walks like a duck and it quacks like a duck, then it must be a duck." Whereas many languages will fail to compile your program if it references an unknown method on a class instance, Python will always attempt to make the method call during execution, raising an AttributeError if the method doesn't exist on the instance's class. Through this mechanism, Python can achieve a degree of polymorphism, which is a programming language feature where objects of different types provide specialized behavior via a consistent method name.

At the advent of object-oriented programming, there was a race to model full systems as cascades of inherited classes. ConsolePrinter inherited from Printer, which inherited from Buffer, which inherited from BytesHandler, and so on. Some of these hierarchies made sense, but many resulted in rigid code that was difficult to update. Trying to make one change could lead to a massive ripple of changes all the way up or down the tree.

Today, the preference has shifted to *composing* behaviors into an object. *Composition* is the converse to decomposition; pieces of functionality are brought together to realize a complete concept. Figure 3.6 contrasts a more rigid inheritance structure with one where objects are composed of many traits. A dog is a quadruped, a mammal, and a canine. With inheritance, you would be forced to create a hierarchy from these. All canines are mammals, so that seems fine, but not all mammals are quadrupeds. Composition frees you from the limitations of a hierarchy while still providing the concept of relatedness between two things.

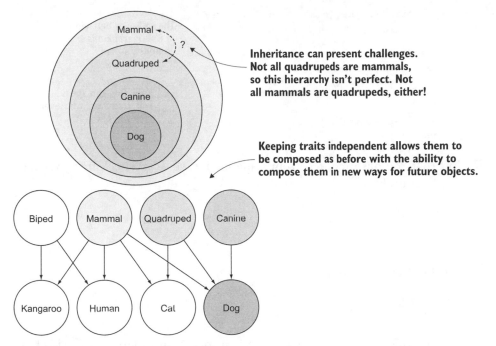

Figure 3.6 Inheritance versus composition

Composition is often done through a language feature called an *interface*. Interfaces are formal definitions of methods and data that a particular class must implement. A class can implement multiple interfaces to broadcast that it has the union of those interfaces' behaviors.

Python lacks interfaces. Oh no! How can you avoid a deep inheritance hierarchy? Fortunately, Python makes this possible through the duck typing system as well as *multiple inheritance*. Whereas many statically typed languages allow a class to inherit from only one other class, Python can support inheritance from an arbitrary number of classes. Something like an interface can be built using this mechanism, and in Python it's often referred to as a *mixin*.

Suppose you want to create a model for a dog that can speak and roll over. You know you'll eventually want to model other animals that can also do tricks, so to make these behaviors into something like an interface, you can name them with a `Mixin` suffix to be clear about your intent. With those behavior mixins in place, you'll be able to make a `Dog` class that can `speak` and `roll_over`, as shown in the following listing, with the freedom to let your future animals `speak` or `roll_over` using the same approach.

Listing 3.4 Multiple inheritance providing interface-like behavior

```
class SpeakMixin:
    def speak(self):
        name = self.__class__.__name__.lower()
```

Speaking behavior is encapsulated in SpeakMixin to show it's composable.

```
        print(f'The {name} says, "Hello!"')
```

**The roll-over behavior
in RollOverMixin is
composable too.**

```
class RollOverMixin:                    ◄─────────┘
    def roll_over(self):
        print('Did a barrel roll!')
```

**Your Dog can speak,
roll_over, and whatever
else you teach it.**

```
class Dog(SpeakMixin, RollOverMixin):   ◄─────────┘
    pass
```

Now that `Dog` has inherited from some mixins, you can check that your dog knows a couple of tricks:

```
dog = Dog()
dog.speak()
dog.roll_over()
```

You should see this output:

```
The dog says, "Hello!"
Did a barrel roll!
```

The fact that the dog knows English is suspect, but otherwise this checks out. We'll take a deeper dive into inheritance and some other related concepts in chapters 7 and 8, so sit tight!

3.6   *Recognizing the wrong abstraction*

Almost as useful as applying abstraction to new code is recognizing when abstractions in existing code aren't working. This could be because new code has proven that the abstraction doesn't fit all use cases, or it could be that you see a way to make the code clearer with a different paradigm. Whatever the case, taking the time to care for the code is a task others will appreciate, even if they don't realize it explicitly.

3.6.1   *Square pegs in round holes*

As I've said, abstraction should be leveraged to make sure things are clearer and easier. If an abstraction causes you to bend over backward just to make something work, consider updating it to remove the friction or replace it with a new approach altogether. I've gotten pretty far into new code trying to make it work with what was in place, only to realize it would be easier to change the environment than adapt to it. The trade-offs here are time and effort, both in rewriting the code and making sure it still works. That up-front time you spend might save everyone time in the long run, though.

If the interface to a third-party package causes friction, and you're not in a position to spend time or effort updating their code, you can always consider creating an abstraction around that interface for your own code to use. This is often called an *adapter* in software, and I liken it to using one of those airport travel plugs in another country. You certainly can't change the electrical plugs in France (without someone getting angry, anyway) and you don't have a French plug for your devices on-hand. So even though the travel plug costs €48 and your first-born, it's less expensive than finding and buying French power supplies for three or four different devices. In software, you can create your own adapter class that has the interface your program expects, with code in each of its methods that makes calls to the incompatible third-party object behind the scenes.

3.6.2 *Clever gets the cleaver*

I've gone on about writing code that's slick, but overly clever solutions can be painful too. If such solutions provide too much magic and not enough granularity, you might find that other developers create their own solutions to get their jobs done, defeating your effort to provide a single working implementation. Robust software must weigh the frequency and impact of use cases to determine which to accommodate; common use cases should be as smooth as possible, whereas rare use cases can be clunky or explicitly unsupported if needed. Your solution should be *just clever enough*, which is an admittedly hard target to hit.

That being said, if something feels awkward or cumbersome, give it some time. If it still feels awkward or cumbersome after a while, ask others if they agree. If they say no but it *still* feels awkward or cumbersome, it's probably awkward or cumbersome. Go forth and make the world a little better with abstraction!

Summary

- Abstraction is a tool for deferring obligatory comprehension of code.
- Abstraction takes many forms: decomposition, encapsulation, programming style, and inheritance versus composition.
- Each approach to abstraction is useful, but context and extent of use are important considerations.
- Refactoring is an iterative process; abstraction that once worked may need to be revisited later.

Designing
for high performance

This chapter covers

- Understanding time and space complexity
- Measuring the complexity of your code
- Choosing data types for different activities in Python

Once you've written working code, there's usually additional work to do. You need your code to not only accomplish its task, but also to accomplish it quickly. The *performance* of your code is how well it utilizes resources like memory and time. Software that performs at an acceptable level, meaning that it utilizes resources efficiently and responds to tasks within a desirable time frame, is said to be *performant*.

Software performance affects real-world people every day, whether they're trying to upload their latest selfies to Instagram or doing real-time market analysis to pick stocks. How performant software should be often comes down to user perception. If something *feels* instantaneous, it might be fast enough.

Software performance can also affect the bottom line. If your software requires you to store something on a disk or in a database, minimizing the amount of storage required will save you money. Software that informs money-making decisions can net you more money if it runs faster. Performance has real-world impact.

> **Human perception**
>
> Humans generally perceive changes faster than 100 ms as instantaneous. If they click a button and the screen responds in 50 ms, they're happy. As responsiveness slows beyond 100 ms, people begin to notice the lag.
>
> For long-running activities like downloading large files, lag can't always be helped. In these cases, accurate progress updates are important because they change the *perception* of progress so it feels faster.

4.1 Hurtling through time and space

If you read around about high-performing software, you're likely to encounter the phrases *time complexity* and *space complexity*. These terms sound like they're straight out of quantum mechanics or astrophysics, but they have a place in software as well.

Time and space complexity are measurements of how much more execution time, memory, or disk storage your software needs as its inputs grow. The faster your software consumes time or space, the higher its complexity.

Complexity isn't meant to be an *exact* quantitative measurement; rather, it helps you understand qualitatively how fast and big your software will be in the worst case. In this section, I'll help you build an intuition for complexity measurements so that you can eke out performance in your work. There is a formal process for determining the complexity of your software, though, and I'll get to that in a bit.

4.1.1 Complexity is a little . . . complex

I won't mince any words about this: measuring complexity can be difficult and is sometimes confusing. It didn't make a whole lot of sense to me in school—I've learned what I know now through repeated practical application. Be ready to do the same yourself.

Complexity determinations are made through a process called *asymptotic analysis*, which involves observing the code and determining the bounds of its worst-case performance.

> **NOTE** Keep in mind that complexity measurements are used to contrast ways of achieving a particular task; they aren't so useful for comparing unrelated tasks. It's useful to compare two algorithms for sorting a list of numbers, for example, but you can't compare a list-sorting algorithm to a search tree. Make sure you compare apples to apples.

The notation used in asymptotic analysis can seem cryptic at first, but it has a plain-English translation. You'll commonly see complexity written in *big O notation*, which signifies the worst-case performance for the code being analyzed. Big O notation looks something like $O(n^2)$—often read as "order n-squared"—where n is the number

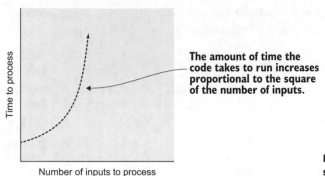

Time to process

The amount of time the code takes to run increases proportional to the square of the number of inputs.

Number of inputs to process

Figure 4.1   *O(n²)* is big O notation shorthand for a *y ∝ x²* relationship.

of inputs and n^2 is the complexity. This is shorthand for "the amount of time the code takes to run increases proportional to the square of the number of inputs," as shown in figure 4.1. $O(n^2)$ is a lot faster to write. I'll use big O notation more in the rest of the chapter.

4.1.2   *Time complexity*

Time complexity is a measure of how quickly your code can perform a task in relation to its inputs. As the number of inputs increases, time complexity tells you at what rate your code will slow down. This can help you reason about how long a task should take as the scale of your inputs grows.

LINEARITY

Linear complexity is one of the most common complexities to arise from code. This complexity is so named because graphing the number of inputs versus time produces a straight line. If you think back to the equation for a line in mathematics, $y = mx + b$, you can think of x as the number of inputs and y as the time it takes your program to execute. There may be some overhead for your program regardless of input (the b, or intercept, in the equation), and each additional input adds some amount of execution time (m, or the slope). This is illustrated in figure 4.2.

Linear complexity is frequent in software because many operations need to do some task for each item in a list: printing a list of names, summing a list of integers, and so on.

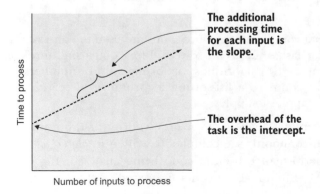

Time to process

The additional processing time for each input is the slope.

The overhead of the task is the intercept.

Number of inputs to process

Figure 4.2   Visualizing a task with linear complexity

As the list grows, the amount of time the computer has to spend grows proportionally. Summing 1,000 integers takes *about* half as long as summing 2,000 integers. For some number of items, n, these kinds of activities are linear with n or, in big O notation, $O(n)$.

You can spot code that's likely to be $O(n)$ in Python by finding `for` loops. A single loop over a list, set, or other sequence is likely to be linear:

```python
names = ['Aliya', 'Beth', 'David', 'Kareem']
for name in names:
    print(name)
```

This remains true even if you perform multiple steps inside the loop:

```python
names = ['Aliya', 'Beth', 'David', 'Kareem']
for name in names:
    greeting = 'Hi, my name is'
    print(f'{greeting} {name}')
```

It *even* remains true if you loop over the same list a set number of times:

```python
names = ['Aliya', 'Beth', 'David', 'Kareem']
for name in names:
    print(f'This is {name}!')

message = 'Let\'s welcome '
for name in names:
    message += f'{name} '
print(message)
```

Although you're looping over the list of names twice, think about it in terms of the equation for a line again. The first loop takes some time, f, per item, and the second loop takes some time, g, per item. The line equation would be something like $y = fx + gx + b$, which is equivalent to $y = (f + g)x + b$. It's still a line, even if it's a steeper one.

This is where the "asymptotic" part of asymptotic analysis comes in. Even though a particular activity may be *steeply* linear, other, more complex operations can still outpace it if the inputs are sufficiently many, as shown in figure 4.3.

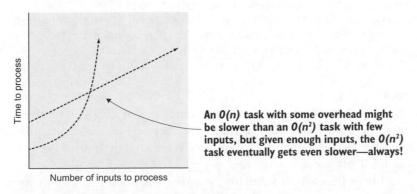

Figure 4.3 Higher-order complexity at large scales

PROPORTIONAL TO THE SQUARE

Another type of time complexity is proportional to the *square* of the inputs ($O(n^2)$). This crops up in cases where, for each item in a list, you need to look at every other item in the list. As you add more inputs, your code has to iterate over the additional items, but it also needs to iterate over those additional items on each of *those* iterations. The increase in execution time is compounded.

You can spot this in Python code by the presence of nested loops. The following code checks if a list has any duplicate items:

The outer loop iterates over every element in the sequence.

```
def has_duplicates(sequence):
    for index1, item1 in enumerate(sequence):
        for index2, item2 in enumerate(sequence):
            if item1 == item2 and index1 != index2:
                return True
    return False
```

The inner loop iterates over every element again, for each element in the outer loop.

Checks if two elements are the same value, but not the same specific element from the sequence

$O(n^2)$ is the *worst case* for this code because even if only the last items are duplicates, or if no duplicates exist, the code still has to iterate over all the inputs before it finishes. If the first two items are duplicates, the code will be much faster because it can stop immediately, but it's useful to examine the worst case to get a better sense for what the code is capable of. Big O notation always measures the worst-case complexity of code for this reason.

> ### Additional notations
>
> It's sometimes useful to calculate not only the *worst* case but also the *average* case and the *best* case. Big Ω (big omega) notation is used for best-case analysis, and big θ (big theta) notation is used to express that the upper and lower bounds are of the specified complexity. Usually these can help you choose the approach best suited to what you are trying to accomplish from a number of choices. The complexity of many algorithms can be found by searching online, such as for "complexity of quicksort". You can also find the time complexity of some common operations in the Python docs (https://wiki.python.org/moin/TimeComplexity).

CONSTANT TIME

The ideal complexity is constant time ($O(1)$), which doesn't depend on the size of the inputs. Nothing can be better than constant time because that would require the software to *speed up* as its input grow! Constant time is realized in some of the data types in Python, which I'll talk more about later.

Some problems that would normally be linear (or worse) can be made constant after up-front computation. That initial computation may itself be nonconstant, but if it allows many subsequent steps to *become* constant, it can be a great trade-off.

4.1.3 Space complexity

Just like time complexity, *space complexity* is a measure of how your code uses disk space or memory as its inputs grow. Space complexity is easy to overlook, though, because it's not always something you observe directly. Sometimes inefficient use of disk space rears its ugly head only when you get a pop up saying you have no disk space left on your computer. It's good to think about space as you write your code so you don't eat up your resources.

> **The garbage man**
>
> Another thing that makes space complexity more difficult in Python is that you don't often manage memory yourself. In some languages, you must explicitly allocate and free up memory, which forces you to manage how your code uses resources. Python uses automatic *garbage collection*, which frees the memory that holds objects that are no longer in use by a running program.

MEMORY

A common way programs use too much memory is by reading large data files fully into memory when they don't have to. Suppose you have a text file containing a row for each person alive today and their favorite color. You'd like to know the number of people who like each color the most. You might consider reading the whole file in as a list of rows and operating on the list:

```
color_counts = {}

with open('all-favorite-colors.txt') as favorite_colors_file:
    favorite_colors = favorite_colors_file.read().splitlines()

for color in favorite_colors:
    if color in color_counts:
        color_counts[color] += 1
    else:
        color_counts[color] = 1
```

Reads the whole file into a list of lines

There are a lot of people on planet Earth. Even if the file only contained one column of favorite colors and each row used 1 byte of data, the file would still be just over 7 GB in size. You might have that much memory on your machine, but the task doesn't require you to have all the row information available at once.

In Python, you can read a file line-by-line in a `for` loop, and on each iteration of the loop, the next line will *replace* the current line in memory. Try updating the code to read one line from the file at a time, and come back when you've got it.

```
color_counts = {}

with open('all-favorite-colors.txt') as favorite_colors_file:
    for color in favorite_colors_file:
```

Reads only one line at a time

```
color = color.strip()                  ◁────  Removes the trailing
                                              newline character
if color in color_counts:                     from each line
    color_counts[color] += 1
else:
    color_counts[color] = 1
```

By reading one line at a time and throwing them out after you get what you need, your memory usage will go only as high as the largest line in the file. Much better! The space complexity has gone from $O(n)$ to $O(1)$.

DISK SPACE

I've run into disk space issues on long-lived applications in the past. These are sometimes hard to see because they don't always cause an issue immediately. It could be weeks or months before you run out of disk space, either because your program writes small amounts of data at a time or simply because you have large storage available.

Many big web applications emit logs of their activity so they can be debugged or analyzed. If you introduce a log statement in your code that gets called 1,000 times per minute in production, this could start eating up disk space quickly. You might want to remove that line, move it somewhere that gets called less frequently, or improve your strategy for storing logs.

Finding opportunities to shift an approach from a higher-order complexity to a lower-order one will almost always yield better performance gains than trying to eke performance out of a particular line of code. Use complexity analysis to understand where these opportunities lie in your software. Read on to see how you can address these opportunities using some of the features built into Python.

4.2   *Performance and data types*

Although your code should be designed with time and space complexity in mind, it will ultimately be built on Python's existing data types. The following sections cover a number of use cases, as well as which data types are best suited for them.

4.2.1   *Data types for constant time*

Remember that the ideal performance is one of constant time, which does not increase as the number of inputs increases. Python's `dict` (dictionary) and `set` (set) types exhibit this behavior when adding, removing, and accessing items. They're quite similar under the hood, with a main difference being that *dictionaries map keys to values,* whereas *sets represent a set of unique, individual items.* Iterating through the items in either of these data types is still $O(n)$ time because it depends on the number of items contained in the object. But fetching specific items or checking if a specific item exists is speedy regardless of the total number of items.

Suppose that instead of counting the world's favorite colors, you're now interested in getting the unique set of all favorite colors so you can check if any colors aren't represented. You can still read the file line-by-line as before, but how might you represent the data and check it for specific colors?

Have a go at representing the data and checking it for specific colors. Then come back here and compare your work to the following listing to see how you did.

Listing 4.1 Using Python's features to minimize space

```
all_colors = set()                                    Iterating over the file is still O(n) time.

with open('all-favorite-colors.txt') as favorite_colors_file:
    for line in favorite_colors_file:
        all_colors.add(line.strip())                  Adding to a set is O(1)
                                                      time, but O(n) space.
print('Amber Waves of Grain' in all_colors)

Membership of the set is an O(1) question.
```

By using a set to hold a list of the unique colors encountered in the file, you can check for specific colors in the set in constant ($O(1)$) time after the loop.

4.2.2 Data types for linear time

The `list` data type in Python exhibits mainly $O(n)$ operations; determining membership in a list or adding a new item to an arbitrary location in a list is slower for lists with more elements. Adding or removing from the *end* of a list takes $O(1)$ time. Lists are useful when the items being stored aren't uniquely identifiable.

The `tuple` type is similar to `list` in terms of performance, with the key difference being that tuples can't be changed after they're created.

4.2.3 Space complexity of operations on data types

Now that you're familiar with the time complexity of some of Python's built-in data structures, I'll teach you a couple of tricks for using them. The data types we've seen so far are all *iterables*—objects that support iteration over their contents (in a `for` loop, for example). Iteration over a set of elements is nearly always going to be $O(n)$ in time complexity; going through every element takes more time if there are more elements. But what about space complexity?

For the data types we've seen so far, all their contents are stored in memory together. If a list has 10 elements, it takes roughly 10 times more space in memory than a list with a single element, as shown in figure 4.4. This means their *space* complexity is also $O(n)$. This can be problematic, the same way reading 7.6 billion records into memory is problematic. If we don't need all that data at once, we might be able to find a more efficient approach.

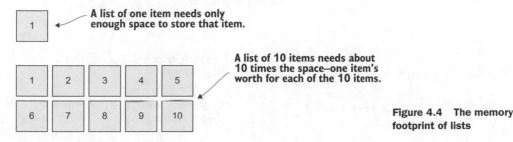

A list of one item needs only enough space to store that item.

A list of 10 items needs about 10 times the space—one item's worth for each of the 10 items.

Figure 4.4 The memory footprint of lists

Enter *generators*. Generators are constructs in Python that produce a single value at a time, pausing until the next value is requested (figure 4.5). This acts a lot like the approach you used earlier to read a file line-by-line. By yielding one value at a time, a generator avoids storing all values it produces in memory at once.

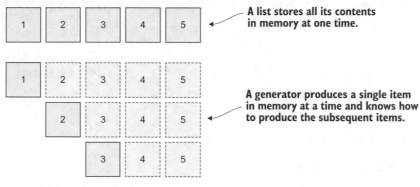

A list stores all its contents in memory at one time.

A generator produces a single item in memory at a time and knows how to produce the subsequent items.

Figure 4.5   Saving space with generators

If you've used the range function in Python before, you've already used a generator. range accepts arguments that specify the bounds of the range you'd like. If range stored all the numbers of the range in memory, code like range(100_000_000) would eat up your available memory in short order. Instead, range stores only the *bounds* of the range and produces values from it one at a time. But how?

To use space efficiently, generators make use of the yield Python keyword. After producing a value, they yield execution back to the calling code. So yield yields a value and then yields execution.

yield works a lot like Python's return statement, except that you can perform operations *after* you yield a value. This can be used to set up for the next value you want to produce. The following listing shows approximately how range behaves under the hood. Note the use of the yield keyword and the increment of the current value *after* yield is used.

Listing 4.2   Using yield to pause and prepare

```
def range(*args):
    if len(args) == 1:          ⟵  Parses arguments to determine
        start = 0                   bounds of the range
        stop = args[0]
    else:
        start = args[0]
        stop = args[1]
                                    yields each value
    current = start                 (one at a time)

    while current < stop:
        yield current          ⟵    Performs the necessary
        current += 1           ⟵    setup for the next value
```

There's a pattern in this implementation you'll see repeated often in generators:

1 Perform the main setup required for producing all values.
2 Create a loop.
3 Yield a value on each iteration of the loop.
4 Update the state for the next iteration of the loop.

Try inspecting the values from your `range` generator now. You can turn it into a list using `list(range(5, 10))`, for example. You can also move forward one value at a time by saving `range(5, 10)` to a variable and making successive calls to `next(my_range)`.

Now that you've got this pattern handy, I'd like you to write your very own generator. Your generator function, `squares`, will take in a list of integers and produce the square of each of them. Give it a shot, and come back to the following listing to see how you did.

> **Listing 4.3 A short generator that yields squared numbers**

```
def squares(items):
    for item in items:
        yield item ** 2
```

The `squares` function ends up being fairly compact because there's no setup or state management to do. I also said that this function accepts a list, but what's kind of cool about it is that you can pass in another generator instead. `squares(range(100_000_000))` works just as well. It will only store one item from the range and one squared result at a time, saving even more space (as shown in figure 4.6).

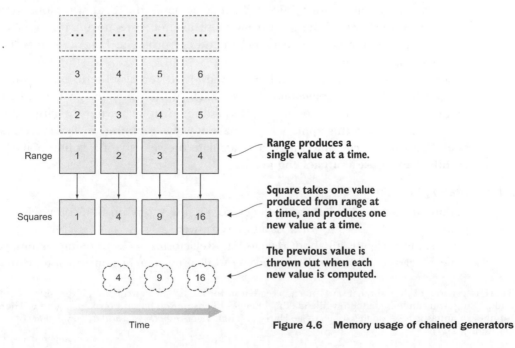

Figure 4.6 Memory usage of chained generators

I recommend making use of generators over lists wherever you can, because you can always build a full list in memory from a generator if needed by writing `list(range(10000))` or `list(squares([1, 2, 3, 4]))`. Using generators will save memory, but it can also save time because the code consuming the values from the generator may not need them all anyway.

> **Lazy evaluation**
>
> The idea of producing one value at a time, and that consuming code may not need all the values you can produce, is often referred to as *lazy evaluation*. It's *lazy* because you'd like to do as little work as possible, and only once you've been asked explicitly to do so. Picture your generators letting out an exaggerated sigh each time they're asked to `yield` a value.

4.3   *Make it work, make it right, make it fast*

The adage "make it work, make it right, make it fast" comes from Kent Beck, the creator of extreme programming. On its face, this could mean that you should first write working code, *then* rework it to be clear and concise, and only *then* make it performant. But I like to think of these three rules as being the steps you take on each small iteration as you write code. Remember that design, implementation, and refactoring all happen in tight cycles as you code.

4.3.1   *Making it work*

This, frankly, is what developers spend a great deal of their time on. You try to turn a problem statement or idea into code that achieves the goal. Developers (myself included) often work all the way through a problem before moving on to refactoring or performance. It can feel like a chicken and egg problem: *How can I make "it" fast if "it" isn't even done yet?*

Just as decomposition is useful for software itself, it is also useful as a tool in breaking down goals into manageable chunks. Each of those smaller goals can be implemented and examined incrementally along the way to achieving the larger goal. It's also much easier in this approach to "make it work," because "it" is a more granular goal. You can sketch some ideas for "calculate the velocity of a falling object" more readily than "make a physics engine."

4.3.2   *Making it right*

Making it work is all about trying to get from point A to point B. If you're clear on the goal of the task, "Does it work?" is a binary answer.

Making it right is all about refactoring. Refactoring seeks to re-implement existing code in a clearer or more well adapted way, while providing the same consistent outcome.[1]

---

[1] There is a school of thought that says you can create tests for the code you write and, if the tests are sufficient and passing, you can lean on them while making changes to ensure you haven't broken anything. There are a number of fantastic texts on this subject. See Harry Percival, *Test-Driven Development with Python*, second edition (O'Reilly, 2017).

Refactoring has no clear "done" moment. You will find yourself iterating while you implement, as well as when you revisit the code to add new functionality. For one metric about when you definitely *should* refactor, Martin Fowler's *rule of three* says that around the time you've implemented a similar thing three times, you should refactor your code to provide an abstraction for that behavior. I like this premise because it suggests a balance around refactoring: don't abstract something immediately, or even after you've duplicated it twice, because it might be premature. Wait to see what use cases arise. They will allow you to generalize the solution more effectively and be sure that it's necessary.

Another aspect to making something right is to use the strengths of the language to your advantage. Take a look at the following code, which determines the most frequent integer in a list:

```python
def get_number_with_highest_count(counts):          ⊲── Determines the number with the
    max_count = 0                                        highest count in a dict that maps
    for number, count in counts.items():                 numbers to counts
        if count > max_count:
            max_count = count
            number_with_highest_count = number
    return number_with_highest_count


def most_frequent(numbers):
    counts = {}
    for number in numbers:                          ⊲── Tallies up the occurrence of
        if number in counts:                             numbers to see which has
            counts[number] += 1                          the highest count
        else:
            counts[number] = 1

    return get_number_with_highest_count(counts)
```

I've made this *work*, but Python has a few tools for making this easier. The first tool helps with the code that increments the count. For each number in the list, it has to check if we've already seen it to know if it can increment the count or if it has to initialize the count. Python has a built-in data type to avoid this extra leg work: the `defaultdict`. You can tell a `defaultdict` the type of the values it stores, and it will default to a sensible value of that type if a new key is accessed:

```python
from collections import defaultdict                 ⊲── Imports defaultdict from
                                                         the collections module

def get_number_with_highest_count(counts):
    max_count = 0
    for number, count in counts.items():
        if count > max_count:
            max_count = count
            number_with_highest_count = number
    return number_with_highest_count
```

```
def most_frequent(numbers):
    counts = defaultdict(int)     ◁——┐
    for number in numbers:
        counts[number] += 1        ◁————

    return get_number_with_highest_count(counts)
```

The counts are integers, so the default type of each value in the defaultdict should be int.

The default value for int is 0, so the first time we see a number, its count will be 0 + 1 = 1.

Not bad—you saved yourself one line of code, and the spirit of the function is a little more clear. But you can do even better. Python also has a helper for counting things in a sequence:

```
from collections import Counter     ◁——┐
```

Counter is also in the collections module.

```
def get_number_with_highest_count(counts):
    max_count = 0
    for number, count in counts.items():
        if count > max_count:
            max_count = count
            number_with_highest_count = number
    return number_with_highest_count


def most_frequent(numbers):
    counts = Counter(numbers)     ◁——┐
    return get_number_with_highest_count(counts)
```

Acts nearly identically to the dict of counts you made manually

You've saved a few more lines, and now the spirit of most_frequent is quite clear: count the unique numbers, and return the one with the highest count. But what about get_number_with_highest_count? It's finding the maximum value in a dictionary that maps numbers to their counts. Python provides two tools that can simplify this function too.

The first is max. max accepts an iterable (lists, sets, dictionaries, and so on) and returns the maximum value from that iterable. In the case of a dictionary, max returns the maximum value of the *keys* by default. The keys of the counts dictionary are the numbers themselves, not the counts. max accepts a second argument, key, which is a function that tells max what part of the iterable to use.

Python will only pass one argument to key: the value from the iterable. In the case of dictionaries, Python iterates over their keys, so the function passed to the key argument for max will only get the numbers but not their counts. You need to tell key that, when given a number, it should index the counts dictionary at that number to get the count value. Writing a separate function in the module won't work because counts won't be available at all in its namespace. How can you get around this?

In functional programming, it's common to pass functions as arguments to other functions, and sometimes those passed functions are short and clear enough that they don't need names. Unlike most of the functions you've probably written in Python, they're *anonymous* functions and are called *lambdas*. Lambdas are indeed functions; they accept arguments and return values. They don't have names, and you can't call them directly, but you can use them as inline arguments to other functions to get things done.

In the case of the `get_number_with_highest_count` function, you can pass a lambda to `max` that accepts a number and returns `counts[number]`. This solves the namespace issue and provides the behavior you want to give to `max`. Let's see how succinct this will make the code:

```python
from collections import Counter


def get_number_with_highest_count(counts):
    return max(
        counts,
        key=lambda number: counts[number]
    )


def most_frequent(numbers):
    counts = Counter(numbers)
    return get_number_with_highest_count(counts)
```

> When iterating over the numbers in counts, uses counts[number] (that number's count) as the comparison value

That's concise, and still clear. Understanding what tools a language has for which activities will often help you produce shorter code.

Shorter isn't always better, of course. You could go further and move the `max` directly into the `most_frequent` function, but when I'm using functions like `max` that aren't always perfectly clear about their behavior, I like having the separate function with a clearer name.

Once you reach a point where the code you've written is working, and it's clear enough about *how* it works that someone else could pick it up and use it, you've made it right.

4.3.3 Making it fast

Tuning the performance of your code can often take as long as writing the code in the first place. Complexity analysis and subsequent improvements require care and a good long look at the data types and operations in your code. You'll need to weigh the time lost to performance tuning against the need to bring your work to market. As mentioned at the beginning of this chapter, you'll also need to decide when the code is performant *enough*. Perfection is the enemy of good enough, as they say, so it's often better to ship something valuable but slow than not to ship anything at all.

If your priority is getting something to market, consider setting some performance milestones for yourself that you can reach iteratively after your initial release. This way, you can focus on making something work, making it work right for ease of future improvement, and shipping your product. You'll likely find new and unexpected bottlenecks by running your code in production.

Your acceptable level of performance will also vary based on your goals. If you are displaying a modal to log in to a site after clicking Log In, it needs to happen instantaneously, or your users will leave. If you're trying to build an annual reporting system so customers can see their sales, they will likely expect to wait a bit.

The *architecture* of the system—all the different services, pages, interactions, and so on—will inform and affect performance too. Bigger systems require more network communication between APIs, databases, and caches. They may also have some processes that happen outside of the user's workflow, like nightly accumulation of metrics for analysis. You can examine other services within this architecture that perform tasks similar to yours to get an idea of the baseline. From there, you can create an informed expectation of your software's performance and strive toward it. The performance of large systems transcends code.

As you write more code, bring what you've learned about the performance of data types and techniques to bear on your software. You can begin to develop a sense for lines of code that might cause performance issues. Nested loops and huge in-memory lists will start to jump out at you.

4.4   Tools

Performance testing in the real world needs to follow an evidence-based approach. This is a direct result of the fact that systems with real users will inevitably experience different behavior; the combination of unexpected inputs, timing, hardware, network latency, and more contribute to a system's performance. As such, poking around your code hoping to stumble on huge performance wins may not be the best use of your time.

4.4.1   timeit

The timeit module in Python is a tool for testing the execution time of code snippets. It can be used from the command line or directly in your code for more control. The timeit module is handy for sanity-checking the performance changes you intend to make.

Imagine you'd like to see how much time it takes to sum the integers from 0 to 999. To time this activity from the command line, you can invoke the timeit module with Python:

```
python -m timeit "total = sum(range(1000))"
```

This will cause timeit to run the summation code many times, ultimately printing some statistics about the execution time:

```
20000 loops, best of 5: 18.9 usec per loop
```

You can conclude from this output that the summation of 0–999 generally takes less than 20 microseconds.

To see how summing 0–4999 affects the outcome, you can change your command and rerun it:

```
python -m timeit "total = sum(range(5000))"
2000 loops, best of 5: 105 usec per loop
```

From this, you can conclude that summing the integers 0–4999 takes a little over five times longer than 0–999.

Keep in mind that timeit is really running your code, and real-world execution has small variations due to many variables. In addition to the code, things like your battery level and CPU clock speed can affect the timing. As such, it's good to run your timing commands a few times to see how stable the measurement is, and to look for significant improvements from that baseline when making changes. So although timeit gives you quantitative measurements, it's best to use it to compare two different implementations qualitatively, focusing on the trend. This is where you'll notice those order-of-magnitude improvements that noticeably speed up your code.

The command-line interface for timeit is great, but it can be cumbersome when you want to test larger or more complex pieces of code. If you need more control over what's being timed, you can use timeit from within your code. If you'd like to time a specific portion of code without timing all of the setup code it requires, you can separate the setup step so its execution time isn't included:

This code sets the stage for the timing test.

```
from timeit import timeit

setup = 'from datetime import datetime'
statement = 'datetime.now()'
result = timeit(setup=setup, stmt=statement)
print(f'Took an average of {result}ms')
```

This code executes within the timer.

timeit produces a timing result, in milliseconds.

This will end up timing only the `datetime.now()` call without timing the `import` needed to make the call.

Suppose you'd like to prove that checking whether an item is in a set is faster than checking if it's in a list. How would you do that using the timeit module? Build your inputs using `set(range(10000))` and `list(range(10000))`, and time the task of finding out if `300` is in them. How much faster is the set?

The timeit module has saved me from going down a rabbit hole a number of times by telling me my hypothesis about speeding up some code was wrong. It's a real time-saver (pun absolutely intended).

4.4.2 CPU profiling

When you were using timeit, the module was *profiling* your code. Profiling means analyzing your code as it runs to gather some metrics about its behavior. The timeit module measured how long your code took to run in total, but another insightful way to measure the performance of your code is through CPU profiling. CPU profiling lets you see which *parts* of your code perform expensive calculations, as well as how often they're called. This kind of output is useful because it helps you understand where you might want to look first when trying to speed up your code.

Suppose you've written a function that isn't too expensive but is called many times in your application. You've also written a function that is expensive but is only called once. If you only have time to fix one, which will it be? Without profiling the code, it's hard to know which will speed up your code the most. You can figure it out using Python's cProfile module.

> **NOTE** If you try to import the cProfile module but get an error, you can use the profile module instead.

The cProfile module prints a few pieces of information about each method or function called while executing your program. For each call, it will show you

- The number of times the call occurred (`ncalls`)
- The time spent in that call alone, not including things it calls in turn (`tottime`)
- The average time spent in that call alone, across the `ncalls` times it was called (`percall`)
- The cumulative time spent in that call, including any time spent in subcalls (`cumtime`)

This information is helpful because it will expose things that are slow—that have a large `cumtime`—but will also expose things that are fast but called many times. The following listing shows a toy program that calls a function 1000 times. The function call takes a random amount of time, up to 10 milliseconds, to execute.

Listing 4.4 Profiling the CPU performance of a Python program

```
import random
import time


def an_expensive_function():
    execution_time = random.random() / 100     ◁── Takes a random amount of
    time.sleep(execution_time)                       time (up to 10 milliseconds)
                                                     to execute


if __name__ == '__main__':
    for _ in range(1000):              ◁── Runs the function
        an_expensive_function()             1000 times
```

Save this program in a cpu_profiling.py module. Then you can profile it from the command line using cProfile:

```
python -m cProfile --sort cumtime cpu_profiling.py
```

Over a large number of calls, you can expect a function that takes 0–10 milliseconds to take about 5 milliseconds on average (percall). Calling it 1000 times (ncalls), you can expect it to take about 5 seconds overall (cumtime). Run cProfile on the program to see if it meets your expectations. You will see a lot of output, but sorting by cumulative time means an_expensive_function calls will be near the top:

```
$ python -m cProfile --sort cumtime cpu_profiling.py
        5138 function calls (5095 primitive calls) in 5.644 seconds

   Ordered by: cumulative time

   ncalls  tottime  percall  cumtime  percall filename:lineno(function)
      4/1    0.000    0.000    5.644    5.644 {built-in method builtins.exec}
        1    0.002    0.002    5.644    5.644 cpu_profiling.py:1(<module>)
     1000    0.003    0.000    5.625    0.006 cpu_profiling.py:5
(an_expensive_function)
     1000    5.622    0.006    5.622    0.006 {built-in method time.sleep}
    ...
```

In this run, an_expensive_function took an average of about 6 milliseconds per call over the span of 1000 calls, leading to a cumulative 5.625 seconds spent inside that function.

When looking at the output of cProfile, you'll want to search for calls with a high percall value or a big jump in cumtime. These characteristics mean the call takes up a good chunk of your program's execution time. Speeding up a slow function can improve the program speed a fair amount, and cutting the execution time of a function that's called thousands of times can be a really big win.

4.5 *Try it out*

Consider the following code. It contains a function, sort_expensive, that has to sort a list of 1000 integers in the range 0–999,999. It also contains a function, sort_cheap, that only has to sort a list of 10 integers in the range 0–999.

Sorting algorithms are generally more expensive than $O(1)$, so the sort_expensive function will take longer than sort_cheap. If you only ran each function once, sort_cheap would surely win. But if you need to run sort_cheap 1,000 times, it's less clear which operation will be fastest.

```
import random


def sort_expensive():
    the_list = random.sample(range(1_000_000), 1_000)
    the_list.sort()


def sort_cheap():
    the_list = random.sample(range(1_000), 10)
    the_list.sort()
```

```
if __name__ == '__main__':
    sort_expensive()
    for i in range(1000):
        sort_cheap()
```

You need to profile the code to understand the performance. See how each task fares using the timeit and cProfile modules.

Summary

- Design for performance both up front and iteratively throughout your development.
- Think carefully about the right data type for the task.
- Prefer generators over lists when you don't need all the values at once, to save on memory usage.
- Use the timeit and cProfile/profile Python modules to test your hypotheses about complexity and performance.

Testing your software

5

I've talked in previous chapters about writing clear code using well-named functions for maintainability, but that's only part of the picture. As you add feature after feature, can you be sure the application still does what you meant it to? Any application you hope will live on long into the future needs some assurances of its longevity. Tests can help you make sure new features are built correctly, and you can run these tests again each time you update your code to make sure it *stays* correct.

Testing can be a strict, formal process for applications that must not fail, like launching shuttles and keeping planes in flight. Such tests are rigorous and often mathematically provable. That's pretty cool, but it goes way beyond what's necessary or practical for most Python applications. In this chapter, you'll learn about the methodology and tools Python developers use to test their code, and you'll get a chance to write some tests yourself.

5.1   *What is software testing?*

Loosely speaking, *software testing* is the practice of verifying that software behaves the way you expect. This can range from making sure a function produces the expected output when given a specific input to making sure your application can handle the stress of 100 users at once. As developers, we constantly do some form of this subconsciously. If you're developing a website, you probably run the server locally and check your changes in the browser as you code. This is a form of testing.

You might think that spending more time validating that your code works means less time shipping software. In the immediate term, this is true, especially as you get acquainted with the tools and processes related to testing. The idea in the long term, though, is that testing will *save* you time by limiting the recurrence of behavior and performance bugs and by providing a scaffolding you can use to confidently refactor code in the future. The more critical a piece of code is to your business, the more time you'll want to spend testing it thoroughly.

5.1.1   *Does it do what it says on the tin?*

One reason to test a piece of software is to determine whether it really does what it claims. A well-named function describes its intent to the reader, but, as they say, the road to hell is paved with good intentions. I can't count the number of times I wrote a function, fully believing it was faithfully carrying out its intended purpose, only to find out later that I'd made a mistake.

Sometimes these mistakes are easy to catch—a typo or exception in an area of code you're familiar with might be easy to track down. The trickier bugs to find are those that don't cause immediate issues but cascade as the application progresses. With good testing, problems can be found early, and you can guard your application from similar issues in the future. A number of categories of testing exist, each focused on identifying particular kinds of problems. I'll cover a few here, but you can be sure this is not an exhaustive list.

5.1.2   *The anatomy of a functional test*

You saw earlier that testing can make sure software produces the right output for a given input. This type of testing is called *functional testing* because it makes sure that a piece of code *functions* correctly. This is in contrast to other types of testing, such as performance testing, which I'll cover in section 5.6.

Although functional testing strategies vary in scale and approach, the basic anatomy of a functional test remains consistent. Because they check that software gives the right output based on a given input, all functional tests need to perform a few specific tasks, including the following:

1 *Prepare the inputs* to the software.
2 *Identify the expected output* of the software.
3 *Obtain the actual output* of the software.
4 *Compare the actual and the expected outputs* to see if they match.

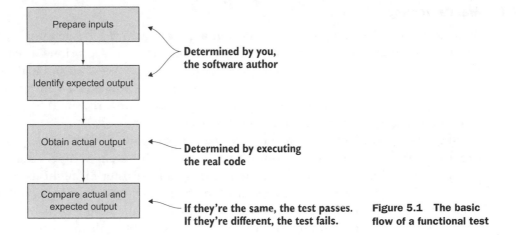

Figure 5.1 The basic flow of a functional test

The preparation of inputs and identification of expected outputs are where most of your work as a developer will be when creating tests, whereas obtaining and comparing the actual output is a matter of executing your code, as shown in figure 5.1.

Structuring your tests this way has another beneficial effect: you can read your tests as a specification of how the code works. This pays off when you revisit code you wrote long ago (or last week, for me). A good test for a `calculate_mean` function might read like this:

> *Given the list of integers* [1, 2, 3, 4], *the expected output of* `calculate_mean` *is* 2.5. *Verify that the actual output of* `calculate_mean` *matches this expectation.*

This format scales to larger functional workflows. In an e-commerce system, the "input" might be clicking a product and then clicking Add to Cart. The expected "output" is the item being added to the cart. A functional test for that workflow would read like this:

> *Given I visit the page for product* 53-DE-232 *and click Add to Cart, I expect to see* 53-DE-232 *in my cart.*

Ultimately, it's nice when your tests not only verify that your code works, but also act as documentation on how to use it. In the next section, you'll see how this recipe for writing a functional test applies to some different testing approaches.

5.2 *Functional testing approaches*

Functional testing takes on many forms in practice. From the constant little checks we do as developers to fully automated tests that get kicked off before every production deployment, there is a spectrum of practices and capabilities. You'll recognize some of the following types of testing, but I recommend reading about each of them to understand the similarities and differences between them.

5.2.1   *Manual testing*

Manual testing is the practice of running your application, giving it some inputs, and checking whether it does what you expect. For example, if you're writing a registration workflow for a website, you would enter a username and password and make sure a new user is created. If you have password requirements, you would want to check that using an invalid password does *not* create a new user. Similarly, you'd test for the case where a user with the username you choose already exists.

Registering on a website is generally a small (and one-time) part of the product experience for most users, but, as you can see, you already have to verify several cases. If any of these things go wrong, your users either can't register or might have their account information overwritten. With this code being so important, relying on manual testing for too long will eventually cause you to miss something. Manually exploring the application for new bugs or new things to test is still a valuable activity, but it should be viewed as a supplement to other types of testing.

5.2.2   *Automated testing*

In contrast to manual testing, *automated testing* allows you to write a great number of tests that can then be executed as many times as you like, without the risk that you'll miss a check when you're trying to leave the office the Friday of a long weekend. If this hypothetical situation seems overly specific, that's because it's not hypothetical. I've lived it.

Automated testing tightens the feedback loop so that you can see quickly whether a change you've made has broken an expected behavior. The time you'll save compared to manual testing will free you up to do more creative exploratory testing of the application. As you uncover things to fix, you should incorporate them into your automated tests. You can think of this as locking in a verification that will make sure the particular bug doesn't happen again. Most of the testing you'll see in the rest of this chapter can be, and often is, automated.

5.2.3   *Acceptance testing*

Closest in nature to the Add to Cart workflow test, *acceptance testing* verifies the high-level requirements of a system. Software that passes these tests is *acceptable* based on the specified requirements. As shown in figure 5.2, acceptance tests answer questions like, "Can the user successfully go through the purchase workflow and buy the product they want?" These are the mission-critical checks for the business—things that keep the lights on.

Acceptance tests are often carried out manually by a business stakeholder, but they can also be automated to a degree with *end-to-end testing*. End-to-end testing makes sure a set of actions can be carried out (from one end to the other) with the appropriate data flowing through where needed. If the workflow is expressed from the viewpoint of the user, it begins to look almost exactly like the Add to Cart workflow.

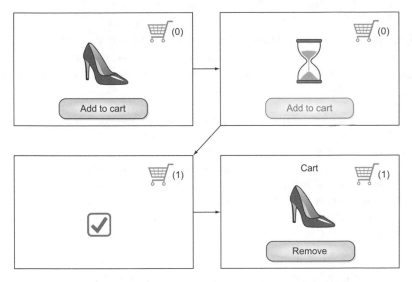

An acceptance test for an e-commerce website might check that a user can visit a product page and successfully add the product to their cart.

This could be implemented as an automated end-to-end test that makes sure the pages each show and pass along the correct information.

Figure 5.2 Acceptance tests verify workflows from a user's perspective.

Testing is for everyone

Libraries like Cucumber (https://cucumber.io) enable you to describe end-to-end tests in natural language as high-level actions, like "click the Submit button." These tests are often much easier to understand than a big mess of code. Writing steps in natural language documents the system in a way most anyone in the organization can understand.

This idea of *behavior-driven development* (BDD) allows you to collaborate with others on end-to-end testing, even if they don't have experience with software development in a coding capacity. BDD is used in many organizations as a way to define the desired outcomes first, only implementing the code to make the tests pass afterward.

End-to-end tests commonly verify areas of high value for the business—if the cart doesn't work, no one can buy products, and you lose revenue—but they are also the most susceptible to breaking because they span such a wide swathe of functionality. If any one step in the workflow doesn't work, the whole end-to-end test fails. Creating a set of tests that vary in granularity will help indicate not only whether the whole workflow is healthy, but also which steps are failing specifically. This allows you to pinpoint problems faster.

End-to-end tests are some of the *least* granular, so what's on the other end of the spectrum?

5.2.4   *Unit testing*

Unit testing is perhaps the most important thing you can take away from this chapter. Unit tests make sure all the little bits of your software are working, and they lay a strong foundation for larger testing efforts like end-to-end testing. I'll show you how to get started with unit testing in Python in section 5.4.

> **DEFINITION**   A *unit* is a small, fundamental piece of software—like the "unit" in "unit circle." What constitutes a unit is the source of much philosophical waxing, but a good working definition is that it's a piece of code that can be isolated for testing. Functions are generally considered units—they can be executed in isolation by calling them with the appropriate inputs. Lines of code within those functions can't be isolated, so they're smaller than a unit. Classes contain many pieces that can be isolated further, so they're generally bigger than a unit, but they are occasionally treated as units.

Unit testing seeks to verify that all the individual units of code in your application work correctly, that each small piece of the software does what it says it does. These are the most fundamental tests you can write and are therefore a great place to get started with testing.

Functions are the most common target of functional unit tests. "Function" is right there in the name, after all. This is because of functions' input-output nature. If you've separated the concerns of your code into small functions, testing them will be a straightforward application of the functional testing recipe.

It turns out that one of the great benefits of structuring your code using separation of concerns, encapsulation, and loose coupling is that it makes code easier to test. Testing can feel tedious, so any opportunity to reduce friction is welcome. The easier the code is to test, the more likely it is that you'll *write* those tests in the first place, so you can reap the reward of confidence in your software. Units are the small, separated pieces you naturally arrive at by sticking with the practices you've learned so far.

Most unit tests in Python compare expected and actual outputs using a simple equality comparison. You can do one of these yourself right now. Open the Python REPL and create this `calculate_mean` function:

```
>>> def calculate_mean(numbers):
...     return sum(numbers) / len(numbers)
```

Now you can test your expectations of this function with a few different inputs, comparing the output to your expected results:

```
>>> 2.5 == calculate_mean([1, 2, 3, 4])
True
>>> 5.5 == calculate_mean([5, 5, 5, 6, 6, 6])
True
```

Try a few other lists of numbers in the REPL now to verify that calculate_mean is giving the right results. Think of useful sets of inputs that might change the behavior of the function:

- Does it work correctly with negative numbers?
- Does it work when the list of numbers contains 0?
- Does it work when the list is empty?

These kinds of curiosities are worth writing tests for. They occasionally uncover questions you haven't accounted for in your code, which gives you an opportunity to address those questions before someone finds out the hard way that a particular use case wasn't considered.

```
>>> 0.0 == calculate_mean([-1, 0, 1])
True
>>> 0.0 == calculate_mean([])
Traceback (most recent call last):
  File "<stdin>", line 1, in <module>
  File "<stdin>", line 2, in calculate_mean
ZeroDivisionError: division by zero
```

Raises an exception for a case you haven't considered yet

You can fix calculate_mean by returning 0 if the list is empty:

```
>>> def calculate_mean(numbers):
...     if not numbers:
...         return 0
...     return sum(numbers) / len(numbers)
>>> 0.0 == calculate_mean([])
True
```

Great—calculate_mean has passed all the cases we've thrown at it. Remember that unit tests are the foundation that enables success in larger testing efforts, like end-to-end testing. To understand that relationship better, we'll look at two other testing categories in the following sections.

5.2.5 Integration testing

Whereas unit tests are all about making sure the individual pieces of your code work as expected, *integration testing* focuses on making sure those units all work in tandem to produce the right behavior (see figure 5.3). You may have 10 fully functional units of software, but if they can't be put together to do what you want, they aren't too useful. Whereas end-to-end workflow tests are usually framed from the perspective of a user, integration tests focus more on the behavior of the code. They're at different levels of abstraction.

Integration testing carries several caveats, though. Because integration tests need to thread multiple pieces of code together, it's common to build tests that are structured much like the code they're testing. This introduces tight coupling between the tests and the code—changes in the code that produce the same outcome might still

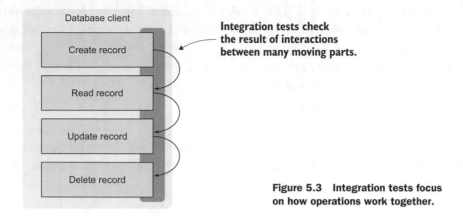

Figure 5.3   Integration tests focus on how operations work together.

cause the tests to break, because the tests are too concerned with *how* the outcome is achieved.

Integration tests may take significantly longer to execute than unit tests. They generally do more than execute some functions and check the output; they might use a database to create and manipulate records, as an example. The interaction being tested is more complex, so the time required to carry it out can grow. For these reasons, integration tests are usually fewer in number than unit tests.

5.2.6   *The testing pyramid*

Now that you've seen manual, unit, and integration testing, let's recap the interplay between them. The idea of a testing pyramid like that in figure 5.4 indicates that you should liberally apply functional tests like unit and integration tests, but be more conservative with long, brittle, and manual tests.[1] Each has merit, and your mileage will

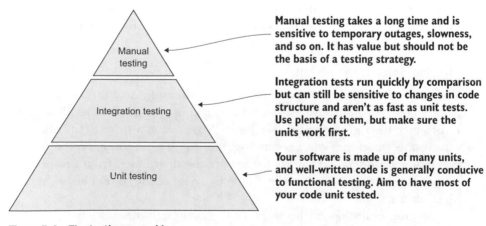

Figure 5.4   The testing pyramid

---

[1]Testing pyramids were first described by Mike Cohn in *Succeeding with Agile* (Addison-Wesley Professional, 2009).

depend on the application and the resources at your disposal, but it's a decent rule of thumb about where to invest time.

You'll get the most bang for your buck by making sure the little pieces of software are all working, then making sure they all work together. Again, automating this process will empower you to use the time you've freed up to think of new ways your software might break. You can then incorporate those ideas as new tests and slowly build confidence that will carry you forward.

5.2.7 Regression testing

Regression testing is less an approach to testing per se, and more a process to follow as you develop your applications. When you write a test, the assumption is that you're saying, "I want to make sure the code keeps working this way." If you change your code in a way that changes the behavior you tested, that would be a *regression*. A regression is a shift to an undesirable (or at least unexpected) state and is usually A Bad Thing.

Regression testing is the practice of running your existing suite of tests after each code change before shipping your code to production. A *test suite* is the collection of tests you've built up over time, either written to verify code as unit/integration tests or to fix things found in exploratory manual testing. Many development teams run these test suites in a *continuous integration* (CI) environment, where changes to an application are frequently combined and tested before being released. A full discussion of CI is beyond the scope of this book, but the idea is to set yourself up for success by running all your tests against all your changes. I highly recommend checking out Travis CI (https://docs.travis-ci.com/user/for-beginners/) or CircleCI (https://circleci.com/docs/2.0/about-circleci/) to learn more.

> ### Version control hooks
> One practice for automating unit tests in source control systems is using a precommit hook. Each time you commit your code, the hook triggers the tests to run. If any failures occur, the commit fails, and you're reminded to fix them before committing your code. Most unit-testing tools should integrate with this approach pretty well. Running the tests again in a continuous integration environment makes sure that they pass just before the code is deployed.

As new features are added, new tests get added to the test suite. These get locked in as regression tests for future changes. Similarly, it's common to add tests for bugs that you find, so that you can build confidence that a particular bug won't reoccur. Like code, test suites won't always be perfect. But leaning on a robust suite to tell you when things go awry can help you focus on other areas, like innovation and performance.

With that, let's see how you can start writing tests in Python.

5.3   Statements of fact

The next step toward creating real tests is to *assert* that a particular comparison holds true. Assertions are statements of fact; if you make an assertion that doesn't hold true, either some assumption you've made is incorrect or the assertion itself is incorrect. If you assert that "you can see the sun on the horizon every morning," it holds true most of the time. But when there are clouds on the horizon, your assertion doesn't hold true. If you update your assumptions to include that the sky is clear, your assertion becomes true again.

Assertions in software are similar. They assert that some expression must hold true, and they fail loudly if that assertion fails. In Python, assertions can be written using the assert keyword. When assertions fail, they raise an AssertionError.

You can test calculate_mean with assertions by adding assert in front of your comparisons. A passing assertion will have no output; a failing one will show you the traceback for the AssertionError:

```
>>> assert 10.0 == calculate_mean([0, 10, 20])
>>> assert 1.0 == calculate_mean([1000, 3500, 7_000_000])
Traceback (most recent call last):
  File "<stdin>", line 1, in <module>
AssertionError
```

This behavior is what many Python testing tools are built on. Using the recipe for a functional test (set up input, identify expected output, obtain actual output, and compare), these tools help you do the comparison and provide valuable context when your assertions fail. Read on to see how two of the most widely used testing tools in Python handle making assertions about your code.

5.4   Unit testing with unittest

Unittest is Python's built-in testing framework. Although it's called unittest, it can also be used for integration testing. Unittest provides features for making assertions about your code, and also the tool for *running* the tests. In this section, you'll see how tests are organized and how to run them, and you'll finally get some practice writing real tests. Let's get to it!

5.4.1   Test organization with unittest

Unittest provides a set of features for performing assertions. You previously saw how to write raw assert statements to test code, but unittest provides a TestCase class with custom assertion methods for more understandable testing output. Your tests will inherit from this class and use methods to make assertions.

I encourage you to use these test classes as a strategy for grouping your tests. The classes are flexible—you can use them to group any tests you like. If you have many tests for a class, putting them in their own TestCase is a good idea. If you have many tests for a single method within a class, you could even create a TestCase only for those. You learned to use cohesion, namespacing, and separation of concerns for code, and you can apply the same ideas to tests.

5.4.2 Running tests with unittest

Unittest provides a test runner that you can use by typing `python -m unittest` in your terminal. When you run the unittest test runner, it will look for tests by

1 Looking in the current directory (and any subdirectories) for modules named `test_*` or `*_test`
2 Looking in those modules for classes that inherit from `unittest.TestCase`
3 Looking in those classes for methods that start with `test_`

Some people like to put their tests as close to the relevant code as possible, making it easier to find tests for a particular module of interest. Others like to put all their tests in a tests/ directory that lives at the root of their project to keep them separate from the code. I've done it both ways and don't have a strong preference myself. Do what works for you, your team, or the community you're writing software with.

5.4.3 Writing your first test with unittest

Now that you've got an idea of how unittest does things, you need something to test. The following listing lays out a class you'll use to get some testing practice.

Listing 5.1   A product class for an e-commerce system

```python
class Product:
    def __init__(self, name, size, color):      ⟵   The product attributes are
        self.name = name                             specified when a Product
        self.size = size                             instance is created.
        self.color = color

    def transform_name_for_sku(self):
        return self.name.upper()

    def transform_color_for_sku(self):
        return self.color.upper()
                                          ⎤   A SKU uniquely identifies
    def generate_sku(self):         ⟵    ⎦   the product attributes.
        """
        Generates a SKU for this product.

        Example:
            >>> small_black_shoes = Product('shoes', 'S', 'black')
            >>> small_black_shoes.generate_sku()
            'SHOES-S-BLACK'
        """
        name = self.transform_name_for_sku()
        color = self.transform_color_for_sku()
        return f'{name}-{self.size}-{color}'
```

This class represents a product for purchase in an e-commerce system. A product has a name and options for size and color, and each combination of these attributes produces a *stock keeping unit* (SKU). A SKU is a unique, internal ID used by companies for pricing and inventory that often uses an all-uppercase format. Place this class definition in a product.py module.

After you've created your product module, you're ready to start writing your first test. Create a test_product.py module in the same directory as product.py. Start by importing unittest and creating an empty `ProductTestCase` class that inherits from the base `TestCase` class:

```
import unittest

class ProductTestCase(unittest.TestCase):
    pass
```

If you run `python -m unittest` at this point, with only product.py and your empty test case in test_product.py, it will say that it ran no tests:

```
$ python -m unittest

----------------------------------------------------------------------
Ran 0 tests in 0.000s

OK
```

It likely found the test_product module and the `ProductTestCase` class, but you haven't written any tests there yet. You can check this by adding an empty test method to the class:

```
import unittest

class ProductTestCase(unittest.TestCase):
    def test_working(self):
        pass
```

Try running the test runner again; you should see that it ran one test this time:

```
$ python -m unittest
.
----------------------------------------------------------------------
Ran 1 test in 0.000s

OK
```

Now you're ready for the real magic. Remember the anatomy of a functional test:

1 Set up the inputs.
2 Identify the expected output.
3 Obtain the actual output.
4 Compare the expected and actual outputs.

If you want to test the `transform_name_for_sku` method from the `Product` class, this recipe becomes

1. Create an instance of `Product` with a name, size, and color.
2. Observe that `transform_name_for_sku` returns `name.upper()`; the expected result is the name in uppercase.
3. Call the `Product` instance's `transform_name_for_sku` method and save it in a variable.
4. Compare the expected result to the saved actual result.

You can write the first three steps using regular code for creating a `Product` instance and getting the value of `transform_name_for_sku`. Using an `assert` statement for the fourth step would work, but `AssertionError` doesn't provide much information in its traceback by default. This is where the custom assertion methods in unittest come into play. The most common one to use for comparing two values is `assertEqual`, which accepts expected and actual values as arguments. It raises an `AssertionError` and provides additional information showing the difference between the two values if they aren't equal. This added context can help you find issues more easily.

Here's what the test might look like on a first pass:

```
import unittest

from product import Product


class ProductTestCase(unittest.TestCase):
    def test_transform_name_for_sku(self):
        small_black_shoes = Product('shoes', 'S', 'black')
        expected_value = 'SHOES'
        actual_value = small_black_shoes.transform_name_for_sku()
        self.assertEqual(expected_value, actual_value)
```

Prepares the setup for transform_name_for_sku: the product with its attributes

Obtains the actual result of generate_ sku for comparison

States the expected result for generate_sku with the given inputs

Uses the special equality assertion method to compare two values

Running the test runner now should still show `Ran 1 test`, and if the test passes (it should), you won't see much additional output.

It's a good idea to see your tests fail to verify that they'll actually catch a problem with your code if one arises. Change the expected value `'SHOES'` to `'SHOEZ'` and run the test again. Now, unittest will raise an `AssertionError` stating that `'SHOEZ'` != `'SHOES'`:

```
$ python -m unittest
F
======================================================================
FAIL: test_transform_name_for_sku (test_product.ProductTestCase)
----------------------------------------------------------------------
Traceback (most recent call last):
  File "/Users/dhillard/test/test_product.py", line 11, in
➥ test_transform_name_for_sku
```

```
        self.assertEqual(expected_value, actual_value)
AssertionError: 'SHOEZ' != 'SHOES'
- SHOEZ
?     ^
+ SHOES
?     ^


----------------------------------------------------------------------
Ran 1 test in 0.001s

FAILED (failures=1)
```

Confident that the test is keeping an eye over your code, you can change it back to the appropriate value and move on to another test.

5.4.4 *Writing your first integration test with unittest*

Now that you've seen what units are and how they can be tested, it's time to look at how the integration of multiple units can be tested. Unit tests are meant to examine the behavior of small pieces of software in isolation, so without integration tests it's difficult to say if these small pieces work together to produce something useful as a whole (see figure 5.5).

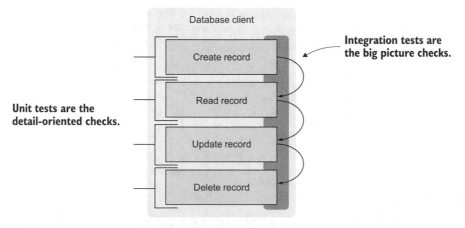

Figure 5.5   Unit tests and integration tests

Now that you can manage products in your inventory with a SKU system, people should be able to start buying them. A new `ShoppingCart` class with the ability to add and remove products would be a good first step. The cart stores products as a dictionary that looks like this:

```
{
    'SHOES-S-BLACK': {          ◁────┐  The keys are the product SKUs.
        'quantity': 2,  ◁──────┐
        ...                     └── A nested dictionary of metadata
                                    about the cart item, like quantity
```

```
    },
    'SHOES-M-BLUE': {
        'quantity': 1,
        ...
    },
}
```

The `ShoppingCart` class contains methods to add and remove a product by managing the data in this dictionary.

```
from collections import defaultdict


class ShoppingCart:
    def __init__(self):
        self.products = defaultdict(lambda: defaultdict(int))

    def add_product(self, product, quantity=1):
        self.products[product.generate_sku()]['quantity'] += quantity

    def remove_product(self, product, quantity=1):
        sku = product.generate_sku()
        self.products[sku]['quantity'] -= quantity
        if self.products[sku]['quantity'] == 0:
            del self.products[sku]
```

Using defaultdict simplifies the logic for checking if a product is already in the cart dictionary.

Adds quantity of a product to the cart

Removes quantity of a product from the cart

The `ShoppingCart` behavior now presents a couple of integration points that should be tested:

- The cart relies on (*integrates with*) the `Product` instance's `generate_sku` method.
- Adding and removing products must work in tandem; a product that's been added must also be able to be removed.

Testing these integrations will look a lot like unit testing; the difference is in how much of your software is executed during the test. Where a unit test generally only executes the code in one method and asserts that the output is as expected, an integration test may run many methods and make assertions about a few things along the way.

In the case of `ShoppingCart`, a useful test would be to initialize the cart, add a product, remove it, and make sure the cart is empty, as shown in the following listing.

Listing 5.2 An integration test for a `ShoppingCart` class

```
import unittest

from cart import ShoppingCart
from product import Product


class ShoppingCartTestCase(unittest.TestCase):
    def test_add_and_remove_product(self):
        cart = ShoppingCart()
```

The test setup is comparable to the earlier unit test.

Creates a cart to add products to

```
          product = Product('shoes', 'S', 'blue')      ◁——— Creates some small blue shoes

          cart.add_product(product)                     ◁——— Adds shoes to the cart
Removes ┌─▷ cart.remove_product(product)
shoes from │
the cart  │   self.assertDictEqual({}, cart.products)   ◁——— The cart should be empty!
```

This test calls the cart's __init__ method, the product's generate_sku method, and the cart's add_product and remove_product methods. There's a lot going on. As you might expect, integration tests are often quite a bit longer as a result.

5.4.5   *Test doubles*

You'll often have to write tests for code that interacts with another system, whether it's a database or an API call. These calls might do destructive things to real data, so calling them for real when you run your tests might have bad consequences. They may also be slow, with the effect being magnified if your test suite executes that area of code multiple times. These other systems may not even be under your control. It often makes sense to imitate them instead of using the real thing.

There are several subtly different ways to imitate these systems with *test doubles*:

- *Faking*—Using a system that behaves a lot like the real one, but avoids expensive or destructive actions
- *Stubbing*—Using a predetermined value as a response instead of getting one from a live system
- *Mocking*—Using a system with the same interface as the real one, but that also records interactions for later inspection and assertions

Faking and stubbing in Python involve writing up your own imitations as functions or classes and telling your code to use them during test execution. Mocking, on the other hand, is most commonly done using the unittest.mock module.

Suppose your code calls an API endpoint to get some tax information for your product sales. You don't want to really use this endpoint in your test because you've seen it take a few seconds to respond. On top of that, it returns dynamic data, so you can't be sure what value you should make assertions about in the test. If the code looks like this:

```
from urllib.request import urlopen


def add_sales_tax(original_amount, country, region):
    sales_tax_rate =
⮑ urlopen(f'https://tax-api.com/{country}/{region}').read().decode()
    return original_amount * float(sales_tax_rate)
```

a unit test with mocking could look like this:

```
import io
import unittest
from unittest import mock

from tax import add_sales_tax


class SalesTaxTestCase(unittest.TestCase):
    @mock.patch('tax.urlopen')
    def test_get_sales_tax_returns_proper_value_from_api(
            self,
            mock_urlopen
    ):
        test_tax_rate = 1.06
        mock_urlopen.return_value = io.BytesIO(
            str(test_tax_rate).encode('utf-8')
        )

        self.assertEqual(
            5 * test_tax_rate,
            add_sales_tax(5, 'USA', 'MI')
        )
```

The mock.patch decorator mocks the object or method specified.

The test function receives the mocked object or method.

The mocked urlopen call will now return the mocked response with the expected test tax rate.

Asserts that the add_sales_tax method calculates the new value from the tax rate returned by the API

Testing in this way allows you to declare, "The code I control behaves in this way given these assumptions," where the assumptions are created using test doubles. If you have fair confidence that the requests library works as it says it does, you can use test doubles to avoid coupling yourself to it. If you need to use a different HTTP client library in the future, or need to change which API you get your tax information from, the test will not have to change.

It's possible to overuse test doubles. I'm most certainly guilty of this from time to time. Usually you'll want to use test doubles to avoid the slow, expensive, or destructive behaviors mentioned before, but sometimes it's tempting to mock your own code to perfectly isolate the unit you're trying to test. This can lead to *brittle* tests that break often when you change your code, in part because they mirror the structure of the implementation too closely. Change the implementation, and you have to change your tests.

Try to write tests that verify what you need but are flexible regarding changes in the underlying implementation. This is loose coupling, once again. Loose coupling applies to test code as much as implementation code.

5.4.6 *Try it out*

How would you test the other methods in the `Product` and `ShoppingCart` classes? Keeping in mind the recipe for functional tests, try adding additional tests for the remaining methods. A thorough test suite will contain assertions for each method and for each different outcome you might expect from the method. You might even find a subtle bug! As a hint, try testing what happens when you remove more things from the cart than it contains.

Some of the values you need to test are dictionaries. Unittest has a special method, assertDictEqual, that provides useful output specific to dictionaries when the test fails.

For short tests like the one you wrote already, you can skip saving the expected and actual values as variables. Enter the expressions directly as arguments to assertEqual:

```
def test_transform_name_for_sku(self):
    small_black_shoes = Product('shoes', 'S', 'black')
    self.assertEqual(
        'SHOES',
        small_black_shoes.transform_name_for_sku(),
    )
```

When you've given it a try, come back and check the following listing to see how you did. Remember to use the unittest test runner after writing or changing a test to see if the test continues to pass.

Listing 5.3   A test suite for Product and ShoppingCart

```
class ProductTestCase(unittest.TestCase):
    def test_transform_name_for_sku(self):
        small_black_shoes = Product('shoes', 'S', 'black')
        self.assertEqual(
            'SHOES',
            small_black_shoes.transform_name_for_sku(),
        )

    def test_transform_color_for_sku(self):
        small_black_shoes = Product('shoes', 'S', 'black')
        self.assertEqual(
            'BLACK',
            small_black_shoes.transform_color_for_sku(),
        )

    def test_generate_sku(self):
        small_black_shoes = Product('shoes', 'S', 'black')
        self.assertEqual(
            'SHOES-S-BLACK',
            small_black_shoes.generate_sku(),
        )


class ShoppingCartTestCase(unittest.TestCase):
    def test_cart_initially_empty(self):
        cart = ShoppingCart()
        self.assertDictEqual({}, cart.products)

    def test_add_product(self):
        cart = ShoppingCart()
        product = Product('shoes', 'S', 'blue')

        cart.add_product(product)
```

```
        self.assertDictEqual({'SHOES-S-BLUE': {'quantity': 1}},
➥ cart.products)

    def test_add_two_of_a_product(self):
        cart = ShoppingCart()
        product = Product('shoes', 'S', 'blue')

        cart.add_product(product, quantity=2)

        self.assertDictEqual({'SHOES-S-BLUE': {'quantity': 2}},
➥ cart.products)

    def test_add_two_different_products(self):
        cart - ShoppingCart()
        product_one = Product('shoes', 'S', 'blue')
        product_two = Product('shirt', 'M', 'gray')

        cart.add_product(product_one)
        cart.add_product(product_two)

        self.assertDictEqual(
            {
                'SHOES-S-BLUE': {'quantity': 1},
                'SHIRT-M-GRAY': {'quantity': 1}
            },
            cart.products
        )

    def test_add_and_remove_product(self):
        cart = ShoppingCart()
        product = Product('shoes', 'S', 'blue')

        cart.add_product(product)
        cart.remove_product(product)

        self.assertDictEqual({}, cart.products)

    def test_remove_too_many_products(self):
        cart = ShoppingCart()
        product = Product('shoes', 'S', 'blue')

        cart.add_product(product)
        cart.remove_product(product, quantity=2)

        self.assertDictEqual({}, cart.products)
```

You can fix the bug in the shopping cart by updating `remove_product` to delete a product from the cart if its quantity is *less than or equal* to 0:

```
if self.products[sku]['quantity'] <= 0:
        del self.products[sku]
```

5.4.7   *Writing interesting tests*

Good tests will use inputs that affect the behavior of the method being tested. SKUs are typically all uppercase, and they usually don't contain spaces either—only letters, numbers, and dashes. But what if the product name contains a space? You'll want to remove the spaces before the name gets put in the SKU. A tank top SKU should start with `'TANKTOP'`, for example.

This is a new requirement, so you can write a new test that describes how the code should behave.

```
def test_transform_name_for_sku(self):
    medium_pink_tank_top = Product('tank top', 'M', 'pink')
    self.assertEqual(
        'TANKTOP',
        medium_pink_tank_top.transform_name_for_sku(),
    )
```

This test fails because the current code returns `'TANK TOP'`. That's okay because you haven't built support for products with spaces in the name yet. Seeing this test fail for the expected reason means that when you write the code to correctly handle spaces, the test should pass.

Thinking of interesting tests like this yourself is valuable because it can surface questions like this earlier in the development process. Then you can survey other stakeholders and ask, "What are all the possible product name formats we might need to support?" If their answer gives you new information, you can incorporate it into the code and the tests to deliver better software.

Now that you understand the benefits of unittest, it's time to learn about pytest.

5.5   *Testing with pytest*

Although unittest is a full-featured and mature framework built into Python, it has a few drawbacks. For some, it feels "un-Pythonic" because it uses `camelCase` instead of `snake_case` for method names (a relic of its JUnit history). Unittest also requires a fair amount of boilerplate that makes the underlying tests a bit more difficult to comprehend.

> **Pythonic code**
>
> Code is often said to be *Pythonic* if it uses the features and common style guidelines for the Python language. Pythonic code uses `snake_case` for variable and method names, list comprehensions instead of simple `for` loops, and so on.

For those who like succinct, straight-to-the-point tests, pytest is an answer (https://docs.pytest.org/en/latest/getting-started.html). Once you've installed pytest, you can get back to the raw `assert` statements you saw earlier. Pytest performs a bit of hidden magic under the hood to make this work, but it produces a smooth experience.

Pytest produces more readable output by default, telling you about the system, the number of tests it finds, the result of individual tests, and a summary of the overall test results:

Information about the system
```
$ pytest
========== test session starts ==========
platform darwin -- Python 3.7.3, pytest-5.0.1, py-1.8.0,
     pluggy-0.12.0
rootdir: /path/to/ecommerce/project          The number of tests
collected 15 items                           pytest discovered

test_cart.py ............    [ 80%]          The status of each test
test_product.py ..          [ 93%]           from each module, with an
test_tax.py .               [100%]           overall progress indicator

======= 15 passed in 0.12 seconds =======    A summary of the full
                                             test suite results
```

5.5.1   *Test organization with pytest*

Pytest does automatic discovery of your tests like unittest does. It will even discover any unittest tests you have lying around. One key difference is that proper pytest test classes are named `Test*` and don't need to inherit from a base class (like `unittest.TestCase`) to work.

The command for running tests with pytest is simpler:

```
pytest
```

Because pytest doesn't require you to inherit from a base class or use any special methods, you don't strictly need to organize your tests into classes. I still recommend it, though, because it remains a good organizational tool. Pytest will include the test class name in failure output and the like, which can help you understand where the tests live and what they're about. On the whole, pytest tests can be organized similarly to those for unittest.

5.5.2   *Converting unittest tests to pytest*

Because pytest will discover your existing unittest tests, you can incrementally convert your tests to pytest as you wish (and *if* you wish, I suppose). For the test suite you've written so far, the conversion looks like this:

- Remove the unittest import from test_product.py.
- Rename the `ProductTestCase` class to `TestProduct` and remove the inheritance from `unittest.TestCase`.
- Replace any `self.assertEqual(expected, actual)` with `assert actual == expected`.

The test case from earlier looks more like the following under pytest.

Listing 5.4   A test case in pytest

```
class TestProduct:                              ◁——— No need to inherit from any base class
    def test_transform_name_for_sku(self):
        small_black_shoes = Product('shoes', 'S', 'black')
        assert small_black_shoes.transform_name_for_sku() == 'SHOES'    ◁——┐
                                                                          │
    def test_transform_color_for_sku(self):                               │
        small_black_shoes = Product('shoes', 'S', 'black')                │
        assert small_black_shoes.transform_color_for_sku() == 'BLACK'     │
                                                                          │
    def test_generate_sku(self):                                          │
        small_black_shoes = Product('shoes', 'S', 'black')                │
        assert small_black_shoes.generate_sku() == 'SHOES-S-BLACK'        │
```

**self.assertEqual goes away; uses
raw assert statements instead**

As you can see, pytest leads to shorter and arguably more readable test code. It also provides its own framework of features that make setting up the environment and dependencies for your tests easier. For a great in-depth look at all pytest has to offer, I highly recommend Brian Okken's book, *Python Testing with pytest: Simple, Rapid, Effective, and Scalable* (Pragmatic Bookshelf, 2017).

You now have some unit and integration testing under your belt; read on to learn briefly about non-functional testing.

5.6   *Beyond functional testing*

You spent the majority of this chapter learning about functional tests. Making code work and making it right both come before making it fast, so functional testing precedes testing the speed of your code. Once you've made sure the code is working, making sure it's performant is a good next step.

5.6.1   *Performance testing*

Performance testing tells you how the changes you make affect things like memory, CPU, and disk usage. In chapter 4, you learned about some of the tools available for performance testing the *units* of your code. You used the timeit module, and that's what I use to see what my options are for specific lines of code and functions. These aren't measurements you'll usually do in an automated way; they're meant for ad hoc comparison of two approaches, and they're quick to write when you're trying to see which of two implementations is faster.

As you develop larger applications with a number of critical operations that need to remain efficient, it may behoove you to integrate some automated performance testing into your process. Automated performance testing looks quite like regression testing in practice; if you deploy a change and notice that the application begins consuming 20% more memory, it's a good sign that you should investigate the change. It's also great for celebrating the moments when you fix a slow piece of code and can watch your app speed up.

Unlike unit testing, which produces binary pass/fail results, performance testing is more qualitative. If you see your application trending slower over time (or a sudden jump after a deployment), that's something to look into. The nature of this kind of testing makes it a bit more difficult to automate and monitor, but solutions are out there.

5.6.2 Load testing

Load testing is a type of performance testing, but it gives you information about how far you can push your application until it falls over. Maybe it consumes too much CPU, memory, or network bandwidth, or it gets too slow for users to use it reliably. Whatever the case, load testing provides metrics you can use to fine-tune the resources you give your application. In more substantial cases, it may motivate you to change the design of part of the system so it's more efficient.

Load testing entails more infrastructure and strategy than something like unit testing. To get a clear picture of performance under load, you need to mimic your production environment closely in both architecture and user behavior. Due to the complexity of application-level load testing, in my mind it sits somewhere above integration testing in the testing pyramid (figure 5.6).

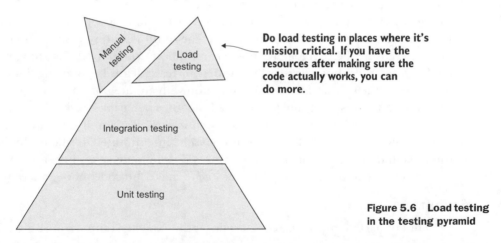

Figure 5.6 Load testing in the testing pyramid

Load testing helps you performance-test your applications in scenarios that more closely mimic real-world user behavior.

5.7 Test-driven development: A primer

A whole school of thought exists around *driving* development using unit and integration testing in software. The general name for these practices is *test-driven development* (TDD). TDD can help you commit to testing up front, so you reap the benefits of testing that we've discussed so far.

5.7.1   *It's a mindset*

For me, the real benefit of TDD is the mindset it puts me in. The stereotype of a quality assurance engineer is that they can always find something in your code to break. This is generally said with some disdain, but I think it's remarkable. Enumerating all the ways a system can blow up is both useful and impressive.

Netflix takes this to an extreme with the idea of chaos engineering. They actively think about the ways systems can fail, but they also introduce some amount of unpredictable failure.[2] This leads to innovative ways of responding to failure.

As you write tests, try to be a chaos engineer. Deliberately try to think of the extremes that your code can endure, and throw them at it. There's a limit, of course—it doesn't make sense for all code to respond predictably to all inputs. But in Python, the exception system allows your code to respond in a predictable way to rare or unexpected situations.

5.7.2   *It's a philosophy*

TDD has a subculture around it, and the only opinions stronger than how to do it correctly are how *not* to do it correctly. It's an art form that produces as many styles and critics as any other movement. I've found it useful to learn how different teams handle the testing aspects of their process; once you do this, you can identify the pieces you like and incorporate them into your own work.

Some TDD literature advocates making sure every line of your code is covered by tests. Although it's good to have strong coverage of the different cases your code can handle, increasing the coverage beyond a certain point can have diminishing returns. Sometimes covering those last few lines with your tests means introducing tighter coupling between the tests and the implementation with an integration test.

If you find that testing some aspect of a function's behavior is awkward or difficult, try to determine if it's because the code's concerns aren't well separated or if it's inherently awkward to test. If awkwardness *must* be incorporated, it's better for it to be in the tests than the real code. Don't refactor code *only* to make testing easier or coverage stronger—do it to make testing easier *and* to make the code more coherent.

Summary

- Functional tests make sure code produces the expected output from a given input.
- Testing saves you time in the long run by catching bugs and making refactoring code easier.
- Manual testing isn't scalable and should be used to supplement automated testing.
- Unittest and pytest are two popular unit and integration testing frameworks for Python.
- Test-driven development puts the tests first, guiding you to a working implementation based on the requirements.

---

[2]To learn more about Netflix's advances in the area of chaos engineering, check out their collection of blog posts on the subject: https://medium.com/netflix-techblog/tagged/chaos-engineering.

Part 3

Nailing down large systems

In part 2, you learned the concepts that form a large part of software design, and in part 3, you'll start to apply them. By building an application from scratch, you'll see how software design concepts can be applied at various points in the development life cycle.

Although designing software that works—and works quickly—may be part of your goal, another part of the goal must be software that you and other developers can understand and maintain. This part of the book will show you that design is an iterative process with some wiggle room; there isn't always a right or wrong answer, and there's rarely a point at which you're "done." You'll learn how to identify pain points in your code so that you can use what you've learned to minimize effort and maximize understanding.

Separation
of concerns in practice

This chapter covers

- Developing an application with separate high-level concerns
- Using specific types of encapsulation to loosen the coupling of different concerns
- Creating a well-separated foundation to enable future extension

In chapter 2, I showed you some of the best practices around separation of concerns in Python. *Separating concerns* means creating boundaries between code that deals with distinct activities to make the code more understandable. You learned how functions, classes, modules, and packages are useful in decomposing code into pieces that are easier to reason about. Although chapter 2 covered several of the tools available for separating concerns, it's helpful to get some experience applying them.

As is true for many, I learn best by doing. As I work through a real project, I often discover connections I didn't see before or find new questions to explore. In this chapter, you'll work through a real application that exhibits a good use case for separating concerns. You'll improve upon it in the chapters to come, and you'll end up with something you can extend for your own personal use.

> **NOTE** This and future chapters make light use of structured query language (SQL), a domain-specific language for manipulating and retrieving data from databases. If you haven't used SQL before, or need a refresher, you might want to run through a tutorial before continuing. Ben Brumm's *SQL in Motion* course (www.manning.com/livevideo/sql-in-motion) is a good primer.

6.1   *A command-line bookmarking application*

In this chapter, you'll develop an application for saving and organizing bookmarks (more specifics on that in a minute).

I'm not a great notetaker. Throughout school and my career, I've struggled to find a way of writing things down for myself that helps me learn and retain information. When I find a great resource that goes through a concept in a novel way or with insightful examples, I've struck gold, but I usually need to dedicate time to read and practice the information in that resource. As a result, I've amassed a great number of bookmarks over the last few years. Maybe I'll have the time to read through them someday!

The default bookmark feature in most browsers is lacking. Although things can be nested in folders and given a title, it's often pretty difficult to recall why you saved something in the first place. A bunch of my bookmarks are code-related articles about testing, performance, new programming languages, and the like. When I find an interesting repository on GitHub, I also use GitHub's "star" feature to save it for later. But GitHub stars are limited too; at the time of writing, they're one big flat list that you can filter only by programming language. Whatever bookmark implementations you might use, they're mostly built on the same foundational principles.

Bookmarks are an example of a small *CRUD* workflow: create, read, update, and delete (figure 6.1). These four operations make up a lot of data-driven tools in the world. You can *create* a bookmark to save for later, and then *read* its information to get the URL. You may want to *update* a bookmark's title if the one you gave it originally was confusing, and you usually *delete* them when you're done with them. This is a pretty good place to start your application.

Because a long description is one of the features missing from some existing bookmark tools, your application will include that off the bat. You'll add a few more features in the following chapters, and do so in a way that will enable you to keep adding features you want.

Figure 6.1   CRUD operations are the basis of many applications that manage user data.

6.2   A tour of Bark

You're going to develop Bark, a command-line bookmarking application. Bark allows you to create bookmarks that, for now, will be made up of a few pieces of information:

- *ID*—A unique, numerical identifier for each bookmark
- *Title*—A short text title for the bookmark, like "GitHub"
- *URL*—A link to the article or website being saved
- *Notes*—An optional, long description or explanation about the bookmark
- *Date added*—A timestamp so you can see how old the bookmark is (in a bid to stave off that pesky procrastination)

Bark will also let you list all bookmarks that have been added and then delete a specific bookmark by its ID. This is all managed through a *command-line interface* (CLI)—an application you interact with in your terminal. On startup, Bark's CLI will present you with a menu of options. Each option, when selected, will trigger an action that will read or modify a database.

> **NOTE**   You won't develop a feature to cover the *update* portion of CRUD for bookmarking in this chapter; you'll get to that in chapter 7.

6.2.1   The benefits of separation: Reprise

Even though the CRUD-like operations Bark supports are fairly common for this kind of application, there's a sizable amount of stuff happening. For an application this big, it's important to remember what benefits separation of concerns will offer:

- *Reduced duplication*—If each piece of your software does one thing, it will be easier to see when two of them do the same thing. You can analyze similar pieces of code to see if it makes sense to combine them into a single source of truth for that behavior.
- *Improved maintainability*—Code is read much more often than it's written. Code that can be understood incrementally because each piece has a clear responsibility allows developers to jump into areas of interest, understand what they need, and jump back out.
- *Ease of generalization and extension*—Code with one responsibility can be generalized to cover that responsibility for a number of use cases, or it can be broken up further to support more varied behavior. Code that does numerous things will have a hard time supporting such flexibility because it's hard to see where changes may have an effect.

Keep these ideas in mind as you work through the exercise in this chapter. My goal is for you to come out of this chapter with something you can continue developing and adding features to. To do this, you'll first think about and then implement a high-level architecture that will support that outcome.

6.3   *An initial code structure, by concern*

I try to start developing applications like Bark with a concise explanation of how it does what it does. This tends to lead me toward an initial architecture.

For example, how does Bark work? What is its concise description? Perhaps the following statement comprises the answers to these questions: *Using a command-line interface, a user chooses options for adding, removing, and listing bookmarks stored in a database.*

Now let's break that down a bit:

- *Command-line interface*—This is a way to present options to a user and understand which options they choose.
- *Choosing options*—Once an option is chosen, some action or business logic happens as a result.
- *Stored in a database*—Data needs to be persisted for later use.

These points represent the high-level layers of abstraction for Bark. The CLI is the *presentation* layer of the application. The database is the *persistence* layer. The actions and *business logic* are kind of like the glue that connects the presentation and persistence layers. Each is a fairly separate concern, as shown in figure 6.2. This kind of *multitier architecture*, where each layer (tier) of an application has freedom to evolve, is used by many organizations. Teams can assemble around each tier based on areas of expertise, and each layer can potentially be reused with other applications if desired.

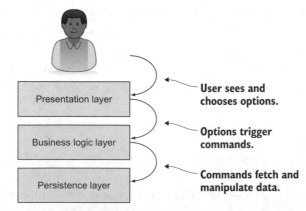

User sees and chooses options.

Options trigger commands.

Commands fetch and manipulate data.

Figure 6.2   A multitier architecture is frequently used in web and desktop applications.

You'll develop each of these layers of Bark as you work through the chapter. Because each is a separate concern, it makes sense to think of them as separate Python modules:

- A database module
- A commands module
- A bark module, which contains the code that actually *runs* the Bark application

We'll start from the persistence layer and work our way up.

> ### Application architecture patterns
>
> Separating applications into layers of presentation, persistence, and actions or rules is a common pattern. Some variations on this approach are so common, they've been given names. *Model-view-controller* (MVC) is a way of *modeling* data for persistence, providing users with a *view* into that data, and allowing them to *control* changes to that data with some set of actions. *Model-view-viewmodel* (MVVM) puts an emphasis on allowing the view and data model to communicate freely. These and other *multitier architectures* are great examples of separation of concerns.

6.3.1   The persistence layer

The persistence layer is the lowest level of Bark (figure 6.3). This layer will be concerned with taking information it receives and communicating it to the database.

You'll be using SQLite, a portable database that stores data in a single file by default (www.sqlite.org/index.html). This is convenient, compared to more complex database systems, because you can start from scratch by deleting the file if something goes wrong.

> **NOTE** Despite being one of the most widely used databases, SQLite is installed on only some operating systems by default. I recommend downloading a precompiled binary for your operating system from the official download page (https://sqlite .org/download.html).

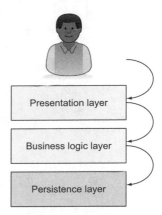

Figure 6.3   The persistence layer deals with data storage—it's the lowest level of the application.

Starting in the database module, you'll create a `Database-Manager` class for manipulating data in the database. Python provides a built-in sqlite3 module, which you can use to get a connection to the database, make queries, and iterate over results. SQLite databases are usually a single file with a .db extension; if you make a sqlite3 connection to a file that doesn't exist, the module will create it for you.

The database module provides most of what you need to manage bookmark data, including the following:

- Creating a table (for initializing the database)
- Adding or deleting a record
- Listing the records in a table
- Selecting and sorting records from a table based on some criteria
- Counting the number of records in a table

How can these tasks be broken down further? Each seems somewhat separate, from the business logic perspective described earlier, but what about at the persistence layer? Most of the activities described can be achieved by constructing an appropriate

SQL statement and executing it. Executing it requires a connection to the database, which requires the path to the database file.

Whereas managing the persistence is a high-level concern, these individual concerns are what you get when you peel open the persistence layer. They should each be separate as well. First things first, though—you need a connection to the database.

Working with databases

Many smart people have produced wonderful and robust packages that make working with databases in Python easier. SQLAlchemy (www.sqlalchemy.org) is a widely used tool for not only interacting with databases, but abstracting data models via an *object-relational mapping* (ORM). An ORM allows you to treat database records as objects in languages like Python, without worrying much about the details of a database at all. The Django web framework also provides an ORM for writing data models.

In the spirit of learning by doing, you'll write the database interaction code yourself in this chapter. It's limited to the scope of Bark, but it can be added to or replaced if you'd like to do more with the rest of the application. If you need to use a database in future projects, consider whether you want to write your database code from scratch or use one of these third-party packages instead.

CREATING AND CLOSING THE DATABASE CONNECTION

While Bark is running, it needs only one connection to the database—it can reuse this connection for all its operations. To make this connection, you can use `sqlite3` `.connect`, which accepts the path of the database file to which it should connect. Again, if the file does not exist, it will be created.

The `__init__` for `DatabaseManager` should

1 Accept an argument containing the path to the database file (Don't hardcode it; separate your concerns!)

2 Use the database file path to create a SQLite connection using `sqlite3` `.connect(path)` and store it as an instance attribute

It's good practice to close the connection to the SQLite database when the program finishes, to limit the possibility of data corruption. For symmetry, the `__del__` for `DatabaseManager` should close the connection with the connection's `.close()` method.

This will serve as the foundation for executing statements.

```python
import sqlite3


class DatabaseManager:
    def __init__(self, database_filename):
        self.connection = sqlite3.connect(database_filename)    ⊲─┐ Creates and stores
                                                                    a connection to the
                                                                    database for later
                                                                    use
    def __del__(self):
        self.connection.close()    ⊲─┐ Cleans up the connection
                                       when done, to be safe
```

EXECUTING STATEMENTS

Your `DatabaseManager` will need a way to execute statements. These statements have a couple of things in common, so encapsulating those aspects into a reusable method will reduce the likelihood of errors from rewriting the same code each time you want to execute a new kind of statement.

Some SQL statements return data; these statements are called *queries*. Sqlite3 manages query results with a concept called a *cursor*. Using a cursor to execute a statement lets you iterate over the results it returns. Statements that aren't queries (`INSERT`, `DELETE`, and so on) don't return any results, but the cursor manages this by returning an empty list.

Write an `_execute` method on `DatabaseManager` that you can use to execute all statements using a cursor, returning a result that you can choose to use where you need to. The `_execute` method should

1 Accept a statement as a string argument
2 Get a cursor from the database connection
3 Execute a statement using the cursor (more on this shortly)
4 Return the cursor, which has stored the result of the executed statement (if any)

Creates the cursor

Uses the cursor to execute the SQL statement

```
def _execute(self, statement):
    cursor = self.connection.cursor()
    cursor.execute(statement)
    return cursor
```

Returns the cursor, which has stored the results

Statements that aren't queries usually manipulate data, and if anything bad happens while they're executing, the data could become corrupted. Databases guard against this with a feature called a *transaction*. If a statement executing within a transaction fails or is otherwise interrupted, the database will roll back to its last known working state. Sqlite3 lets you use the connection object to create a transaction via a *context manager*, a Python block using the `with` keyword that provides some special behavior when the code enters and exits the block.

Update `_execute` to put the `cursor` creation, execution, and return inside a transaction, like the following:

```
def _execute(self, statement):
    with self.connection:
        cursor = self.connection.cursor()
        cursor.execute(statement)
        return cursor
```

This creates a database transaction context.

This happens within the database transaction.

Using `.execute` inside a transaction will get you where you need to go, functionally speaking. But it's a good security practice to use placeholders for real values in SQL statements to prevent users from doing malicious things with specially crafted queries.[1] Update _execute to accept two things:

- A SQL statement as a string, possibly containing placeholders
- A list of values to fill in the placeholders in the statement

The method should then execute the statement by passing both arguments to the cursor's execute, which accepts the same arguments. It should look something like the following snippet:

```
def _execute(self, statement, values=None):    ◄───  values is optional; some statements
        with self.connection:                         don't have placeholders to fill in.
            cursor = self.connection.cursor()
            cursor.execute(statement, values or [])  ◄───  Executes the statement,
            return cursor                                    providing any passed-in
                                                             values to the placeholders
```

Now you have a database connection and the ability to execute arbitrary statements on that connection. Remember that the connection is managed for you automatically when you create a DatabaseManager instance, so you don't need to think about how it's opened and closed, unless you want to change it. Now, statement execution is managed within the _execute method, so you also don't need to think about *how* a statement is executed; you only need to tell it *what* statement to execute. This is the power of separating your concerns.

Now that you've got these building blocks, it's time to develop some database interactions.

CREATING TABLES

One of the first things you'll need is a database table in which to store your bookmark data. You'll have to *create* this table using a SQL statement. Because the concerns of connecting to the database and executing statements are now abstracted, the work of creating a table includes the following:

1. Determine the column names for the table.
2. Determine the data type of each column.
3. Construct the right SQL statement to create a table with those columns.

Remember that each bookmark has an ID, title, URL, optional notes, and the date it was added. The data type and constraints for each column follow:

- *ID*—The ID is the *primary key* of the table, or the main identifier of each record. It should automatically increment each time a new record is added, using the AUTOINCREMENT keyword. This column is an INTEGER type; the rest are TEXT.
- *Title*—The title is required because it's hard to skim your existing bookmarks if they're only URLs. You can tell SQLite the column can't be empty by using the NOT NULL keyword.

---

[1] See the Wikipedia article on SQL injection: https://en.wikipedia.org/wiki/SQL_injection.

- *URL*—The URL is required, so it gets NOT NULL as well.
- *Notes*—Notes for a bookmark are optional, so only the TEXT specifier is necessary.
- *Date*—The date the bookmark was added is required, so it gets NOT NULL.

A table creation statement in SQLite uses the CREATE TABLE keywords, followed by the table name, the list of columns, and their data type information in parentheses. Because you'll want Bark to create the table on startup if it doesn't already exist, you can use CREATE TABLE IF NOT EXISTS.

Based on the previous descriptions of the bookmark columns, what would the SQL statement look like for creating a bookmarks table? See if you can write it out, then come back to check your work against the following listing.

Listing 6.1   The creation statement for a bookmarks table

```
CREATE TABLE IF NOT EXISTS bookmarks
(
    id INTEGER PRIMARY KEY AUTOINCREMENT,
    title TEXT NOT NULL,
    url TEXT NOT NULL,
    notes TEXT,
    date_added TEXT NOT NULL
);
```

The main ID of each record, which increments automatically as records are added

NOT NULL requires a column to be populated with a value.

You can now write your method for creating tables. Each column is identified by a name, like title, that maps to a data type and constraints, like TEXT NOT NULL, so a dictionary seems like an appropriate Python type for representing columns. The method needs to

1 Accept two arguments: the name of the table to create, and a dictionary of column names mapped to their data types and constraints
2 Construct a CREATE TABLE SQL statement like the one shown earlier
3 Execute the statement using DatabaseManager._execute

Try writing the create_table method now, and then check back to see how it compares to the following listing.

Listing 6.2   Creating a SQLite table

```
def create_table(self, table_name, columns):
    columns_with_types = [
        f'{column_name} {data_type}'
        for column_name, data_type in columns.items()
    ]
    self._execute(
        f'''
        CREATE TABLE IF NOT EXISTS {table_name}
        ({', '.join(columns_with_types)}),
        '''
    )
```

Constructs the column definitions, with their data types and constraints

Constructs the full create table statement and executes it

A note on generalization

Right now, you need only the `bookmarks` table for Bark. I've already argued in this book that early optimization is a no-no, and the same is true for generalization. So why make a general-use `create_table` method?

When I start building a method with hardcoded values, I check to see if it's much work to parameterize those values with arguments to the method. For example, replacing the string `'bookmarks'` with a `table_name` string argument isn't much work. The columns and their data types follow similarly. Using this approach, the `create_table` method can be made general enough to create most any table you'll need.

You'll use this method later on to create a `bookmarks` table, which is what Bark will interact with to manage bookmarks as you develop the application.

ADDING RECORDS

Now that you can create a table, you need to be able to add bookmark records to it. This is the "C" in CRUD (figure 6.4).

SQLite expects the `INSERT INTO` keyword, followed by the table name, to indicate the intent to add a new record to the table. This is followed by the list of columns you're supplying values for in parentheses, the `VALUES` keyword, and then the values you're supplying in parentheses. A record insert statement in SQLite looks like this:

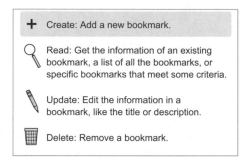

Figure 6.4   Creation is the most basic operation necessary for CRUD, so it's the crux of many systems.

```
INSERT INTO bookmarks
(title, url, notes, date_added)
VALUES ('GitHub', 'https://github.com',
➡ 'A place to store repositories of code', '2019-02-01T18:46:32.125467');
```

Remember that it's a good practice to use placeholders instead, as in the _execute method earlier. What parts of the preceding query should use placeholders?

1   `bookmarks`
2   `title`, `url`, and so on
3   `'GitHub'`, `'https://github.com'`, and so on
4   All of the above

Only places where literal values go can use placeholders in statements, so 3 is the correct answer. An `INSERT` statement for the `bookmarks` table, with placeholders, looks like this:

```
INSERT INTO bookmarks
(title, url, notes, date_added)
VALUES (?, ?, ?, ?);
```

To construct this statement, you'll need to write an add method in DatabaseManager that

1 Accepts two arguments: the name of the table, and a dictionary that maps column names to column values
2 Constructs a placeholder string (a ? for each column specified)
3 Constructs the string of the column names
4 Gets the column values as a tuple (A dictionary's .values() returns a dict_values object, which happens not to work with sqlite3's execute method.)
5 Executes the statement with _execute, passing the SQL statement with placeholders and the column values as separate arguments

Write the add method now, and check back with the following listing to see how it compares.

> Listing 6.3 Adding a record to a SQLite table

```
def add(self, table_name, data):
        placeholders = ', '.join('?' * len(data))
        column_names = ', '.join(data.keys())        ◁——  The keys of the data are
        column_values = tuple(data.values())    ◁            the names of the columns.

        self._execute(
            f'''
            INSERT INTO {table_name}
            ({column_names})
            VALUES ({placeholders});
            ''',
            column_values,          ◁——
        )
```

The keys of the data are the names of the columns.

.values() returns a dict_values object, but execute needs a list or tuple.

Passes the optional values argument to _execute

USING CLAUSES TO LIMIT ACTION SCOPE

To insert records into a database, all you need is the info to be inserted, but some database statements are used in tandem with one or more additional *clauses*. Clauses affect which records the statement will operate on. Using a DELETE statement without a clause, for example, could end up deleting all the records in the table. You don't want that.

WHERE clauses can be appended to several kinds of statements to limit the statement's effect to records matching that criteria. You can combine multiple WHERE criteria using AND or OR. In Bark, for example, each bookmark record has an ID, so you can limit a statement to acting on a particular record by its ID with a clause like WHERE id = 3.

This kind of limiting is useful both for queries (to search for specific records) and for regular statements. Clauses will be useful when you need to delete specific records.

DELETING RECORDS

After a bookmark has outlived its usefulness, you need a way to delete it (figure 6.5). To delete a bookmark, you can issue a DELETE statement to the database, using a WHERE clause to specify a bookmark by its ID.

In SQLite, the statement to delete the bookmark with an ID of 3 looks like this:

```
DELETE FROM bookmarks
WHERE ID = 3;
```

As in the create_table and add methods, you can represent the criteria as a dictionary that maps column names to the values you want to match. Write a delete method that

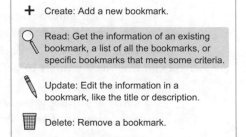

+ Create: Add a new bookmark.

Read: Get the information of an existing bookmark, a list of all the bookmarks, or specific bookmarks that meet some criteria.

Update: Edit the information in a bookmark, like the title or description.

Delete: Remove a bookmark.

Figure 6.5   Delete is the counterpart of create, so most systems cover this operation as well.

1 Accepts two arguments: the table name to delete records from, and a dictionary mapping column names to the value to match on. The criteria should be a required argument, because you don't want to delete all your records.
2 Constructs a string of placeholders for the WHERE clause.
3 Constructs the full DELETE FROM query and executes it with _execute.

Check your results against the following listing.

Listing 6.4   Deleting records in SQLite

```
def delete(self, table_name, criteria):
        placeholders = [f'{column} = ?' for column in criteria.keys()]
        delete_criteria = ' AND '.join(placeholders)
        self._execute(
            f'''
            DELETE FROM {table_name}
            WHERE {delete_criteria};
            ''',
            tuple(criteria.values()),
        )
```

The criteria argument isn't optional here; all records would be deleted without any criteria.

Uses the values argument of _execute as the values to match against

SELECTING AND SORTING RECORDS

You can add and remove records from a table now, but how can you retrieve them? Aside from creating and deleting information, you'll want to be able to read what you've already stored (figure 6.6).

You can create a query statement in SQLite using SELECT * FROM bookmarks (the * means "all columns") and some criteria:

```
SELECT * FROM bookmarks
WHERE ID = 3;
```

+ Create: Add a new bookmark.

Read: Get the information of an existing bookmark, a list of all the bookmarks, or specific bookmarks that meet some criteria.

Update: Edit the information in a bookmark, like the title or description.

Delete: Remove a bookmark.

Figure 6.6   Reading existing data is usually a necessary part of a CRUD application.

Additionally, you can sort these results by a specific column using an ORDER BY clause:

```
SELECT * FROM bookmarks
WHERE ID = 3
ORDER BY title;
```

This orders the results by the title column in ascending order.

Again, you should use placeholders where there are literal values in the query:

```
SELECT * FROM bookmarks
WHERE ID = ?
ORDER BY title;
```

Your select method will look somewhat similar to the delete method, except that criteria can be optional. (It will fetch all records by default.) It should also accept an optional order_by argument that specifies a column to sort the results by (the default is the primary key of the table). Using delete as a guide, write select now and come back to compare with the following listing when you're done.

Listing 6.5 A method for selecting SQL table data

```
def select(self, table_name, criteria=None, order_by=None):
    criteria = criteria or {}

    query = f'SELECT * FROM {table_name}'

    if criteria:
        placeholders = [f'{column} = ?' for column in criteria.keys()]
        select_criteria = ' AND '.join(placeholders)
        query += f' WHERE {select_criteria}'

    if order_by:
        query += f' ORDER BY {order_by}'

    return self._execute(
        query,
        tuple(criteria.values()),
    )
```

Criteria can be empty by default, because selecting all records in the table is all right.

Constructs the WHERE clause to limit the results

Constructs the ORDER BY clause to sort the results

This time, you want the return value from _execute to iterate over the results.

You've now created a database connection; written an _execute method for executing arbitrary SQL statements with placeholders in a transaction; and written methods to add, query, and delete records. This is about all you'll need for manipulating a SQLite database for the moment. You just finished a database manager in fewer than 100 lines of code. Nice work.

Next, you'll develop the business logic that interacts with the persistence layer.

6.3.2 The business logic layer

Now that the persistence layer for Bark is in place, you can work on the layer that figures out what to put in and get out of the persistence layer (figure 6.7).

When a user interacts with something in the presentation layer of Bark, Bark needs to trigger something to happen in the business logic and ultimately in the persistence layer. It might be tempting to do something like the following:

```
if user_input == 'add bookmark':
    # add bookmark
elif user_input == 'delete bookmark #4':
    # delete bookmark
```

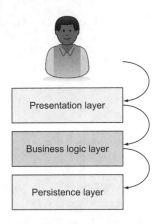

But this would couple the text presented to the user with the actions that need to be triggered. You would have new conditions for each menu option, and if you wanted multiple options to trigger the same command, or you wanted to change the text, you would have to refactor some code. It would be nice if the presentation layer were the only place that knows about the menu option text displayed to the user.

Figure 6.7   The business logic layer determines when and how data is read from or written to the persistence layer.

Each action is kind of like a *command* that needs to be *executed* in response to a user's menu choice. By encapsulating the logic of each action as a command object, and providing a consistent way to trigger them via an execute method, these actions can be decoupled from the presentation layer. The presentation layer can then point menu options to commands without worrying about how those commands work. This is called the *command pattern*.[2]

You'll develop each of the CRUD actions and some peripheral functionality as commands in the business logic layer.

CREATING THE BOOKMARKS TABLE

Now that you're working in the business logic layer, create a new "commands" module to house all the commands you're going to write. Because most of the commands will need to make use of the DatabaseManager, import it from the database module and create an instance of it (called db) to be used throughout the commands module. Remember that its __init__ method requires the file path to a SQLite database; I suggest calling it bookmarks.db. Leaving out any leading path will create the database file in the same directory as the Bark code.

Because you'll need to initialize the bookmarks database table if it doesn't already exist, start by writing a CreateBookmarksTableCommand class whose execute method creates the table for your bookmarks. You can make use of the db.create_table method you wrote earlier to create your bookmarks table. Later in the chapter, you'll trigger this command to run when Bark starts up. Check your work against the following listing.

---

[2]See Wikipedia's "Command pattern" article for more on this pattern: https://en.wikipedia.org/wiki/Command _pattern.

Listing 6.6   A command for creating a table

```
db = DatabaseManager('bookmarks.db')
```
◁ — **Remember, sqlite3 will automatically create this database file if it doesn't exist.**

```
class CreateBookmarksTableCommand:
    def execute(self):
        db.create_table('bookmarks', {
            'id': 'integer primary key autoincrement',
            'title': 'text not null',
            'url': 'text not null',
            'notes': 'text',
            'date_added': 'text not null',
        })
```

This will eventually be called when Bark starts up. (pointing to `def execute(self):`)

Creates the bookmarks table with the necessary columns and constraints (pointing to `db.create_table`)

Notice that the command is only aware of its duties (calling persistence layer logic) and the interface of its dependency (`DatabaseManager.create_table`). This is loose coupling, thanks in part to separating the persistence logic and (eventually) the presentation logic. You should be seeing the benefits of separation of concerns more and more clearly as you work through these exercises.

ADDING BOOKMARKS

To add a bookmark, you'll need to pass data received from the presentation layer on to the persistence layer. The data will be passed as a dictionary mapping column names to values. This is a great example of code relying on a shared interface rather than the specifics of an implementation. If the persistence layer and the business logic layer agree on a data format, they can each do what they need to, as long as the data format stays consistent.

Write an `AddBookmarkCommand` class that will perform this operation. This class will

1 Expect a dictionary containing the title, URL, and (optional) notes information for a bookmark.

2 Add the current datetime to the dictionary as `date_added`. To get the current time in UTC, in a standardized format with wide compatibility, use `datetime.datetime.utcnow().isoformat()`.[3]

3 Insert the data into the bookmarks table using the `DatabaseManager.add` method.

4 Return a success message that will eventually be displayed by the presentation layer.

Check your work against the following listing.

Listing 6.7   A command for adding a bookmark

```
from datetime import datetime

...
```

---

[3]See Wikipedia's article on "ISO 8601" for more information on this time format: https://en.wikipedia.org/wiki/ISO_8601.

```
class AddBookmarkCommand:
    def execute(self, data):
        data['date_added'] = datetime.utcnow().isoformat()
        db.add('bookmarks', data)
        return 'Bookmark added!'
```

Adds the current datetime as the record is added

Using the DatabaseManager.add method makes short work of adding a record.

You'll use this message in the presentation layer later.

You've now written all the business logic needed for creating bookmarks. Next, you'll want to be able to list the bookmarks you've added.

LISTING BOOKMARKS

Bark needs to be able to show you the bookmarks you've saved—without that, Bark wouldn't be of much use. You're going to write a `ListBookmarksCommand` that will provide the logic for displaying the bookmarks in the database.

You'll want to make use of the `DatabaseManager.select` method to get the bookmarks from the database. By default, SQLite sorts records by their order of creation (that is, by the primary key of the table), but it might also be useful to sort bookmarks by date or title. In Bark, bookmarks' IDs and dates sort identically because they both strictly increase as you add bookmarks, but it's good practice to sort explicitly by the column of interest in case that changes.

`ListBookmarksCommand` should do the following:

- Accept the column to order by, and save it as an instance attribute. You can set the default value to `date_added` if you like.
- Pass this information along to `db.select` in its `execute` method.
- Return the result (using the cursor's `.fetchall()` method) because `select` is a query.

Write the command to list bookmarks, and come back to check your work against the following listing.

Listing 6.8   A command to list existing bookmarks

```
class ListBookmarksCommand:
    def __init__(self, order_by='date_added'):
        self.order_by = order_by

    def execute(self):
        return db.select('bookmarks', order_by=self.order_by).fetchall()
```

db.select returns a cursor you can iterate over to get the records.

You can create a version of this command for sorting by date or by title.

Now you've got enough functionality to add bookmarks and view existing ones. The last step for managing bookmarks is a command for deleting them.

DELETING BOOKMARKS

Similar to adding a new bookmark, the deletion of a bookmark requires some data to be passed from the presentation layer. This time, though, the data is simply an integer value representing the ID of the bookmark to delete.

Write a `DeleteBookmarkCommand` command that accepts this information in its `execute` method and passes it to the `DatabaseManager.delete` method. Remember that `delete` accepts a dictionary mapping column names to values to match against; here, you'll want to match the given value in the `id` column. Once the record is deleted, return a success message for use in the presentation layer.

Come back and check your work against the following listing.

Listing 6.9   A command to delete bookmarks

```
class DeleteBookmarkCommand
:
    def execute(self, data):
        db.delete('bookmarks', {'id': data})
        return 'Bookmark deleted!'
```

> delete accepts a dictionary of column name, match value pairs.

QUITTING BARK

There's one piece of polish left: a command for exiting Bark. A user could use the usual Ctrl-C method of stopping the Python program, but an option to exit is a little nicer.

Python provides the `sys.exit` function for stopping program execution. Write a `QuitCommand` whose `execute` method exits the program using this approach, then come back and check your work against the following listing.

Listing 6.10   A command to exit the program

```
import sys

...

class QuitCommand
:
    def execute(self):
        sys.exit()
```

> This should immediately exit Bark.

Now you can wipe the sweat from your brow . . . not because you're done, but because you'll be developing the presentation layer next.

6.3.3   *The presentation layer*

Bark uses a command-line interface (CLI). Its presentation layer (the part the user sees, as shown in figure 6.8) is text in a terminal. Depending on the application, a CLI can run until the completion of a specific task, or it can keep running until the user explicitly exits. Because you wrote `QuitCommand`, you might guess that you'll be doing the latter.

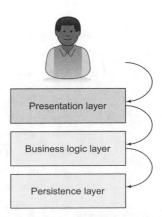

Figure 6.8   The presentation layer shows users what actions can be taken and a way to trigger them.

The presentation layer of Bark contains an infinite loop:

1   Clears the screen
2   Prints the menu options
3   Gets the user's choice
4   Clears the screen and executes the command corresponding to the user's choice
5   Waits for the user to review the result, pressing Enter when they're done

Now that you're working on the presentation layer, you'll need to create a new bark module. It's a good practice to put code for command-line applications into an `if` *name* `== '`*main*`'` : block; this will make sure you don't unintentionally execute the code in the module by importing the bark module somewhere. If you start with a Hello, World! type of program, you can do a quick check to make sure things are set up properly.

Start with the following in your bark module:

```
if __name__ == '__main__':
    print('Welcome to Bark!')
```

Try running `python bark.py` in your terminal; you should see `Welcome to Bark!` as a result. Now you can start hooking up the presentation layer to some business logic.

DATABASE INITIALIZATION

Remember that Bark needs to initialize the database, creating the bookmarks table if it doesn't already exist. Import the commands module and update your code to execute the `CreateBookmarksTableCommand`, as shown in the following snippet. After making this update and running `python bark.py`, you won't see any text output, but you should see that a bookmarks.db file is created.

```
import commands


if __name__ == '__main__':
    commands.CreateBookmarksTableCommand().execute()
```

It may seem small, but you've just accomplished something pretty remarkable. This represents a full pass through all the layers of your *multitier architecture*. The presentation layer (the act of running bark.py, so far) has triggered a command in the business logic, which, in turn, set up a table in the persistence layer fit for storing bookmarks. Each layer knows just enough about its surroundings to do its job; things are well separated and loosely coupled. You'll experience this a few more times as you start adding menu options to Bark that trigger more commands.

MENU OPTIONS

When you start Bark, it should present you with a menu of options that looks something like this:

```
(A)  Add a bookmark
(B)  List bookmarks by date
(T)  List bookmarks by title
(D)  Delete a bookmark
(Q)  Quit
```

Each option has a keyboard shortcut and a descriptive title. If you look carefully, each of these options corresponds to one of the commands you wrote earlier. Because you wrote the commands using the command pattern, each command can be triggered the same way as the others—using its execute method. Commands differ only in what setup and input they require, and then from the presentation layer's perspective they do whatever they do.

Based on what you've learned about encapsulation, how would you go about hooking up the items in the presentation layer to the business logic they control?

1 Use conditional logic to call the right Command class's execute method based on the user input.
2 Make a class that pairs the text to be displayed to the user and the command it triggers.

I recommend choice 2. To hook each menu option up to the command it should trigger, you can create an Option class. The class's __init__ method can accept the name to display to the user in the menu, an instance of the command to execute when chosen by the user, and an optional preparation step (to get additional input from the user, for example). All of these can be stored as instance attributes.

When chosen, an Option instance needs to

1 Run the specified preparation step, if any.
2 Pass the return value from the preparation step, if any, to the specified command's execute method.
3 Print the result of the execution. These are the success messages or bookmark results returned from the business logic.

An Option instance should be represented as its text description when shown to the user; you can use __str__ to override the default behavior. Abstracting this work from the rest of the code that gets and validates user input allows you to keep your concerns separate.

Try writing the Option class, then check the following listing to see how you've done.

Listing 6.11 Connecting menu text to business logic commands

An instance of the command to execute / **The name displayed in the menu**

```
class Option:
    def __init__(self, name, command, prep_call=None):
        self.name = name
        self.command = command
        self.prep_call = prep_call
```

The optional preparation step to call before executing the command

choose will be called when the option is chosen by the user.

```
    def choose(self):
        data = self.prep_call() if self.prep_call else None
        message = self.command.execute(data) if data
    else self.command.execute()
        print(message)

    def __str__(self):
        return self.name
```

Calls the preparation step if specified

Executes the command, passing in the data from the preparation, if any

Represents the option as its name instead of the default Python behavior

With the `Option` class in place, now is a good time to start hooking up more of the business logic you created earlier. Remember that you need to do a few things with each option:

1 Print the keyboard key for the user to enter to choose the option.
2 Print the option text.
3 Check if the user's input matches an option and, if so, choose it.

What Python data structure would work well to hold all your options?

1 `list`
2 `set`
3 `dict`

Each keyboard key maps to a menu option, and you need to check the user's input against the available options, so you need to keep those pairings stored somehow. Choice 3 is a good one because a `dict` can provide keyboard key and option pairs that you can also iterate over, with the dictionary's `.items()` method, for printing the option text. I also recommend using `collections.OrderedDict` specifically, to ensure that your menu options will always be printed in the order you specify.

Add your options dictionary after `CreateBookmarksTableCommand` now, adding an item for each menu option. Once the dictionary is in place, create a `print_options` function that iterates over the options and prints them in the format you saw earlier:

```
(A) Add a bookmark
(B) List bookmarks by date
(T) List bookmarks by title
(D) Delete a bookmark
(Q) Quit
```

Check your work with the following listing.

Listing 6.12   Specifying and printing menu options

```
def print_options(options):
    for shortcut, option in options.items():
        print(f'({shortcut}) {option}')
    print()
```

```
...

if __name__ == '__main__':
    ...

    options = {
        'A': Option('Add a bookmark', commands.AddBookmarkCommand()),
        'B': Option('List bookmarks by date',
    commands.ListBookmarksCommand()),
        'T': Option('List bookmarks by title',
    commands.ListBookmarksCommand(order_by='title')),
        'D': Option('Delete a bookmark', commands.DeleteBookmarkCommand()),
        'Q': Option('Quit', commands.QuitCommand()),
    }
    print_options(options)
```

After you've added the menu options, running Bark should print all of the options you added. You can't yet trigger them; for that, you'll need to get some user input.

USER INPUT

With our overall goal of threading presentation to business logic to persistence, what remains to be added is a bit of interactivity with Bark users. The approach for getting the user's desired option goes like this:

1 Prompt the user to enter a choice, using Python's built-in input function.
2 If the user's choice matches one of those listed, call that option's choose method.
3 Otherwise, repeat.

What approach might you use in Python to get this repeating behavior?

1 A while loop
2 A for loop
3 A recursive function call

Because there isn't a definitive end state for getting the user's input (they might enter an invalid choice four billion times), a while loop (option 1) makes the most sense. *While* the user's choice is invalid, keep prompting them. You can take it easy on them by accepting the upper- and lowercase versions of each option if you like.

Write a get_option_choice function, and use it after printing the options to get the user's choice. Then call that option's choose method. Try it out, then compare your work with the following listing.

Listing 6.13   Getting a user's choice of menu option

```
def option_choice_is_valid(choice, options):
    return choice in options or choice.upper() in options

def get_option_choice(options):
```

The choice is valid if the letter matches one of the keys in the options dictionary.

Gets an initial choice from the user

```
choice = input('Choose an option: ')
while not option_choice_is_valid(choice, options):
    print('Invalid choice')
    choice = input('Choose an option: ')
return options[choice.upper()]

if __name__ == '__main__':
    ...

    chosen_option = get_option_choice(options)
    chosen_option.choose()
```

While the user's choice is invalid, keep prompting them.

Returns the matching option once they've made a valid choice

At this point, you can run Bark, and some of the commands, like listing bookmarks and quitting, will respond to your input. But a couple of options require some additional preparation, as I alluded to earlier. You need to supply a title, description, and so on to add a bookmark, and you need to specify the ID of a bookmark to delete it. Much like you got user input for the menu option to choose, you'll need to prompt the user for this bookmark data.

Here's another opportunity to encapsulate some behavior. For each piece of information you need, you should

1 Prompt the user with a label—"Title" or "Description", for example
2 If the information is required and the user presses Enter without entering any info, keep prompting them

Write three functions—one to provide the repeating prompt behavior, and two that use it to get information for adding or deleting a bookmark. Then add each information-fetching function as the prep_call to the appropriate Option instance. Check your results against the following listing to see how you did, or if you get stuck.

Listing 6.14   Gathering bookmark information from the user

```
def get_user_input(label, required=True):
    value = input(f'{label}: ') or None
    while required and not value:
        value = input(f'{label}: ') or None
    return value

def get_new_bookmark_data():
    return {
        'title': get_user_input('Title'),
        'url': get_user_input('URL'),
        'notes': get_user_input('Notes', required=False),
    }

def get_bookmark_id_for_deletion():
    return get_user_input('Enter a bookmark ID to delete')

if __name__ == '__main__':
```

A general function for prompting users for input

Gets initial user input

Continues prompting while the input is empty, if required

Function to get the necessary data for adding a new bookmark

The notes for a bookmark are optional, so don't keep prompting.

Gets the necessary information for deleting a bookmark

```
    ...
    'A': Option('Add a bookmark', commands.AddBookmarkCommand(),
➥ prep_call=get_new_bookmark_data),
    ...
    'D': Option('Delete a bookmark', commands.DeleteBookmarkCommand(),
➥ prep_call=get_bookmark_id_for_deletion),
```

If all is well, you should now be able to run Bark and add, list, or delete bookmarks! Congratulations on a job well done.

> ### Nerding out
>
> We just covered a heck of a lot of stuff, but I want to point out something I find exciting. Because of the way you've built Bark, if you want to add new functionality, there's a clear roadmap:
>
> 1 Add any new database manipulation methods you may need to database.py.
> 2 Add a command class that performs the business logic you need in commands.py.
> 3 Hook up the new command to a new menu option in bark.py.
>
> How cool is that? Separating concerns allows you to clearly see which areas of code you need to augment when adding new functionality.

Before finishing up this chapter, there are a couple of remaining pieces of polish to attend to.

CLEARING THE SCREEN

Clearing the screen just before printing the menu or executing a command will make it easier to see the current context the user is in. To clear the screen, you can defer to your operating system's command-line program for clearing the terminal text. The command for clearing the screen is clear on many operating systems, but it's cls on Windows. You can figure out if you're on Windows by checking os.name—on Windows this is 'nt'. (Windows NT is to Windows 10 as macOS is to Mojave.)

Write a clear_screen function that makes the appropriate call using os.system, as in the following code:

```
import os


def clear_screen():
    clear = 'cls' if os.name == 'nt' else 'clear'
    os.system(clear)
```

Call this just before calling print_options, and just before calling the .choose() method of the user's selected option:

```
if __name__ == '__main__':
    ...

    clear_screen()
    print_options(options)
    chosen_option = get_option_choice(options)
    clear_screen()
    chosen_option.choose()
```

This will be most helpful when the menu and command results get printed over and over again, which is the final piece of this puzzle.

APPLICATION LOOP

The last step is to run Bark in a loop so that users can perform several actions in a row. To do this, create a loop method and move everything but the database initialization from the if __name__ == '__main__' block into it. Back in the if __name__ == '__main__' block, call loop inside a while True: block. At the end of loop, add a line to pause and wait for the user to press Enter before proceeding.

```
                              ┌─ Everything that happens for
                              │  each menu > option > result
                              │  loop goes here.
                                                    ┌─ Prompts the user to press
def loop():                                         │  Enter and reviews the
    # All the steps for showing/selecting options   │  result before proceeding
    ...                                              │  (_ means "unused value")
    _ = input('Press ENTER to return to menu') ◄────┘

if __name__ == '__main__':
    commands.CreateBookmarksTableCommand().execute()

    while True:     ◄──── Loops forever (until the user chooses the
        loop()            option corresponding to QuitCommand)
```

Now Bark will give the user a way to return to the menu after each interaction, and the menu gives them an option to exit. This covers all the bases. What do you think? I think it's about time to start using Bark.

Summary

- Separation of concerns is a tool for achieving more readable, maintainable code.
- End-user applications are often separated into persistence, business logic, and presentation layers.
- Separation of concerns works closely with encapsulation, abstraction, and loose coupling.
- Applying effective separation of concerns allows you to add, change, and delete functionality without affecting the surrounding code.

Extensibility and flexibility

This chapter covers

- Using inversion of control to make code flexible
- Using interfaces to make code extensible
- Adding new features to your existing code

At many established organizations, your day-to-day work as a developer involves not only writing new applications, but updating existing ones. When you're tasked with adding a new feature to an existing application, your goal is to *extend* the functionality of that application, introducing new behavior by adding code.

Some applications are *flexible* to this kind of change and can adapt to shifting requirements. Others may fight you tooth and nail. In this chapter, you'll learn strategies for writing software that's flexible and extensible by adding an "Import GitHub stars" feature to Bark.

7.1 What is extensible code?

Code is said to be *extensible* if adding new behaviors to it has little or no impact on existing behaviors. Said another way, software is extensible if you can add new behavior without changing existing code.

127

Think about a web browser like Google Chrome or Mozilla Firefox. You've probably installed something in one of these browsers to block advertisements or to easily save the article you're reading to a notes tool like Evernote. Firefox calls these installable pieces of software *add-ons*, whereas Chrome calls them *extensions*, and both are examples of a *plugin system*. Plugin systems are implementations of extensibility. Chrome and Firefox weren't built with ad blockers or Evernote in mind *specifically*, but they were designed to allow for such extensions to be built.

Massive projects like web browsers succeed when they can cater to the needs of hundreds of thousands of users. It would be a massive feat to predict all those needs in advance, so an extensible system allows for solutions to those needs to be built after the product is brought to market. You won't always need to be so forward-looking, but drawing on some of the same concepts will help you build better software.

As with many facets of software development, extensibility is a spectrum and something you'll iterate on. By practicing concepts like separation of concerns and loose coupling, you can improve your code's extensibility over time. As the extensibility of your code improves, you'll find that adding new features becomes faster because you can focus almost entirely on that new behavior without worrying about how it will affect the features around it. This also means you'll have an easier time maintaining and testing your code, because features are more isolated and therefore less likely to introduce tricky bugs because of intermingled behavior.

7.1.1   Adding new behaviors

In the last chapter, you wrote the beginnings of the Bark application. You used a multitier architecture to separate the concerns of persisting, manipulating, and displaying bookmark data. You then built a small set of features on top of those layers of abstraction to make something useful. What happens when you're ready to add new functionality?

In an ideal extensible system, adding new behavior involves adding new classes, methods, functions, or data that encapsulate the new behavior without changing existing code (figure 7.1).

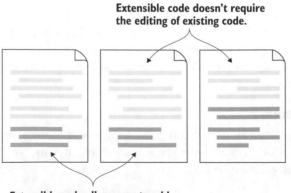

Extensible code doesn't require the editing of existing code.

Extensible code allows you to add a new feature by adding new code.

Figure 7.1   Adding new behavior to extensible code

Code that isn't extensible requires many edits throughout the code to add a new feature.

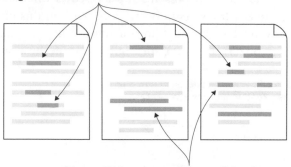

Often, additions are made to conditional expressions or by adding new `else` cases, making the code harder to understand over time.

Figure 7.2   Adding new behavior to code that isn't extensible

Compare this with a less extensible system, where new functionality may require adding conditional statements to a function here, a method there, and so on (figure 7.2). That breadth of changes and their granularity is sometimes referred to as *shotgun surgery*, because adding a feature requires peppering changes throughout your code like the pellets from a shotgun round.[1] This often points to a mixing of concerns or an opportunity to abstract or encapsulate in a different way. Code that requires these kinds of changes is not extensible; creating new behavior is not a straightforward endeavor. You need to go searching through the code for exactly the right lines to update.

Toward the end of the last chapter, I noted that adding a new feature to Bark is a relatively simple matter:

- Adding new data persistence logic in the database module, if needed
- Adding new business logic to the command module for the underlying functionality
- Adding a new option in the bark module to handle user interaction

TIP   Duplicating some code and updating that new copy to do what you need is a perfectly valid approach to extension. I use this approach occasionally on my way to making the original code more extensible. By creating a duplicate version, altering it, and seeing how the two versions differ, I can more easily refactor that duplicated code back into a single, multipurpose version later. If you try to deduplicate code without a thorough understanding of all the ways it's being used, you risk assuming too much and making your code inflexible to future changes. So remember, duplication is better than the wrong abstraction.

---

[1]Read more about shotgun surgery and other code smells in "An Investigation of Bad Smells in Object-Oriented Design," *Third International Conference on Information Technology: New Generations* (2006), https://ieeexplore.ieee .org/document/1611587.

If Bark is close to ideal in doing the three activities, you should only need to add code, without affecting code that's already present. You'll discover whether this is the case when you start writing the GitHub stars importer a bit later in this chapter. But because real systems are rarely ideal, you'll still find yourself needing to make changes to existing code regularly (figure 7.3). How does flexibility apply in these situations?

You'll still have to edit existing code every now and then; software is a continuous, iterative process.

Shoot for extending your code as often as is feasible given your time constraints.

Figure 7.3   How extensibility looks in practice

7.1.2   *Modifying existing behaviors*

There are a number of reasons you might need to change code you or someone else has already written. You might need to change the code's behavior, such as when you're fixing a bug or addressing a change in requirements. You might need to refactor to make the code easier to work with, keeping the behavior consistent. In these cases, you aren't necessarily looking to *extend* the code with new behavior, but the *flexibility* of the code still plays a big role.

Flexibility is a measure of code's resistance to change. Ideal flexibility means that any piece of your code can be easily swapped out for another implementation. Code that requires shotgun surgery in order to change is *rigid*; it fights against changes by making you work hard. Kent Beck wittily said, "For each desired change, make the change easy (warning: this may be hard), then make the easy change."[2] Breaking down the code's resistance first—through practices like decomposition, encapsulation, and so on—paves the way to enabling you to make the specific change you originally intended.

In my own work, I make little, continuous refactorings in the area of code I'm working in. For example, the code you work in may contain a complicated set of if/else statements, as in listing 7.1. If you need to change a behavior in this set of conditionals, it's likely you'll need to read most of it to understand where the change

---

[2]Kent Beck on Twitter (September 25, 2012), https://twitter.com/kentbeck/status/250733358307500032.

should be made. And if the change you want to make applies to the body of each conditional, you'll need to apply the change many times over.

Listing 7.1   A rigid mapping of conditions to outcomes

```
if choice == 'A':
    print('A is for apples')
elif choice == 'B':
    print('B is for bats')
...
```

This conditional needs to be updated properly for each choice.

The concerns of mapping an option to a message and printing the message are mixed.

How could this be improved?

1 Extract information from the conditional checks and bodies into a `dict`.
2 Use a `for` loop to check against each available choice.

Because each choice maps to a specific outcome, extracting the mapping of behaviors into a dictionary (option 1) would be the right approach. By mapping the letter for the choice to the word that goes in the message, a new version of the code can retrieve the right word from the mapping regardless of the choice picked. You no longer need to keep adding `elif` statements to a conditional and defining the behavior for the new case. You can instead add a single new mapping from the chosen letter to the word you'll use in the message, printing only at the end, as in listing 7.2. The mapping of choices to messages acts like *configuration*—information a program uses to determine how to execute. Configuration is often easier to understand than conditional logic.

Listing 7.2   A more flexible way to map conditions to outcomes

```
choices = {
    'A': 'apples',
    'B': 'bats',
    ...
}
print(f'{choice} is for {choices[choice]}')
```

Extracting the mapping of choices to messages makes adding a new option simpler.

The outcome is centralized, and printing behavior is separated somewhat.

This version of the code is more readable. Whereas the example in listing 7.1 required you to understand the conditions and what each condition does, the version here is more clearly structured as a set of choices and a line that prints information about a specific choice. Adding more choices and changing the message that gets printed is also easier, because they've been separated. This is all in the pursuit of loose coupling.

7.1.3   *Loose coupling*

Above all, extensibility arises from loosely coupled systems. Without loose coupling, most changes in a system will require the shotgun surgery variety of development. Suppose you'd written Bark without the layers of abstraction around the database and the business logic—something like the following listing. This version is difficult to read, in part because of its physical layout (note the deep nesting) and also because so much is happening in one glob of code.

Listing 7.3   A procedural approach to Bark

```
if __name__ == '__main__':
    options = [...]

    while True:
        for option in options:
            print(option)           ◁──  Deep nesting is a strong hint that
                                          concerns need further separation.
        choice = input('Choose an option: ')

        if choice == 'A':       ◁────  if/elif/else are difficult to reason about.
            ...
            sqlite3.connect(...).execute(...)    ◁──  Database behavior is repetitive
        elif choice == 'D':                           and mixed with user interaction.
            ...
            sqlite3.connect(...).execute(...)
```

This code would work, but consider trying to implement a change that affects how you connect to the database, or a change to the underlying database altogether. It would be a major pain. This code has many interdependent pieces all talking to each other, so adding new behavior would mean figuring out the right place to add another `elif`, writing some raw SQL, and so on. Because you would incur these costs each time you wanted to add new behavior, this system would not scale well.

Imagine the atoms in a solid piece of iron—they're tightly packed, firmly holding onto each other. That makes iron *rigid*, and it resists being bent or reshaped. But blacksmiths figured out how to overcome this by melting the iron, which loosens up the atoms so they can flow around each other freely. Even as it cools, the iron is *malleable*, or able to move and flex without breaking.

This is what you want from your code, as shown in figure 7.4. If each piece is only loosely coupled to any other piece, those pieces can move around more freely without breaking something unexpectedly. Letting the code get too tightly packed together, and permitting it to rely heavily on the code around it, will allow your code to settle into a solid form that's hard to reshape.

The loose coupling you've used writing Bark means that new database functionality can be added with new methods on the `DatabaseManager` class or with focused changes to an existing (centralized) method. New business logic can be encapsulated in new `Command` classes, and adding to the menu is a matter of creating a new option in the `options` dictionary in the bark module and hooking it up to a command. This sounds a bit like the browser plugin systems I described earlier. Bark doesn't expect to handle any *specific* new features, but they can be added with a known quantity of effort.

Loosely coupled pieces of code can move around and change their shape freely, just like the molecules in a liquid.

Tightly coupled pieces of code rely on the code around them. Changing one piece is difficult because the other pieces must move to accommodate it.

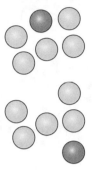

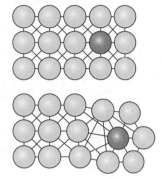

Figure 7.4 Flexibility contrasted with rigidity

This recap of loose coupling shows how what you've learned so far can help you design flexible code. Now I'll teach you a few new techniques for getting even deeper flexibility.

7.2 Solutions for rigidity

Rigidity in code is a lot like stiff joints. As software gets older, the code that gets used the least tends to be the most rigid, and it requires some care to loosen it up again. Specific kinds of rigid code require specific kinds of care, and you should regularly examine code for opportunities to keep it flexible through refactoring.

In the next few sections, you'll learn some specific ways to reduce rigidity.

7.2.1 Letting go: Inversion of control

You learned earlier that composition provides benefits over inheritance by allowing objects to reuse behaviors without confining them to a particular inheritance hierarchy. When you separate your concerns into many smaller classes and want to compose those behaviors back together, you can write a class that uses instances of those smaller classes. This is a common practice in object-oriented codebases.

Imagine you're working in a module that deals with bicycles and their parts. You open up the bicycle module and see the code in the following listing. As you read to understand what the code is doing, try to assess how well it follows practices like encapsulation and abstraction.

Listing 7.4 A composite class that depends on other, smaller classes

```
class Tire:
    def __repr__(self):
        return 'A rubber tire'
```

Small classes to be used for composition

```
class Frame:
    def __repr__(self):
        return 'An aluminum frame'


class Bicycle:                              ⟵┐ Bicycle creates the
    def __init__(self):                        parts it needs.
        self.front_tire = Tire()
        self.back_tire = Tire()
        self.frame = Frame()
                                            ⟵┐ A method to print all
    def print_specs(self):                     of the bicycle's parts
        print(f'Frame: {self.frame}')
        print(f'Front tire: {self.front_tire}, back tire: {self.back_tire}')
                                            ⟵┐ Creates the bicycle
if __name__ == '__main__':                     and prints its specs
    bike = Bicycle()
    bike.print_specs()
```

Running this code will print out the specs of your bicycle:

```
Frame: An aluminum frame
Front tire: A rubber tire, back tire: A rubber tire
```

This will certainly get you a bicycle. The encapsulation looks good; each part of the bicycle lives in its own class. The levels of abstraction make sense too; there's a `Bicycle` at the top level, and each of its parts is accessible a level down from that. So what's wrong? Can you see anything that might be difficult to do with this code structure?

1 Adding new parts to a bicycle
2 Upgrading parts of a bicycle

Adding new parts to a bicycle (option 1) turns out not to be very difficult. You can create an instance of a new part and store it on the `Bicycle` instance in the `__init__` method, the same as the others. Upgrading (changing) the parts of a `Bicycle` instance dynamically (option 2) turns out to be hard in this structure because the classes for those parts are hardcoded into the initialization.

You could say that the `Bicycle` *depends on* the `Tire`, `Frame`, and other parts it needs. Without them, the bicycle can't function. But if you want a `CarbonFiberFrame`, you have to crack open the `Bicycle` class's code to update it. Because of this, `Tire` is currently a *rigid* dependency of `Bicycle`.

Inversion of control says that instead of creating instances of dependencies in your class, you can pass in existing instances for the class to make use of (figure 7.5). The *control* of dependency creation is *inverted* by giving the control to whatever code is creating a `Bicycle`. This is powerful.

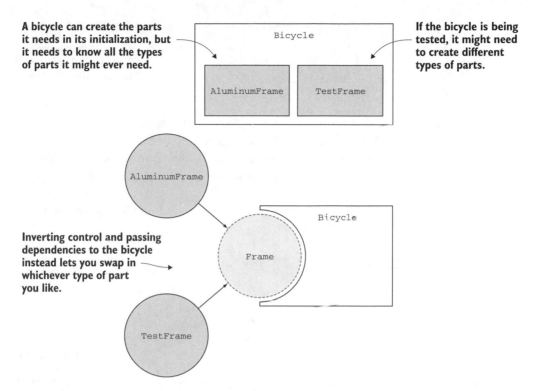

A bicycle can create the parts it needs in its initialization, but it needs to know all the types of parts it might ever need.

If the bicycle is being tested, it might need to create different types of parts.

Inverting control and passing dependencies to the bicycle instead lets you swap in whichever type of part you like.

Figure 7.5   Using inversion of control to gain flexibility

Try updating the `Bicycle.__init__` method to accept an argument for each of its dependencies, and pass them into the method. Come back to the following listing to see how you did.

Listing 7.5   Using inversion of control

```python
class Tire:
    def __repr__(self):
        return 'A rubber tire'


class Frame:
    def __repr__(self):
        return 'An aluminum frame'


class Bicycle:
    def __init__(self, front_tire, back_tire, frame):
        self.front_tire = front_tire
        self.back_tire = back_tire
        self.frame = frame

    def print_specs(self):
        print(f'Frame: {self.frame}')
```

The dependencies are passed into the class upon initialization.

```
        print(f'Front tire: {self.front_tire}, back tire: {self.back_tire}')

if __name__ == '__main__':
    bike = Bicycle(Tire(), Tire(), Frame())
    bike.print_specs()
```

> The code that creates a Bicycle supplies it with the appropriate instances.

This should give you the same result as before. It may seem like all you did was shift the issue around, but it has enabled a degree of freedom in your bicycles. Now you can create any fancy tire or frame you wish and use it in place of the basic versions. As long as your `FancyTire` has the same methods and attributes as any other tire, `Bicycle` won't care.

Try creating a new `CarbonFiberFrame` and upgrading your bicycle to use it. Come back to the following listing to see how you did.

Listing 7.6   Using a new kind of frame for a bike

```
class CarbonFiberFrame:
    def __repr__(self):
        return 'A carbon fiber frame'

...

if __name__ == '__main__':
    bike = Bicycle(Tire(), Tire(), CarbonFiberFrame())
    bike.print_specs()
```

> A carbon fiber frame can be used as easily as a regular frame.

> You should now see a carbon fiber frame in the printed specs.

This ability to swap out dependencies with minimal effort is valuable in testing your code; to truly isolate behavior in your classes, you will occasionally want to replace a real implementation of a dependency with a test double. Having a rigid dependency on `Tire` forces you to mock the `Tire` class for each of your `Bicycle` tests to achieve isolation. Inversion of control frees you from this constraint, letting you pass in a `MockTire` instance, for example. This way, you won't forget to mock something, because you must pass *some* kind of tire to the `Bicycle` instances you create.

Making testing easier is one of the big reasons to follow the principles you've learned in this book. If your code is hard to test, it may be hard to understand as well. If it's easy to test, it may be easy to understand. Neither is certain, but they're correlated.

7.2.2   *The devil's in the details: Relying on interfaces*

You saw that `Bicycle` *depends* on `Tire` and other parts, and much of your code will inevitably have dependencies like this. But another way rigidity manifests is when your high-level code relies too strongly on the details of lower-level dependencies. I mentioned that a `FancyTire` could be put on a bicycle *as long as* it has the same methods and attributes as any other tire. More formally, any object can be swapped in if it has a tire *interface*.

The `Bicycle` class doesn't have much knowledge about (or interest in) the details of a *specific* tire. It only cares that a tire has a particular set of information and behavior; otherwise, tires are free to do what they like.

This practice of sharing agreed-upon interfaces (in contrast with class-specific details) between high- and low-level code will give you the freedom to swap implementations in and out. Remember that in Python the presence of duck typing means that strict interfaces aren't required. You decide which methods and attributes comprise a particular interface. It's up to you as a developer to make sure your classes adhere to the interfaces their consumers expect.

In Bark, `Command` classes in the business logic provide an `execute` method as part of their interface. The presentation layer uses this interface when a user selects an option. The implementation of a particular command can change as much as it needs to, and no change is required in the presentation layer as long as the interface stays the same. You would only need to change the presentation layer if, for example, the `Command` classes' `execute` methods required an additional argument.

This gets back to cohesion as well. Code that is closely related will not need to rely on interfaces; it's close enough together that inserting an interface will feel forced. On the other hand, code that's already in different classes or modules has already been separated, so using shared interfaces instead of directly reaching into other classes is most likely the way to go.

7.2.3 *Fighting entropy: The robustness principle*

Entropy is the tendency for organization to dissolve into disorganization over time. Code often starts out small, neat, and understandable, but it tends toward complexity over time. One reason this happens is because code often grows to accommodate different kinds of inputs.

The *robustness principle*, also known as Postel's Law, states: "Be conservative in what you do, be liberal in what you accept from others." The spirit of this statement is that you should provide only the behavior necessary to achieve the desired outcome, while being open to imperfect or unexpected input. This isn't to say you should accept any input under the sun, but being flexible can ease development for consumers of your code. By mapping a possibly large range of inputs to a known, smaller range of outputs, you can direct the flow of information toward a more limited, expected range (figure 7.6).

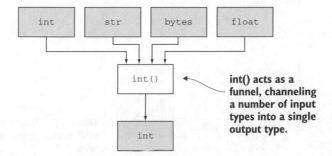

int() acts as a funnel, channeling a number of input types into a single output type.

Figure 7.6 Reducing entropy when mapping inputs to outputs

Consider the built-in `int()` function, which converts its input to an integer. This function works for inputs that are already integers:

```
>>> int(3)
3
```

It also works for strings:

```
>>> int('3')
3
```

And it even works for floating-point numbers, returning just the whole number part:

```
>>> int(6.5)
6
```

`int` accepts multiple data types and funnels them all to an integer return type, raising an exception only if it's truly unclear how to proceed:

```
>>> int('Dane')
ValueError: invalid literal for int() with base 10: 'Dane'
```

Spend some time understanding the range of inputs that consumers of your code might reasonably expect to supply, and then rein in that input so that you return only what the rest of your system expects. This will provide flexibility for those consumers at the entry points of the system, while keeping the number of situations the underlying code must handle manageable.

7.3 *An exercise in extension*

Now that you understand what goes into an extensible and flexible design, you can apply those concepts by adding functionality to Bark. Right now, Bark is a rather manual tool—you can add bookmarks, but it's a one-at-a-time thing, and users have to enter all the URLs and descriptions themselves. It's tedious work, especially if they already have a pile of bookmarks saved in a different tool.

You're going to build a GitHub stars importer for Bark (figure 7.7). This new import option in the presentation layer must do the following:

1 Prompt the Bark user for the GitHub username to import stars from.
2 Ask the user whether to preserve the timestamps of the original stars.
3 Trigger a corresponding command.

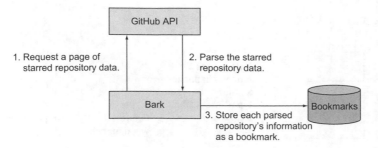

Figure 7.7 The flow for a GitHub stars importer for Bark

The command that gets triggered must use the GitHub API to fetch the star data.[3] I recommend installing and using the requests package (https://github.com/psf/requests).

The star data is paginated, so the process will look something like the following:

1 Get the initial page of star results. (The endpoint is https://api.github.com/users/{github_username}/starred.)
2 Parse the data from the response, using it to execute an `AddBookmarkCommand` for each starred repository.
3 Get the `Link: <...>; rel=next` header, if present.
4 Repeat for the next page if there is one; otherwise, stop.

NOTE To get the timestamps for GitHub stars, you have to pass an `Accept: application/vnd.github.v3.star+json` header in your API requests.

From the user's perspective, the interaction should look something like the following:

```
$ ./bark.py
(A) Add a bookmark
(B) List bookmarks by date
(T) List bookmarks by title
(D) Delete a bookmark
(G) Import GitHub stars
(Q) Quit

Choose an option: G
GitHub username: daneah
Preserve timestamps [Y/n]: Y
Imported 205 bookmarks from starred repos!
```

It turns out that Bark, as written, isn't *perfectly* extensible, particularly regarding bookmark timestamps. Currently, Bark forces the timestamp to be the time the bookmark is created (using `datetime.datetime.utcnow().isoformat()`), but you want the option to preserve the timestamps of GitHub stars. You can improve this by using inversion of control.

Try updating the `AddBookmarkCommand` to accept an optional timestamp, using its original behavior as the fallback. Check the following listing to see how you did.

Listing 7.7 Inverting control of the timestamp for a bookmark

```
class AddBookmarkCommand:                              Adds an optional timestamp
                                                       argument to execute
    def execute(self, data, timestamp=None):    ◁─┘
        data['date_added'] = timestamp or datetime.utcnow().isoformat()   ◁─┐
        db.add('bookmarks', data)
        return 'Bookmark added!'                   Uses the passed-in timestamp if provided,
                                                     using the current time as a fallback
```

---

[3]Learn about GitHub's starred repositories API at http://mng.bz/lony.

You've now improved the flexibility of AddBookmarkCommand, and it's extensible enough to handle what you need for the GitHub stars importer. You won't need any new functionality at the persistence layer, so you can focus on the presentation and business logic for this new feature. Give it a shot and come back to check your work against the following two listings.

Listing 7.8   A GitHub stars import command

```
class ImportGitHubStarsCommand:
    def _extract_bookmark_info(self, repo):        ⟵  Given a repository dictionary,
        return {                                       extract the needed pieces to
            'title': repo['name'],                     create a bookmark.
            'url': repo['html_url'],
            'notes': repo['description'],
        }

    def execute(self, data):
        bookmarks_imported = 0

        github_username = data['github_username']              The URL for the
        next_page_of_results =                                 first page of star
➥ f'https://api.github.com/users/{github_username}/starred'  ⟵  results

        while next_page_of_results:             Gets the next page of results,
            stars_response = requests.get(      using the right header to tell
                next_page_of_results,         ⟵  the API to return timestamps
                headers={'Accept': 'application/vnd.github.v3.star+json'},
            )
            next_page_of_results =
➥ stars_response.links.get('next', {}).get('url')  ⟵  The Link header with
                                                        rel=next contains the
            for repo_info in stars_response.json():     link to the next page,
                repo = repo_info['repo']                if available.

                if data['preserve_timestamps']:
                    timestamp = datetime.strptime(
                        repo_info['starred_at'],
                        '%Y-%m-%dT%H:%M:%SZ'      ⟵  Formats the timestamp
                    )                                in the same format that
                else:                                existing Bark bookmarks
                    timestamp = None                 use

                bookmarks_imported += 1
                AddBookmarkCommand().execute(      ⟵  Executes an
                    self._extract_bookmark_info(repo),  AddBookmarkCommand,
                    timestamp=timestamp,                populating with the
                )                                       repository data

        return f'Imported {bookmarks_imported} bookmarks from starred repos!'  ⟵
                                                    Returns a message indicating
                                                    how many stars were imported
```

Annotations: **Continues getting star results while more pages of results exist** (pointing to `while next_page_of_results:`). **The info about the starred repository** (pointing to `repo = repo_info['repo']`). **The timestamp when the star was created** (pointing to `repo_info['starred_at'],`).

Listing 7.9   A GitHub stars import option

```
...

def get_github_import_options():          ◁──┐   A function to get the GitHub
    return {                                      username to import stars from
        'github_username': get_user_input('GitHub username'),
        'preserve_timestamps':            ◁──┐
            get_user_input(                       Whether or not to retain the time
                'Preserve timestamps [Y/n]',      when the star was originally created
                required=False
            ) in {'Y', 'y', None},        ◁──┐   Accepts "Y", "y", or just pressing
    }                                             Enter as the user saying "yes"


def loop():
    ...


    options = OrderedDict({               ──┐   Adds the GitHub import option
        ...                                      to the menu with the right
        'G': Option(                      ◁──┘   command class and function
            'Import GitHub stars',
            commands.ImportGitHubStarsCommand(),
            prep_call=get_github_import_options
        ),
    })
```

> ## More practice
>
> If you'd like some more experience extending Bark, try implementing the ability to edit an existing bookmark.
>
> You'll need to add a new method to `DatabaseManager` for updating records. Updating a record requires the user to specify which record to update (similar to delete) as well as the column name and the new value to use. You can use what you've already written in `add`, `select`, and `delete` as a guide.
>
> The presentation layer must prompt the user for the ID of the bookmark to update, the column to update, and the new value to use. This will hook up to a new `Edit-BookmarkCommand` in the business logic layer.
>
> This is all stuff you're a pro at now, so give it a shot! My version is in the source code for this chapter (see https://github.com/daneah/practices-of-the-python-pro).

You should be seeing how adding behavior to an extensible system is a low-friction activity. It's a joy to be able to focus almost entirely on accomplishing the desired behavior, composing pieces of the existing infrastructure to hook up the rest of the plumbing. There's a rare moment as a developer when you might feel like the conductor of an orchestra, slowly layering the strings, woodwinds, and percussion together into a wonderful harmony. If your orchestra produces more of a cacophony from time to time, don't get disheartened. Find the points of rigidity causing dissonance, and see how you can free yourself up, using what you've learned.

In the next chapter, you'll learn more about inheritance and the occasions where it's an appropriate solution.

Summary

- Build code so that adding new features means adding new functions, methods, or classes without editing existing ones.
- Inversion of control allows other code to customize behavior to its needs without changing the low-level implementation.
- Sharing agreed-upon interfaces between classes instead of giving them detailed knowledge about each other reduces coupling.
- Be deliberate about what input types you want to handle, and be strict about your output types.

The rules (and exceptions) of inheritance

8

If you've written your own classes or used a class-based framework in Python, you've almost certainly encountered *inheritance*. Classes can inherit from other classes, ending up with their parent class's data and behavior. In this chapter, you'll learn the details of inheritance in Python, where it works well, and where it should be avoided.

8.1 The inheritance of programming past

Inheritance was conceived of in the early days of computer programming, but although it has existed for a long time, folks still have spirited debates about when and how it should be used. For much of the history of object-oriented programming, inheritance was the name of the game. Many applications sought to model the real world as a carefully curated hierarchy of objects, in the hopes that it would lead to some kind of obvious, neat structure. This paradigm was so embedded into object-oriented programming practices that the two concepts—object-oriented programming and inheritance—were nearly inseparable.

8.1.1   *The silver bullet*

Though inheritance is sometimes the right tool to reach for, it has been used on occasion as the hammer for every nail—the elusive "silver bullet." Much like a silver bullet, however, a paradigm that meets every need is a work of fiction.

The ubiquity of class inheritance in object-oriented programming quietly sowed frustration for many developers, and over time more and more people renounced object-oriented programming altogether. This is an unfortunate outcome. Object orientation has a number of benefits for mental modeling of problems. Inheritance even has its place when modeling the right hierarchies. Although inheritance isn't the solution to every data modeling problem you'll encounter, it *is* the right solution for a specific set of use cases, which you'll learn more about later in this chapter.

Before we get to that, though, it's important for you to understand how class inheritance led to so much frustration.

8.1.2   *The challenges of hierarchies*

Object-oriented programming is all about the separation, encapsulation, and classification of information and behaviors. I work with a number of librarians who have forgotten more than I'll ever know about classification—these folks work to identify relationships between things, creating taxonomies or even ontologies to categorize things.[1] This works well for organizing raw information, but it can introduce pain once software behavior is involved. As software grows, it becomes difficult to keep parent-child relationships between classes straight.

> **NOTE** _Parent_ classes are referred to as *superclasses* in Python (and in many other languages). *Child* classes are referred to as *subclasses*. I'll use this nomenclature throughout the rest of the chapter.

A class inherits all of its superclass's information and behavior, and it can then override them to do something different (figure 8.1). This is probably the tightest cou-

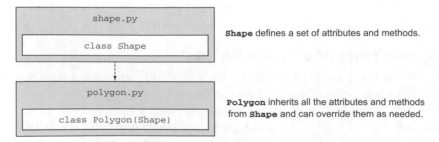

Figure 8.1   Inheritance with one superclass and one subclass

---

[1]For more on ontology in the context of information science, see the Wikipedia article: https://en.wikipedia.org/wiki/Ontology_(information_science).

pling that exists in programming. A class is fully coupled to its superclass because everything it knows and does by default is tied to that superclass.

Seeing this coupling is *very difficult* when class hierarchies grow, because if you're looking at a particular class, it isn't obvious whether another class is inheriting from it or not. This leads to bugs because of unintended changes in behavior, as depicted in figure 8.2.

To analogize, in quantum physics it's possible for two particles to be *entangled* in such a way that changes to one will effect the same change in the other, regardless of how far apart they are in space. This "spooky action at a distance," as Einstein called it, means that you can't reliably determine the state of a particle, because that state could change at any moment because of a change in its twin particle's state. This is exciting for physics, but in software it's a big danger. By changing one class, you may inadvertently end up changing—or worse, breaking—the functionality in another subclass you were unaware of. It's like the movie *Butterfly Effect*. (Spoiler alert: It doesn't go well for Ashton Kutcher's character.)

Developers frequently use inheritance to reuse code, but this presents challenges later on. With a deep hierarchy, classes at different levels may override or supplement their superclasses' behavior. Before too long, you'll find yourself traversing up and down your classes trying to follow the flow of information. I've said before that what

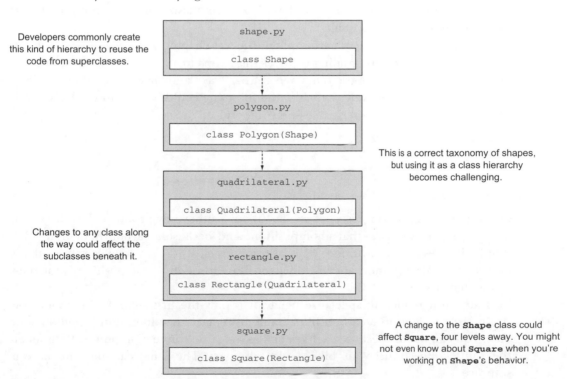

Developers commonly create this kind of hierarchy to reuse the code from superclasses.

shape.py

class Shape

polygon.py

class Polygon(Shape)

This is a correct taxonomy of shapes, but using it as a class hierarchy becomes challenging.

quadrilateral.py

class Quadrilateral(Polygon)

Changes to any class along the way could affect the subclasses beneath it.

rectangle.py

class Rectangle(Quadrilateral)

square.py

class Square(Rectangle)

A change to the **Shape** class could affect **Square**, four levels away. You might not even know about **Square** when you're working on **Shape**'s behavior.

Figure 8.2 How deep inheritance hierarchies can lead to more bugs

we do as developers should increase our understanding and reduce cognitive load; deep hierarchies work against this goal. So why are we still using inheritance?

8.2   The inheritance of programming present

Because of the pains caused by complicated hierarchies, inheritance has gotten a bad reputation. It isn't innately evil, though. It's simply been used too often and for the wrong reasons.

8.2.1   What is inheritance for, really?

Though many still reach for inheritance to reuse code in some class, that's not what it's for. Inheritance is for *specialization of behavior*. Put another way, you should fight the urge to subclass only to reuse code. Create subclasses to make a method return a different value or work differently under the hood.

In this sense, subclasses should be treated as *special cases* of their superclass. They will reuse code from the superclass, but only as a natural result of the idea that an instance of the subclass *is* an instance of the superclass.

When a class *B* inherits from a class *A*, we often say *B* "is-an" *A*. This is to stress that instances of *B* are in fact instances of *A*, and as such should look like an *A* (more on this in a bit). Contrast this with composition, where if an instance of class *C* uses an instance of a class *D*, we say that *C* "has-a" *D* to emphasize that *C* is composed of *D* (among other things, potentially).

Think back to the `Bicycle` example in the last chapter. You introduced multiple types of bicycle frames, upgrading the `AluminumFrame` to a `CarbonFiberFrame` and the `Tire` to a `FancyTire`. Suppose that `CarbonFiberFrame` and `FancyTire` inherited from `Frame` and `Tire`, respectively. Which of the following could be said about the way you modeled bicycles using inheritance and composition?

1   A `Tire` has-a `Bicycle`.
2   A `Bicycle` has-a `Tire`.
3   A `CarbonFiberFrame` is-a `Frame`.
4   A `CarbonFiberFrame` has-a `Frame`.

Because a tire isn't composed of a bike (it's the other way around), 1 is incorrect, whereas 2 makes sense—that's composition. And because a carbon fiber frame *is* a frame (it doesn't *have* a frame), 4 is also incorrect, whereas 3 makes sense—that's inheritance. Again, inheritance is for specialization, whereas composition is for reusable behaviors (figure 8.3).

Using inheritance to specialize behavior is only the first step. Think about how you're able to swap in a carbon fiber frame to replace the aluminum frame on your bike. You can do this because each frame has the same connection points. Without all the right connections, your bike could fall apart. The same can be said of your software.

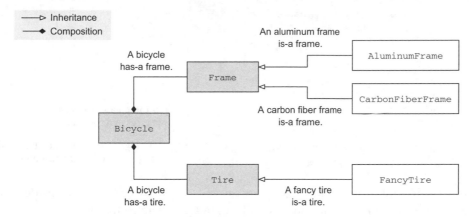

Figure 8.3 How inheritance and composition work together

8.2.2 *Substitutability*

Barbara Liskov, Institute Professor at MIT, developed a principle outlining the concept of *substitutability* as it relates to inheritance. The Liskov substitution principle states that in a program, any instance of a class must be replaceable by an instance of one of its subclasses without affecting the correctness of the program.[2] *Correctness* in this context means the program remains error-free and achieves the same basic outcomes, though the precise result may be different or achieved in a different manner. Substitutability arises from subclasses strictly adhering to their superclasses' interface.

It's not difficult to stray from this principle in Python. Consider the following listing, which is perfectly valid Python code that models slugs and snails (two types of gastropod). The Snail inherits from Slug (snails and slugs are the same, aside from the shell), and you might even say the Snail is specializing the Slug by adding information about its shell. But the Snail is breaking substitutability, because a program that is using a Slug can't replace it with a Snail without adding the shell_size argument to the __init__ method, as shown in the following listing.

> **Listing 8.1 A subclass that breaks substitutability**

```
class Slug:
    def __init__(self, name):
        self.name = name

    def crawl(self):                          Snail inherits from Slug.
        print('slime trail!')
                                              Using a different instance
                                              creation signature is a common
class Snail(Slug):                            way to violate substitutability.
    def __init__(self, name, shell_size):
```

---

[2]For more on the Liskov substitution principle, see the Wikipedia article: https://en.wikipedia.org/wiki/Liskov
_substitution_principle.

```
        super().__init__(name)
        self.name = name
        self.shell_size = shell_size


def race(gastropod_one, gastropod_two):
    gastropod_one.crawl()
    gastropod_two.crawl()


race(Slug('Geoffrey'), Slug('Ramona'))
race(Snail('Geoffrey'), Snail('Ramona'))
```

You can create two Slug instances and race them.

Trying to use Snail without a shell_size argument raises an exception.

You could pull more tricks out of your sleeve to make this work, but consider that this might be a better case for composition. A snail *has-a* shell, after all.

I like to think about substitutability by examining the *role* a particular set of classes fills. If each class in a hierarchy can fulfill the role in question, they're likely substitutable. If a subclass changes any of its method signatures or raises an exception as part of its specialization, it may not fulfill that role, and this might be a hint that the class hierarchy should be arranged differently.

8.2.3   *The ideal use case for inheritance*

Sandi Metz, a Ruby programmer who originally came from the Smalltalk community (Smalltalk being a programming language written in part by Alan Kay, one of the pioneers of object-oriented programming), laid out a great set of ground rules about when to use inheritance:[3]

- The problem you're solving has a shallow, narrow hierarchy.
- Subclasses are at the leaves of the object graph; they don't make use of other objects.
- Subclasses use (or specialize) *all* the behavior of their superclass.

I'll talk through each of these in a little more detail.

SHALLOW, NARROW HIERARCHY

The *shallow* part of this rule addresses the problem with deep inheritance hierarchies you learned earlier: deeply nested class hierarchies can lead to difficult management and the introduction of bugs. Keeping the hierarchy small and contained makes it easier to reason about when necessary (figure 8.4).

The *narrow* part of this rule means that no class in the hierarchy should have too many subclasses. As the number of subclasses grows, it becomes difficult to know which ones provide which specialization, and other developers may duplicate subclasses if they can't find the one they're looking for.

---

[3]See Sandi Metz, "All the Little Things," *RailsConf 2014*, www.youtube.com/watch?v=8bZh5LMaSmE for more.

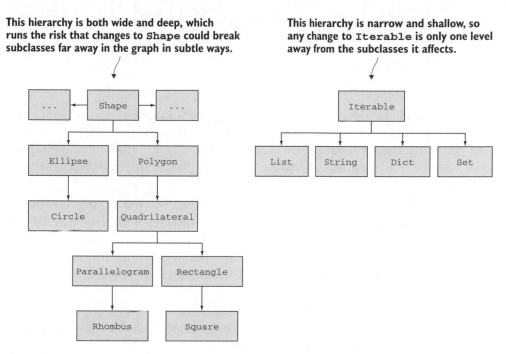

This hierarchy is both wide and deep, which runs the risk that changes to `Shape` could break subclasses far away in the graph in subtle ways.

This hierarchy is narrow and shallow, so any change to `Iterable` is only one level away from the subclasses it affects.

Figure 8.4   Narrow, shallow inheritance hierarchies can be reasoned about more effectively.

SUBCLASSES AT THE LEAVES OF THE OBJECT GRAPH

You can think of all the objects in your software as nodes in a graph, with each object pointing to other objects it inherits from or makes use of through composition. When using inheritance, a class may point to other objects, but its *subclasses* generally shouldn't have any further dependencies. Subclasses are for *specializing* behavior, but if a subclass has a unique dependency that the superclass or any other subclasses don't have, composition might be a better way to accomplish that portion of the task. This is a good check to make sure that your subclasses are specializing behavior without adding much new coupling.

SUBCLASSES USE ALL THE BEHAVIOR OF THEIR SUPERCLASS

This is an outcome of the "is-a" relationship you learned about earlier. If a subclass *doesn't* use all of its superclass's behavior, is it *really* an instance of the superclass? Consider a class that represents a bird:

```
class Bird:
    def fly(self):
        print('flying!')
```

You might subclass this so that `fly` does something different for certain kinds of birds:

```
class Hummingbird(Bird):
    def fly(self):
        print('zzzzzooommm!')
```

What happens when you get to a penguin, or a kiwi, or an ostrich? None of these birds fly at all. One possible solution is to override `fly` in this way:

```
class Penguin(Bird):
    def fly(self):
        print('no can do.')
```

You could also override `fly` to do nothing (`pass`) or raise an exception of some kind. This goes against the substitutability principle, though. Any code that *knows* it's dealing with a `Penguin` will be unlikely to call `fly` at all, so that behavior isn't being used. Again, composition of the flying behavior into classes that need it might be a better choice here.

EXERCISE

Now that you know some of the things to look for, try applying the rules for inheritance and composition to the `Bicycle` example. The bicycle module can be found in the source code for this chapter(see https://github.com/daneah/practices-of-the-python-pro).

How well does the `Bicycle` example follow the rules for inheritance that Metz describes? See if you can tell whether the objects in the bicycle module do or do not follow each of the rules.

Come back here to see how you did:

- `Frame` and `Tire` both have a narrow, shallow hierarchy; they each have one level below them, with at most two subclasses.
- The different types of tires and frames don't depend on any other objects.
- The different types of tires and frames use or specialize all the behavior of their superclasses.

Success! The model you created uses inheritance properly where needed, and uses composition to bring different pieces together into a whole. Read on to see what tools Python provides for inspecting and using inheritance.

8.3 *Inheritance in Python*

Python provides a set of tools for examining classes and their inheritance structure, along with a number of ways to approach inheritance and composition. This section will cover each of them so that when you do use inheritance, you'll have the know-how to debug and test your code.

8.3.1 *Type inspection*

One of the most common things you'll want to know when debugging your code is what type of object you're dealing with on a particular line. Python's dynamic typing means this isn't always immediately obvious, so it's a good thing to inspect.

Type checking

The latest versions of Python support *type hinting*, which is a way to tell developers and automated tooling what types of objects a function or method expects. Tools can check for calls that might violate these types, without executing your code. Note that Python doesn't enforce the types during execution; this feature is strictly a development aid.

The basic way to check the type of an object is to use the built-in `type()` function. `type(some_object)` will tell you which class that object is an instance of:

```
>>> type(42)
<class 'int'>
>>> type({'dessert': 'cookie', 'flavor': 'chocolate chip'})
<class 'dict'>
```

Although this is useful, you'll also frequently want to know if an object is an instance of a particular class or any of its subclasses. Python provides the `isinstance()` function for this purpose:

```
>>> isinstance(42, int)
True
>>> isinstance(FancyTire(), Tire)
True
```

Any classes you reference will need to be imported into the namespace.

Lastly, if you only need to know whether a class is a subclass of another, Python gives you the `issubclass` function:

```
>>> issubclass(int, int)
True
>>> issubclass(FancyTire, Tire)
True
>>> issubclass(dict, float)
False
```

> **NOTE** `issubclass` is somewhat confusingly named. Because it considers a class to be a subclass of itself, it will return `True` even if the two classes you provide are in fact the same class.

These tools can come in handy in real code occasionally, but their presence is often a red flag, because changing behavior based on the data type is precisely what subclasses of behavior are for. These built-in functions are good for inspecting objects from the outside, but Python also provides useful features for handling inheritance *within* classes.

8.3.2   Superclass access

Suppose you're creating a subclass and you need to specialize its behavior in a way that depends on its superclass's original behavior. How can you do that in Python? You can use the built-in `super()` function, as shown in the following listing, which forwards any method or attribute accesses to the superclass.

Listing 8.2   Using `super()` to access superclass behavior

```
class Teller:
    def deposit(self, amount, account):
        account.deposit(amount)
```

```
class CorruptTeller(Teller):          ⟵—— A corrupt teller is-a teller.
    def __init__(self):
        self.coffers = 0
                                                 The corrupt teller overrides
                                                 the default deposit behavior.
    def deposit(self, amount, account):  ⟵
        self.coffers += amount * 0.01            ⟵
        super().deposit(amount * 0.99, account)  ⟵   The corrupt teller skims a
                                                     little off the top for himself.
                    He deposits the rest the way any teller
                       does, but using a different amount.
```

Code that uses super() can become particularly confusing if substitutability is broken. Overriding methods to take different numbers of arguments, and passing only some of them along using super(), can lead to confusion and poor maintainability. Substitutability becomes particularly important in the case of *multiple inheritance* in Python.

8.3.3   *Multiple inheritance and method resolution order*

Up to now, I've mostly been discussing *single* inheritance, where a subclass has precisely one superclass. But Python also supports the idea of *multiple inheritance*, where a subclass may have two or more direct superclasses, as shown in figure 8.5.

Multiple inheritance has uses within plugin architectures or when you want to implement multiple interfaces in one class. For example, an aquatic vehicle has the interfaces of both a boat and a car.

You can inherit from multiple classes in a subclass by providing more than one in the class definition, as shown in listing 8.3. Place this code in a "cats" module to give it

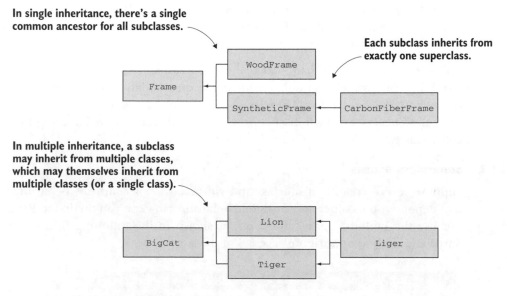

Figure 8.5   Single and multiple inheritance

a try for yourself. Can you guess what `print(liger.eats())` does before running this code?

Listing 8.3 Multiple inheritance in Python

```
class BigCat:
    def eats(self):
        return ['rodents']


class Lion(BigCat):          ←——┐  Lion is-a BigCat through
    def eats(self):                 single inheritance.
        return ['wildebeest']


class Tiger(BigCat):         ←——┐  Tiger also is-a BigCat
    def eats(self):                 through single inheritance.
        return ['water buffalo']


class Liger(Lion, Tiger):    ←——┐  Liger uses multiple inheritance;
    def eats(self):                 it is-a Lion and it is-a Tiger.
        return super().eats() + ['rabbit', 'cow', 'pig', 'chicken']


if __name__ == '__main__':
    lion = Lion()
    print('The lion eats', lion.eats())
    tiger = Tiger()
    print('The tiger eats', tiger.eats())
    liger = Liger()
    print('The liger eats', liger.eats())
```

Does the liger eat the prey you expected?

```
The liger eats ['wildebeest', 'rabbit', 'cow', 'pig', 'chicken']
```

Because `Liger` inherits both from `Lion` and `Tiger`, you might have expected it would eat the same prey they eat, at a minimum. `super()` works a bit differently under multiple inheritance. When `super().eats()` is called, Python starts searching for the definition of `eats()` that it should use. Python does this through a process called *method resolution order*, which determines the list of classes Python will search, in order.

These are the steps for method resolution order:

1 Generate a depth-first ordering of the superclasses, from left to right. For `Liger` this is `Lion` (leftmost parent), `BigCat` (the only parent of `Lion`), `object` (the implicit parent of `BigCat`), `Tiger` (the next parent of `Liger`), `BigCat`, and `object` (see figure 8.6).

2 Remove any duplicates. The list becomes `Liger`, `Lion`, `BigCat`, `object`, and `Tiger`.

3 Move each class so that it appears after all of its subclasses. The final list is `Liger`, `Lion`, `Tiger`, `BigCat`, `object`.

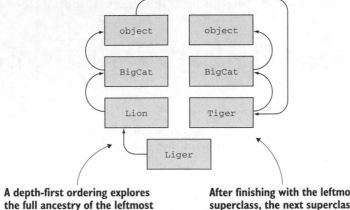

A depth-first ordering explores the full ancestry of the leftmost superclass of `Liger` (`Lion`) first.

After finishing with the leftmost superclass, the next superclass (`Tiger`) is explored.

Figure 8.6   The depth-first ordering for a class inheritance hierarchy

How does this look for `Liger`? The full process is shown in figure 8.7.

When you ask for `super().eats()`, Python will work its way through the method resolution order until it finds an `eats()` method on one of the classes (other than the one you called `super()` from). As you can see, it finds `Lion` first, which returns `['wildebeest']`. `Liger` then adds its own list of prey animals, resulting in the list you saw in the output.

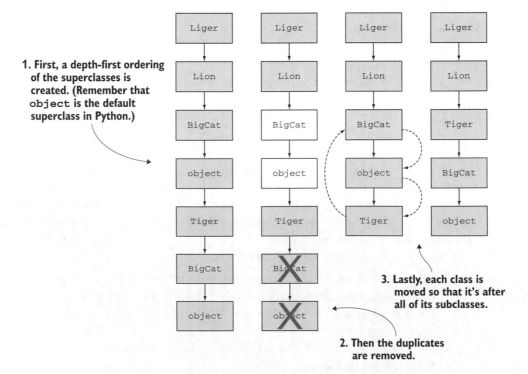

1. First, a depth-first ordering of the superclasses is created. (Remember that `object` is the default superclass in Python.)

3. Lastly, each class is moved so that it's after all of its subclasses.

2. Then the duplicates are removed.

Figure 8.7   How Python determines the method resolution order for a class

> ### Inspecting the method resolution order
>
> You can see the method resolution order for any class by using its `__mro__` attribute:
>
> ```
> >>> Liger.__mro__
> (<class '__main__.Liger'>, <class '__main__.Lion'>,
> ➥ <class '__main__.Tiger'>, <class '__main__.BigCat'>, <class 'object'>)
> ```

You *can* make multiple inheritance work as you expected by practicing *cooperative* multiple inheritance. In cooperative multiple inheritance, each class commits to having the same method signatures (substitutability) and to calling `super().some_method()` from within its own `some_method()`. The presence of `super()` in each method means Python will keep going through the method resolution order even after it finds a method. This ensures that no class blocks execution or breaks things with an unexpected interface. The classes play nicely together.

Try updating the `Lion` and `Tiger` classes to call `super().eats()`, the same way the `Liger.eats()` method does. Rerun the code and come back here to check if it matches the following output.

```
The liger eats ['rodents', 'water buffalo', 'wildebeest', 'rabbit', 'cow',
➥ 'pig', 'chicken']
```

Although multiple inheritance isn't something you're likely to use every day, it's important to know how to tackle it when you see it. As your software grows, the likelihood that you'll need to make use of different paradigms increases, so come prepared.

8.3.4 Abstract base classes

Up to now, I've fibbed to you a bit about interfaces being unavailable in Python. You first needed to get a handle on when and how to use inheritance and composition effectively, but now is a good time to delve a bit deeper.

Abstract base classes in Python are a way of using something that looks like inheritance to achieve something that's effectively an interface. An abstract base class, like a formal interface in other languages, outlines which methods and attributes its subclasses *must* implement. This gets back to the idea of fulfilling roles mentioned earlier, in section 8.2.2. You can't create an instance of an abstract base class directly; it acts as a template for how other classes behave.

Python provides the abc module for easing the creation of abstract base classes. The abc module provides a couple of helpful constructs:

- You can inherit from the ABC class to indicate that your class is an abstract base class.
- You can mark methods defined in your abstract base class as abstract using the `@abstractmethod` decorator. (Decorators are outside the scope of this book, but you can think of `abstractmethod` as a label for a method you define.) This enforces the rule that these methods must be defined in any subclass of your abstract class.

Suppose you're modeling a food chain, and you want to make sure all the predator classes adhere to an interface that includes an `eat` method for eating prey. You can create an abstract base class, `Predator`, that defines this method and its signature. Then you can subclass `Predator`, and any subclass that doesn't define `eat` will raise an exception, as noted in the following listing.

Listing 8.4   Using abstract base classes to enforce an interface

Inheriting from ABC makes this class an abstract base class.

```
from abc import ABC, abstractmethod
```

This indicates that the method must be defined on any subclasses.

```
class Predator(ABC):
    @abstractmethod
    def eat(self, prey):
        pass
```

This method signature can be checked by IDEs in any subclasses.

Abstract methods have no default implementation.

```
class Bear(Predator):
    def eat(self, prey):
        print(f'Mauling {prey}!')
```

States your intent to implement the interface by subclassing the abstract base class

This method must be defined, or an exception will be raised.

```
class Owl(Predator):
    def eat(self, prey):
        print(f'Swooping in on {prey}!')


class Chameleon(Predator):
    def eat(self, prey):
        print(f'Shooting tongue at {prey}!')


if __name__ == '__main__':
    bear = Bear()
    bear.eat('deer')
    owl = Owl()
    owl.eat('mouse')
    chameleon = Chameleon()
    chameleon.eat('fly')
```

TIP   If you're using an IDE, it can warn you if you have the wrong method signature. Python won't check this at runtime, but it may still raise an error for the usual mistakes, like too many or too few arguments.

Try creating a new `Predator` without the `eat` method, and then try creating an instance of it at the end of the module. You should see a `TypeError` mentioning that the instance couldn't be created because it didn't define an implementation for the abstract method `eat()`.

Now try adding a method to the `Bear` class that makes it roar. What do you expect to happen?

1 A `TypeError` is raised when the instance is created because `Predator` doesn't define `roar` as an abstract method.

2 A `RuntimeError` is raised when `roar()` is called because `Predator` doesn't define `roar` as an abstract method.

3 It works like any normal class method.

Defining additional methods on a subclass of an abstract base class works just fine (option 3). An abstract base class enforces that its subclasses *minimally* implement the methods it defines, but additional behavior is fine because the subclass still implements the desired interface. It's also possible to put additional behavior into the base class itself and receive it in subclasses like normal inheritance. Steer away from that practice, though, because putting real behavior in a class that claims to be abstract could confuse whoever reads the code.

Abstract base classes are a nice supplement to Python's duck typing; if you need additional protections and guarantees around the interfaces to which your classes must adhere, they're there for you. I don't find myself reaching for them often, though. Composition via inversion of control is usually enough for me. Try using both and see which makes more sense to you and your code.

Now that you've got a good handle on the different aspects of inheritance, let's take a look at Bark to see what opportunities it holds for inheritance and composition.

8.4 Inheritance and composition in Bark

Bark hasn't made use of inheritance so far. See how far you can get without it? But as you've learned, inheritance can help you out when used correctly. In this last section, you'll see how you can use it to make Bark more robust.

8.4.1 Refactoring to use an abstract base class

Interfaces are a way to declare that a class implements a specific set of methods and attributes, and you just learned that abstract base classes can be used to augment the idea of interfaces in Python. Which of the following adhere to an interface in Bark?

1 Commands in the commands module

2 Database statement execution in the database module

3 Options in the bark module

Options in the bark module all behave similarly, but there isn't a distinct *class* for each option, only distinct *instances* of `Option`. This doesn't look like an interface. Database statement execution is similarly contained within a single class. Commands (option 1) make use of interfaces; each command class implements an `execute()` method that is called when the command is triggered.

To make sure all your future commands remember to implement the `execute()` method, I'd like you to refactor the commands module to use an abstract base class.

You can call this base class Command, and it should define the execute() method as an abstractmethod that raises NotImplementedError by default. Each of the existing command classes should then inherit from Command.

Note that the existing command classes all implement execute() already, so they're covered on that front. But there are a few different signatures for the execute() method, which you learned isn't good for substitutability or when dealing with abstract base classes. Some are called with a data argument, whereas others take no arguments. Think about how you could normalize the methods so they have the same signature. Which of the following would work?

1 Remove the data argument from the execute() methods that accept it.
2 Add data as an optional keyword argument to the execute() methods that don't already accept it.
3 Make all execute() methods accept a variable number of positional arguments (*args).

Removing the data argument (option 1) would stop you from being able to act on the data inside the commands, which would remove a fair amount of functionality from Bark. Although option 3 would work, it's often best to be explicit about the arguments you accept until you need flexibility to handle widely differing numbers of arguments. Right now, execute() always needs one or zero arguments, so I'd choose to go the route of adding data as an argument to each of them (option 2).

Try creating the Command abstract base class and inheriting from it for your commands. As you go along, try renaming execute() methods temporarily or changing their signatures to see how your IDE (or Bark) reacts to the broken interface. Come back to the following listing to see how you did.

Listing 8.5 An abstract base class for the command pattern

```
from abc import ABC, abstractmethod        ◁─── Imports the tools needed from abc


class Command(ABC):          ◁─┐ Defines the Command
    @abstractmethod            │ base class
    def execute(self, data):       ◁─── Defines execute as an abstract
                                         method that accepts a data argument


class CreateBookmarksTableCommand(Command):   ◁─── Each command inherits from Command.
    def execute(self, data=None):     ◁─┐
        ...                             │ Adds the data argument (None by
                                        │ default, so callers can omit it)


class AddBookmarkCommand(Command):   ◁─┐
    ...                                │ Commands that already accept a data
                                       │ argument need only inherit from Command.
```

Because `execute()` has a consistent signature, you can also simplify a line in the bark module where an option triggers a command in the `choose()` method:

```
class Option:
    ...

    def choose(self):
        ...
        message = self.command.execute(data)
```

Always passes data to execute

Bark should continue to work exactly as it did before. Adding the abstract base class here just makes it a little safer when creating future commands. If you decide that your commands need to implement additional methods or accept additional arguments in the future, you can start by adding them to `Command`, and your IDE can help you find the places that need to be updated. It's a handy way to develop.

8.4.2 *A final check on your inheritance work*

You've successfully used inheritance to make your use of composition a bit more robust. Check one more time if your code passes Metz's tests for good use of inheritance:

- *Commands have a shallow, narrow hierarchy.* Seven command classes wide, each one level of hierarchy deep.
- *Commands don't know about other objects.* They do make use of the database connection object, but that's a piece of global state that adheres to a database interface.
- *Commands use or specialize all of the functionality from their superclass.* `Command` is an abstract class with no behavior itself.

Excellent. You're using inheritance where it makes sense and adds value, without forcing that structure onto things that don't need it. This kind of critical examination is valuable as you continue to write and refactor code.

Continue on to the next chapter to learn how to keep classes maintainable by keeping them small.

Summary

- Use inheritance to represent true is-a relationships (good for specialization of behavior).
- Use composition for has-a relationships (good for reuse of code).
- Method resolution order is key to keeping multiple inheritance straight.
- Abstract base classes provide interface-like control and safety in Python.

Keeping
things lightweight

9

This chapter covers
- Using complexity measurements to identify code to refactor
- Python language features for breaking up code
- Using Python language features to support backward compatibility

In your software development, you'll remain vigilant about separating concerns, but you'll generally wait until a sensible organization presents itself in order to avoid creating the wrong abstractions. This means your classes will generally grow bit by bit until they become unruly.

This is quite like the art of training a bonsai tree; you need to give the tree time to grow, and only after it tells you where it's headed can you encourage it down that path. Trimming the tree too often can stress it, and forcing it into an unnatural shape may stunt its ability to thrive.

In this chapter, you'll learn how to prune your code to keep it healthy and thriving.

9.1 How big should my class/function/module be?

Many an online forum on software maintenance contains questions of this nature. I sometimes wonder if we keep asking because we think eventually we can transcend to some new plane of understanding, where the answer was obvious all along. Each ensuing discussion thread contains a mix of opinions, anecdotes, and occasional data points.

The desire to find a final answer to this question isn't inherently bad; it's useful to have guidelines and waypoints so you can recognize when you should invest time in your code. But it's also important to understand the strengths and weaknesses of the metrics that we use to approach this question.

9.1.1 Physical size

Some folks attempt to prescribe a line limit for functions, methods, and classes. This metric seems nice because it's readily measurable: "My function is 17 lines long." I take issue with this approach because it can force a developer to break up a function that is otherwise perfectly understandable, increasing cognitive load.

If you draw a line in the sand at five lines, a six-line function is suddenly out of the question. This encourages developers to play "code golf," trying to fit the same amount of logic into fewer lines. Python enables this kind of game too:

```python
def valuable_customers(customers):
    return [customer for customer in customers if customer.active and
➥ sum(account.value for account in customer.accounts) > 1_000_000]
```

Were you able to make sense of that code immediately? It's not awful, but does mashing it into one line add value?

Take a look at a rewritten version, where each clause is given its own line:

```python
def valuable_customers(customers):
    return [
        customer
        for customer in customers
        if customer.active
        and sum(account.value for account in customer.accounts) > 1_000_000
    ]
```

Breaking things up logically gives someone reading your code a chance to digest each clause, forming a mental model of what's happening as they go.

Another form of the line-limit rule I've seen is that "a class should fit on one screen." This shares some of the pain points with its stricter version, while at the same time being less measurable due to different screen sizes and resolutions.

The spirit of these metrics is to "keep it simple," with which I agree. But there are other ways to define "simple."

9.1.2 Single responsibility

A more open-ended measurement of the size of a class, method, or function is how many different things it does. As you've learned from separation of concerns, the ideal number is one. For functions and methods, this means performing a single calculation or task. For classes, it means dealing with a single, focused facet of some larger business problem.

If you spot a function performing two tasks or a class that contains two distinct areas of focus, that's a strong signal of an opportunity to separate them. But there may be times when what feels like a single task is still complex enough to warrant breaking down further.

9.1.3 *Code complexity*

One of the more robust ways of understanding the cognitive and maintenance impact of code is through its *complexity*. Like time and space complexity, code complexity is a quantitative measurement of the characteristics of your code, not just a subjective measure of how confused you get by reading it.

Complexity measurement tools are a great thing to have in your tool belt. I find that they often accurately point out code I would have trouble reading and understanding as a human. In the next few sections, I'll show you what code complexity looks like, along with some tools for measuring it.

MEASURING CODE COMPLEXITY

A common measure of complexity is *cyclomatic* complexity. Although the name sounds scarily scientific, measuring cyclomatic complexity involves determining the number of execution paths through a function or method. The structure (and therefore, complexity) of a function is affected by the number of conditional expressions and loops it contains.

The higher the complexity score is for a function or method, the more conditionals and loops you should expect it to contain. The specific score isn't always terribly useful; its trend over time, and how it changes in response to alterations you make in the code, is what will help you write more maintainable software. Seek to drive your complexity scores down over time, and consider pieces of code with high complexity when determining where to invest refactoring time.

You can measure the complexity of a function yourself. By creating a graph of the *control flow*, or the path the code takes as it executes, you can count the number of nodes and edges in the graph and calculate the cyclomatic complexity. The following are represented as nodes in the control flow graph of a program:

- The "start" of the function (where the control flow enters)
- `if`/`elif`/`else` conditions (each one is its own node)
- `for` loops
- `while` loops
- The "end" of a loop (where you draw the execution path back to the start of the loop)
- `return` statements

Consider the function in the following listing, which accepts a sentence as either a string or a list of words and determines whether the sentence has any long words in it. It contains a loop and multiple conditional expressions.

Listing 9.1   A function with conditionals and a loop

```
def has_long_words(sentence):
    if isinstance(sentence, str):          ◄──┐  Splits words in sentence if
        sentence = sentence.split(' ')        │  it's a string (conditional)

    for word in sentence:                  ◄────  Does work for each word (loop)
        if len(word) > 10:    ◄──┐
            return True           │  Returns True if a long word
                                  │  is found (conditional)
    return False
```

Returns
False if
no words
were long

The edges are arrows that follow the different execution paths your code can take. Cyclomatic complexity, *M*, for a function or method is equal to the number of edges minus the number of nodes, plus two. You can add nodes and edges for the lines of code that aren't inside a conditional block or a loop if it helps you diagram a function, but they won't affect the overall complexity—they each add one node and one edge, which cancel out in the math.

The `has_long_words` function has one conditional to check if the input is a string, a loop for each word in the sentence, and a conditional inside the loop to check if a word is long. Its diagram is shown in figure 9.1. By diagramming the control flow and simplifying the graph as plain nodes and edges, you can count them up and plug the results into the cyclomatic complexity equation. In this case, the graph of `has_long_words` has 8 nodes with 10 edges, so its complexity is $M = E - N + 2 = 10 - 8 + 2 = 4$.

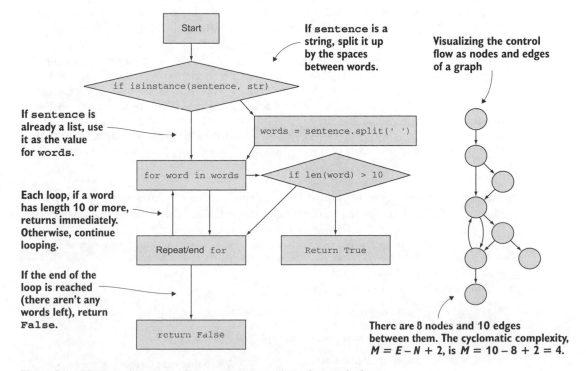

Figure 9.1   Diagramming control flow to measure cyclomatic complexity

Most sources recommend shooting for a complexity of 10 or lower for a given function or method. This corresponds roughly to how much developers can reasonably understand at once.

In addition to helping you understand the health of your code, cyclomatic complexity is useful in testing. Recall that cyclomatic complexity measures the number of execution paths a function or method has. Consequently, this is also the minimum number of distinct test cases you would need to write to cover each execution path. This follows from the fact that each `if`, `while`, and so on requires you to prepare a different set of preconditions to test what happens in one case or the other.

Remember that perfect test coverage doesn't guarantee that your code actually works; it only means your tests caused that part of the code to run. But making sure you cover the execution paths of interest is usually a good idea. Untested branches of execution are usually what people are referring to when they talk about "edge cases," a term with negative connotations that usually means "a thing we didn't think of." The excellent Coverage package by Ned Batchelder (https://coverage.readthedocs.io) can print branch coverage metrics for your tests.

Halstead complexity

For some applications, reducing the risk of shipping defective software is as big a priority as maintainability. Although reducing branches in your code tends to make it more readable and understandable, it hasn't been proven to reduce the number of bugs in software. Cyclomatic complexity predicts the number of defects about as well as the number of lines of code does. But there's at least one set of metrics out there that tries to address the defect rate.

Halstead complexity attempts to measure quantitatively the ideas of level of abstraction, maintainability, and defect rate. Measuring Halstead complexity involves inspecting a program's use of the programming language's built-in operators and how many variables and expressions it contains. It's beyond the scope of this book, but I recommend reading more about it. (The Wikipedia article is a good place to start: https://en.wikipedia.org/wiki/Halstead_complexity_measures.) Radon (https://radon.readthedocs.io) can measure the Halstead complexity of your Python programs if you're interested in exploring.

Recall the code you wrote to import GitHub stars in Bark (reproduced in the following listing). Try to diagram the control flow and calculate the cyclomatic complexity.

Listing 9.2   The code for importing GitHub stars in Bark

```
def execute(self, data):
    bookmarks_imported = 0

    github_username = data['github_username']
    next_page_of_results =
➥ f'https://api.github.com/users/{github_username}/starred'

    while next_page_of_results:              ◁─┐  A loop that code further
        stars_response = requests.get(          │  down will come back to
```

```
            next_page_of_results,
            headers={'Accept': 'application/vnd.github.v3.star+json'},
        )
        next_page_of_results = stars_response.links.get('next', {}).get('url')

        for repo_info in stars_response.json():        ◁─┐  Another loop that code further
            repo = repo_info['repo']                       down will come back to

            if data['preserve_timestamps']:
                timestamp = datetime.strptime(
                    repo_info['starred_at'],
                    '%Y-%m-%dT%H:%M:%SZ'
                )
            else:                           ◁─┐  Another branch
                timestamp = None                 of execution

            bookmarks_imported += 1
            AddBookmarkCommand().execute(
                self._extract_bookmark_info(repo),
                timestamp=timestamp,
            )

    return f'Imported {bookmarks_imported} bookmarks from starred repos!'
```

One branch of execution → (points to `if data['preserve_timestamps']:` block)

The point that returns to the for, or, if complete, to the while → (points to `bookmarks_imported += 1` through `)` block)

When you're done, come back and check your work against the solution in figure 9.2.

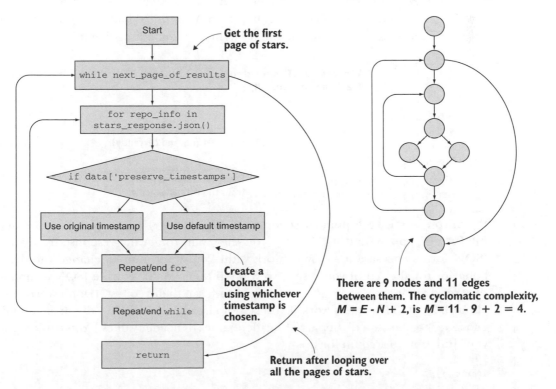

Figure 9.2 The cyclomatic complexity of a function from the Bark application

Fortunately, you won't need to diagram each function and method you write. A number of tools out there, like SonarQube (www.sonarqube.org) and Radon (https://radon.readthedocs.io), can measure these for you. These tools can even be integrated into your code editors so that you can break up complex code as you develop.

Now that you've learned some of the ways to discover when code has grown complex, you can get some practice breaking down that complexity.

9.2   Breaking down complexity

I have some mildly bad news: recognizing that code is complex is the easy part. The next challenge is understanding how to deal with specific kinds of complexity. Throughout the rest of this chapter, I'll point out some common patterns of complexity I've seen during my travels with Python, and I'll show you the options you have for tackling them.

9.2.1   Extracting configuration

I'll start with an example you've already seen in this book: as your software grows, certain areas of the code need to continue adapting to new requirements.

Imagine you're building a web service that indecisive users can query to see what they should eat for lunch. If a user goes to your service's /random endpoint, they should get a random food, like pizza, in return. Your initial handler function accepts the user's request as an argument, and it might look something like this:

```
import random                   ┌─ A list of foods (This could go
                                │  in a database eventually.)
FOODS = [          ◁────────────┘
    'pizza',
    'burgers',
    'salad',              ┌─ The function accepts the user's
    'soup',              │   HTTP request (unused currently).
]
                         │
def random_food(request):  ◁────┤   ┌─ Returns a random food
    return random.choice(FOODS)  ◁──┴── from the list, as a string
```

When your service gets popular (people are *all* indecisive), some users want to build a full-fledged app around it. They tell you they want to get the response from you in JSON format because it's easy to work with. You don't want to change the default behavior for the rest of your users, so you tell them you'll return a JSON response if they send an Accept: application/json header in their request. (Don't worry much about how HTTP headers work if you're not already familiar with them; assume that request.headers is a dictionary of header names to header values.) You could update your function to account for this:

```
import json
import random

...
```

```
def random_food(request):
    food = random.choice(FOODS)          Chooses the food at random and
                                         stores it for use momentarily

    if request.headers.get('Accept') == 'application/json':
        return json.dumps({'food': food})          Returns {"food": "pizza"}, for
    else:                                          example, if the request has the
        return food                                Accept: application/json header
                Continues returning "pizza",
                for example, by default
```

Think about this change in terms of cyclomatic complexity; what is the complexity before and after the change?

1 1 before, 2 after
2 2 before, 2 after
3 1 before, 3 after
4 2 before, 1 after

Your initial function had no conditionals or loops, so the complexity was 1. Because you've added only one new condition (the case when the user requests JSON), the complexity has gone from 1 to 2 (option 1).

An increase of complexity by 1 to handle a new requirement isn't terrible to start with. But if you continue on that trajectory for long, increasing complexity linearly with each requirement, you'll soon be dealing with hairy code:

...

```
def random_food(request):
    food = random.choice(FOODS)          Each additional requirement is a new
                                         condition, increasing complexity.
    if request.headers.get('Accept') == 'application/json':
        return json.dumps({'food': food})
    elif request.headers.get('Accept') == 'application/xml':
        return f'<response><food>{food}</food></response>'
    else:
        return food
```

Do you remember how to solve this? As a hint, observe that the conditionals are mapping a value (the value of the `Accept` header) to another value (the response to return). What data structure makes sense?

1 `list`
2 `tuple`
3 `dict`
4 `set`

A Python dictionary (option 3) maps values to other values, so it's a good fit for refactoring this code. Remodeling the execution flow as a configuration of header values to response formats, and then choosing the right one based on the user's request, will simplify things.

Try extracting the different header values and response types into a dictionary, using the default behavior as the fallback if the user doesn't request a response format (or requests an unknown format). Check your work against the following listing when you're done.

Listing 9.3   An endpoint with extracted configuration

```
...            Extracted from the previous if/elif conditions

def random_food(request):                              Gets the requested response
    food = random.choice(FOODS)                        format if available; otherwise, falls
                                                        back to returning the plain string
    formats = {
        'application/json': json.dumps({'food': food}),
        'application/xml': f'<response><food>{food}</food></response>',
    }

    return formats.get(request.headers.get('Accept'), food)
```

Believe it or not, this new solution is reduced back to a cyclomatic complexity of 1. And even if you continue adding entries to the formats dictionary, no additional complexity is added. This is the kind of gain I talked about in chapter 4; you've gone from a linear algorithm to a constant one.

Extracting configuration into a map also makes code much more readable, in my experience. Trying to sift through a number of if/elif conditions is tiresome, even when they're all fairly similar. In contrast, a dictionary's keys are generally scannable. If you know the key you're looking for, it's quick to spot.

Can we do even better?

9.2.2   *Extracting functions*

With the growing cyclomatic complexity defeated, two other things are still growing in tandem within the random_food function:

- The code that knows *what* to do (format the response as JSON, XML, and so on)
- The code that knows *how to decide* what to do (based on the Accept header values)

This is an opportunity to separate concerns. As I've advocated a few times in this book, extracting some functions here could be helpful. If you look at each item in the formats dictionary, you'll notice that the value is a function of the food variable. Each of these values could be a function that accepts a food argument and returns the formatted response that will go back to the user, as shown in figure 9.3.

Try changing your random_food function to use these separated response-format functions. The dictionary will now map formats to the function that can return the response for that format, and random_food will call that function with the food value.

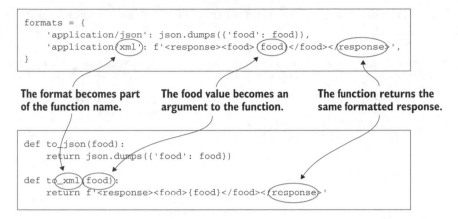

Figure 9.3 Extracting inline expressions as functions

If no function is available after calling `formats.get(…)`, you should fall back to a function that returns the `food` value unchanged; this can be done using a lambda. Check the following listing when you're done.

Listing 9.4 A service endpoint with response-formatting functions

```
def to_json(food):                    ⟵—— The extracted formatting functions
    return json.dumps({'food': food})


def to_xml(food):
    return f'<response><food>{food}</food></response>'


def random_food(request):
    food = random.choice(FOODS)

    formats = {                            Maps data formats
        'application/json': to_json,       to their respective
        'application/xml': to_xml,    ⟵—┘  formatting functions now
    }

    format_function = formats.get(    ⟵—┐  Gets the appropriate formatting
        request.headers.get('Accept'),  ⟵┘ function if available
        lambda val: val               ⟵——— Uses a lambda as the fallback to
    )                                       return the unchanged food value
    return format_function(food)   ⟵—┐
            Calls the formatting function
            and returns its response   ┘
```

To fully separate the concerns, you can now extract `formats` and the business of getting the right function from it into its own function, `get_format_function`. This function accepts the user's `Accept` header value and returns the right formatting function. Try that out now and refer to the following listing when you're done to check your work.

Listing 9.5   Separating concerns into two functions

```
def get_format_function(accept=None):          ◁──┐ Determines which formatting
    formats = {                                    │ function to use
        'application/json': to_json,
        'application/xml': to_xml,
    }

    return formats.get(accept, lambda val: val)

                                    ┌── random_food is three
def random_food(request):      ◁──┘    short steps now.
    food = random.choice(FOODS)
    format_function = get_format_function(request.headers.get('Accept'))   ◁──┐
    return format_function(food)
                                    Previously mixed concerns are
                                    abstracted to function calls now.
```

You may be thinking this code is more complex; you now have four functions compared to your initial one. But you've achieved something here: each of these functions has a cyclomatic complexity of 1, is quite readable, and has a nice separation of concerns.

You've also got something *extensible* on your hands, because when you need to handle new response formats, the process is as follows:

1 Add a new function to format the response as desired.
2 Add the mapping of the required `Accept` header value to the new formatting function.
3 Profit.

You can create new business value just by adding new code and updating configuration. This is the ideal.

Now that you know some tricks for functions, I want to show you a few for classes.

9.3   *Decomposing classes*

Classes can grow unruly like functions, and perhaps at a faster rate. But it feels somehow more scary to break down a class than it does a function. Functions feel like building blocks, but classes feel like completed products. This is a mental barrier I often struggle to suppress.

You should have the confidence to decompose classes as frequently as functions. Classes are just another tool at your disposal. When you find that a class starts growing in complexity, it's usually due to a mixing of concerns. Once you identify a concern that feels like its own object, you've got enough to start breaking it down.

9.3.1 Initialization complexity

I often see classes that have complex initialization procedures. For better or worse, these classes are usually complex because they deal with complex data structures. Have you ever seen a class like the following?

Listing 9.6 A class with complex domain logic in its construction

```
class Book:
    def __init__(self, data):
        self.title = data['title']          ◁── Extracts some fields from
        self.subtitle = data['subtitle']        the passed-in data

        if self.title and self.subtitle:
            self.display_title = f'{self.title}: {self.subtitle}'
        elif self.title:
            self.display_title = self.title
        else:
            self.display_title = 'Untitled'
```

Complexity arising from the domain logic of your business →

When the domain logic you're dealing with is complex, your code is more likely to reflect that. In these cases, it's more important than ever for developers to rely on useful abstractions to make sense of it all.

I've talked about extracting functions and methods as a useful way to break down code. One approach you could take here is to extract the logic for `display_title` into a `set_display_title` method that you could call from the __init__ method, as shown in the following listing. Try creating a book module and adding the `Book` class to it, extracting a setter method for `display_title`.

Listing 9.7 Using a setter to simplify class construction

```
class Book:
    def __init__(self, data):
        self.title = data['title']
        self.subtitle = data['subtitle']
        self.set_display_title()            ◁── Calls the extracted function

    def set_display_title(self):            ◁── Extracted function
        if self.title and self.subtitle:        sets display_title.
            self.display_title = f'{self.title}: {self.subtitle}'
        elif self.title:
            self.display_title = self.title
        else:
            self.display_title = 'Untitled'
```

This has cleaned up the __init__ method, but a couple of issues arise from this approach:

- Getters and setters are generally discouraged in Python because they can clutter up a class.

- It's good practice to set all necessary attributes to some initial value directly inside __init__, but display_title is set in a different method.

You could fix the latter by setting display_title to 'Untitled' by default, but this can be misleading. A reader might conclude the display title is typically (or even *always*) 'Untitled', if they don't read carefully.

There is one approach that can give you the readability benefit of extracting a method, without suffering these drawbacks. It involves creating a function that returns the value for display_title.

But wait! If you think about how you use Book, it might be something like this:

```
...

book = Book(data)
return book.display_title
```

How can you make the display_title logic a function without having to update the second line to return book.display_title() instead? Fortunately, Python provides a tool for this occasion. The @property decorator can be used to signify that a method on a class should be accessible as an attribute.

Create a display_title *method* now, decorated with @property, that uses the existing logic to return the proper display title. Compare your changes with the following listing when you're done.

> **NOTE** Methods can be used as properties only if self is their only argument, because when you access the attribute, you can't pass any arguments to it.

Listing 9.8   Using @property to simplify class construction

```python
class Book:
    def __init__(self, data):
        self.title = data['title']
        self.subtitle = data['subtitle']

    @property                              ◁── A property is a function that can
    def display_title(self):                    be referenced as an attribute.
        if self.title and self.subtitle:
            return f'{self.title}: {self.subtitle}'
        elif self.title:
            return self.title
        else:
            return 'Untitled'
```

Using @property, you can still reference book.display_title as an attribute, but all its complexity is abstracted into its own function. This reduces the complexity of the __init__ method, making it more readable at the same time. I make frequent use of @property in my own code.

NOTE Because properties are methods, repeatedly accessing them means that the methods are called each time. This is often okay, but it can have performance impacts for properties that are expensive to calculate.

What should you do when there's enough functionality to abstract a whole *class* worth of methods?

9.3.2 Extracting classes and forwarding calls

When you extracted `get_format_function` from `random_food` in section 9.2.2, you still *called* the extracted function from its original location. When dealing with classes, something similar will need to happen if you want to maintain *backward compatibility*. Backward compatibility is the practice of evolving your software without breaking the implementation consumers previously relied on. If you change the arguments of a function, the name of a class, and so on, consumers will need to update their code if they want it to continue working. To avoid these problems, you could take a hint from the post office's mail forwarding system.

When you move to a new address, you can tell the post office to forward your mail (figure 9.4). People who send you mail at your old address don't need to know your new address immediately because the post office will intercept the mail and direct it to you automatically. Each time you receive a piece of mail addressed to your old residence, you can notify the sender of your new address so they can update their records. Once you're confident you aren't receiving mail made out to the old address any longer, you can stop the post office forwarding.

When you extract one class from another, you'll want to continue providing the previously existing functionality for a while, despite changing things under the hood, so that consumers don't need to immediately worry about upgrading their software. As with your mail, you can continue accepting calls in one class and pass them along to another class under the hood. This is known as *forwarding*.

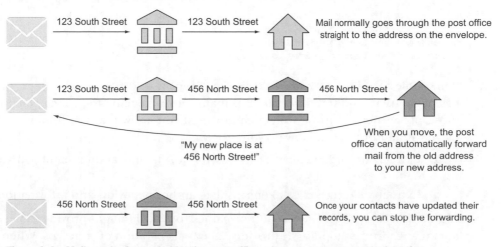

Figure 9.4 Mail can be forwarded by the post office when you move to a new location.

Suppose your `Book` class has grown to keep track of the author information. This feels natural at the start; what is a book without its author? But as the class takes on more functionality, the author starts to feel like a separate concern. As shown in the following listing, methods soon exist for the author's name as it should be displayed on a website, as well as how it should be displayed in a research paper citation.

Listing 9.9   A `Book` class too concerned with author details

```python
class Book:
    def __init__(self, data):
        # ...

        self.author_data = data['author']          # Stores the author as a
                                                    # dictionary from the data

    @property
    def author_for_display(self):                  # Displays the author,
        return f'{self.author_data["first_name"]}  # such as "Dane Hillard"
{self.author_data["last_name"]}'

    @property
    def author_for_citation(self):                 # Gets the citation-suitable author
        return f'{self.author_data["last_name"]},  # name, such as "Hillard, D"
{self.author_data["first_name"][0]}.'
```

Suppose you'd been using this `Book` class like so:

```python
book = Book({
    'title': 'Brillo-iant',
    'subtitle': 'The pad that changed everything',
    'author': {
        'first_name': 'Rusty',
        'last_name': 'Potts',
    }
})


print(book.author_for_display)
print(book.author_for_citation)
```

Being able to reference `book.author_for_display` and `book.author_for_citation` has been great, and you'd like to keep that. But referencing the `author` dictionary in those properties is starting to feel clumsy, and you know that you'll want to do a lot more with authors soon. How do you proceed?

1 Extract an `AuthorFormatter` class for formatting author names in different ways.
2 Extract an `Author` class to encapsulate author behaviors and information.

Although a class for formatting author names (option 1) might provide value, extracting an `Author` class (option 2) provides a better separation of concerns. When several methods in a class share a common prefix or suffix, especially one that doesn't match the name of the class, there might be a new class waiting to be extracted. Here, author_ is a sign that an Author class might make sense. It's time to try your hand at extracting a class.

Create an Author class (either in the same module or imported from a new module). This Author class should contain all the same information as before, but in a more structured manner. The class should

- Accept author_data as a dictionary in __init__, storing each relevant value (first name, last name, and so on) from the dictionary as an attribute
- Have two properties, for_display and for_citation, that return the properly formatted author string

Remember that you also want Book to keep working for users, so you want to keep the existing author_data, author_for_display, and author_for_citation behaviors on Book for now. By initializing an Author instance with author_data, you can *forward* calls from Book.author_for_display to Author.for_display, and so on. This way, Book will let Author do most of the work, keeping only a temporary system in place to make sure calls keep working. Give it a try now, and come back to the following listing to see how you did.

Listing 9.10   Extracting an Author class from the Book class

```python
class Author:
    def __init__(self, author_data):
        self.first_name = author_data['first_name']     # What was previously stored
        self.last_name = author_data['last_name']        # only as a dictionary is now
                                                         # structured attributes.

    @property
    def for_display(self):                               # The Author-level properties are
        return f'{self.first_name} {self.last_name}'     # simpler than the originals.

    @property
    def for_citation(self):
        return f'{self.last_name}, {self.first_name[0]}.'


class Book:                                              # Continues storing author_data until
    def __init__(self, data):                            # consumers don't need it anymore
        # ...

        self.author_data = data['author']               # Stores an instance of Author
        self.author = Author(self.author_data)          # for forwarding calls

    @property
    def author_for_display(self):                        # Replaces previous logic with
        return self.author.for_display                   # forwarding to the Author instance

    @property
    def author_for_citation(self):
        return self.author.for_citation
```

Do you notice that even though the code now has more lines, each line has been simplified? And looking at the classes, it's a bit easier to tell what kind of information they contain. Eventually, much of the code still in `Book` will also be removed, at which point `Book` will be leveraging composition of the `Author` class to provide information about its authors.

If you want to be *really* nice to your consumers as you decompose a class, you can also leave them hints so they know they should switch to the new code. For example, you want the consumers of `Book` to move from `book.author_for_display` to `book.author.for_display` so that you can remove the forwarding. Python has a built-in system for this kind of messaging, called `warnings`.

One type of warning is specifically a `DeprecationWarning`, which you can use to let people know that something should no longer be used. This warning generally prints a message in a program's output telling the user they should make a change. A deprecation warning can be produced as follows:

```
import warnings

warnings.warn('Do not use this anymore!', DeprecationWarning)
```

You can help consumers upgrade their code smoothly by adding a `DeprecationWarning` to each method you eventually want to remove.[1] Try adding them to the author-related properties in the `Book` class now. You can say something useful like `'Use book.author.for_display instead'`. If you run the code now, you should see warning messages in the output that look like the following:

```
/path/to/book.py:24: DeprecationWarning: Use book.author.for_display instead
```

Congratulations! You've extracted a new class, breaking down the complexity of a class that outgrew itself. You did it in a backward-compatible way, leaving hints for users so they know what's coming and how to fix it. This resulted in more structured, more readable code with separate concerns and strong cohesion. Well done, you.

Summary

- Code complexity and separate concerns are better metrics than physical size for breaking up code.
- Cyclomatic complexity measures the number of execution paths through your code.
- Extract configuration, functions, methods, and classes freely to break down complexity.
- Use forwarding and deprecation warnings to temporarily support the new and old ways of doing things.

---

[1]See Brett Slatkin, "Refactoring Python: Why and how to restructure your code," *PyCon 2016*, www.youtube.com/watch?v=D_6ybDcU5gc, for a treasure trove of deprecation and extraction tricks.

Achieving loose coupling

10

This chapter covers

- Recognizing the signs of tightly coupled code
- Strategies for reducing coupling
- Message-oriented programming

Loose coupling is what allows you to make changes in different areas of your code without worrying that you'll break something elsewhere. It allows you to work on one feature while your coworker tackles another. It's also the foundation for other desirable characteristics, like extensibility. Without loose coupling, the job of maintaining your code can quickly grow out of hand.

In this chapter, you'll see some of the pains of tight coupling and learn how to address them.

10.1 Defining coupling

Because the idea of coupling plays such a big role in effective software development, it's important to get a solid grip on what it means. What is coupling exactly? You can think of it as the connective tissue between the different areas of your code.

10.1.1 *The connective tissue*

Coupling can be a tricky concept at first because it's not necessarily tangible. It's a kind of mesh that runs throughout your code (figure 10.1). Where two pieces of code have high interdependency, that mesh is tightly woven and taut. Moving either piece of code around requires the other to move around too. The mesh between areas with little or no interdependence is flexible—maybe it's made of rubber bands. You'd have to change the code in this looser part of the mesh much more drastically for it to impact the code around it.

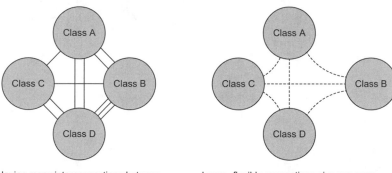

Having many interconnections between classes makes it difficult to change one without requiring changes to the others.

Loose, flexible connections give you more leeway to make changes that are less likely to affect the surrounding code.

Figure 10.1   Coupling is a measure of the interconnectedness of distinct pieces of software.

I like this analogy because it doesn't say that tight coupling is inherently *bad* in all cases. Rather, it focuses on the ways tight and loose coupling differ and helps you get a sense of the resulting outcomes for your code—tight coupling usually means more work when you want to shuffle things around. It also implies that coupling is a continuum rather than a binary, all-or-nothing thing.

Although coupling is measured along a continuum, there *are* common ways it manifests. You can learn to recognize these and reduce coupling in your software as you see fit. First, though, I want to give you a more fine-grained definition of tight and loose coupling.

10.1.2 *Tight coupling*

Coupling between two pieces of code (modules, classes, and so on) is considered tight when those pieces of code are interconnected. But what does interconnectedness look like? In your code, several things create interconnections:

- A class that stores another object as an attribute
- A class whose methods call functions from another module
- A function or method that does a lot of procedural work using methods from another object

Anytime a class, method, or function needs to carry a lot of knowledge about another module or class, that's tight coupling. Consider the code in the following listing. The `display_book_info` function needs to know all the different pieces of information that a `Book` instance contains.

```
class Book:
    def __init__(self, title, subtitle, author):
        self.title = title
        self.subtitle = subtitle
        self.author = author


def display_book_info(book):
    print(f'{book.title}: {book.subtitle} by {book.author}')
```

A book stores several pieces of info as attributes.

This function has knowledge of all the book's attributes.

If the `Book` class and the `display_book_info` function live in the same module, this code might be tolerable. It operates on related information, and it's together in one place. But as your codebase grows, you may eventually find functions like `display_book_info` in one module operating on classes from other modules.

Tight coupling isn't inherently bad. Occasionally, it's just trying to tell you something. Because `display_book_info` operates only on info from `Book` and does something book-related, the function and the class have *high cohesion*. It's *so* tightly coupled to `Book` that it makes sense for you to move it inside the `Book` class as a method, as shown in the following listing.

```
class Book:
    def __init__(self, title, subtitle, author):
        self.title = title
        self.subtitle = subtitle
        self.author = author

    def display_info(self):
        print(f'{self.title}: {self.subtitle} by {self.author}')
```

Function moved to a method whose only necessary argument is self (still a Book)

All references to book change to self.

In general, tight coupling is problematic when it exists between two separate concerns. Some tight coupling is a sign of high cohesion that isn't structured well.

You may have seen or written code similar to listing 10.3. Imagine you've got a search index to which your users can submit queries. The search module provides functionality for cleaning up those queries to make sure they produce consistent results from the index. You write a main procedure that gets a query from the user, cleans it up, and prints the cleaned-up version.

```
import re


def remove_spaces(query):
```

Turns ' George Washington ' into 'George Washington'

```
        query = query.strip()
        query = re.sub(r'\s+', ' ', query)
        return query
```

```
                                          Turns 'Universitätsstraße' ("University
                                          Street") into 'universitätsstrasse'
    def normalize(query):    ◁─────
        query = query.casefold()
        return query
                                                            Gets a query
                                                            from the user
    if __name__ == '__main__':
        search_query = input('Enter your search query: ')   ◁─┘
        search_query = remove_spaces(search_query)   ◁──────     Removes spaces and
        search_query = normalize(search_query)                   normalizes casing
        print(f'Running a search for "{search_query}"')   ◁─     Prints the
                                                                 cleaned-up query
```

Is the main procedure tightly coupled to the search module?

1 No, because it could easily do that work itself.
2 Yes, because it calls some of the functions inside the search module.
3 Yes, because it would likely have to change if you changed the way cleaning queries works.

You can effectively identify coupling by assessing the likelihood that any given change to a module will require a change to the code that uses it (option 3). Although the main procedure *could* do the work the cleaning functions do, it's important to discuss coupling as it currently exists in your code. Option 1 is hypothetical and doesn't help you achieve this. Calling a few functions from a module (option 2) is sometimes a sign of coupling, but the more important metric is how likely a change to the search module will require changes to the main procedure.

Suppose your users report that they're still getting inconsistent results from minor changes to their queries. You do some investigation and realize it's because some users like to put quotes around their queries, thinking it will make them more specific, but your search index treats quotes literally, matching only records that contain the quotes as written. You decide to discard the quotes before running the query.

The way things are currently written, this would involve adding a new function to the search module *and* updating all the places where you clean queries to ensure they call the new function, as shown in the following listing. Those points in the code are all tightly coupled to the search module.

Listing 10.4   **Tight coupling causing changes to ripple outward**

```
    def remove_quotes(query):    ◁──    A new function for
        query = re.sub(r'"', '', query)     removing quotes
        return query
```

```
    if __name__ == '__main__':
```

```
...
search_query = remove_quotes(search_query)   ◁──── Calls the new function
...                                                  anywhere you normalize
                                                     queries
```

Read on to understand what *loose* coupling is and how it can help you in situations like this.

10.1.3 Loose coupling

Loose coupling is the ability of two pieces of code to interact to accomplish a task without either relying heavily on the details of the other. This is often achieved through the use of shared abstractions. You learned about interfaces in earlier chapters, and you used a shared abstraction in Bark to achieve the command pattern.

Loosely coupled code implements and uses interfaces; at the extreme end, it uses *only* interfaces for intercommunication. Python's dynamic typing allows us to relax this a bit, but there's a philosophy here I'd really like to emphasize to you.

If you begin to think about the intercommunication between pieces of your code in terms of the *messages* that objects send to each other (figure 10.2), rather than focusing on the objects themselves, you'll begin to identify cleaner abstractions and stronger cohesion. What are messages? Messages are the questions you ask of an object or the things you tell it to do.

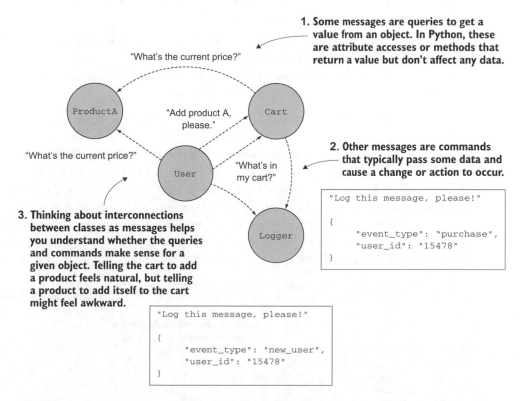

Figure 10.2   Imagining interconnections between classes as the messages they send and receive

Take another look at the main procedure of your query cleaner in the following listing. You achieve each transform on the query by calling a function to get a new query. Each of these is a message you're sending.

Listing 10.5   Calling functions from a module

Tells the search module to remove spaces

```
if __name__ == '__main__':
    search_query = input('Enter your search query: ')
    search_query = remove_spaces(search_query)
    search_query = remove_quotes(search_query)
    search_query = normalize(search_query)
    print(f'Running a search for "{search_query}"')
```

Tells the search module to remove quotes

Tells the search module to normalize the casing

What you've written achieves the task—cleaning the query—but how do the messages feel to you? Does calling the various functions from the search module feel like a lot of hoops to jump through? If I saw this code, I might say to myself, "I just want the cleaned-up query. I don't care how!" Going through the paces of calling each function is tedious, especially if you're cleaning queries throughout your code.

Think about this in terms of the message or messages you'd *like* to send. A cleaner approach might be to send a single message: "Here's my query; clean it please." What approach might you take to achieve this?

1 Combine the query-cleaning functions into a single function to remove spaces and quotes and normalize casing.
2 Wrap the existing function calls in another function you can call anywhere.
3 Use a class to encapsulate the query-cleaning logic.

Any of these could work. Because separation of concerns is generally a good idea, option 1 might not be the best choice because it combines several concerns into a single function. Wrapping the existing functions into another (option 2) would keep the concerns separate while providing a single entry point for the cleaning behavior, which is good. Encapsulating that logic further into a class (option 3) could make sense later on, if you need the cleaning logic to maintain information between steps.

Try refactoring the search module to make each transform function private, providing a `clean_query(query)` function that performs all the cleaning and returns the cleaned query. Come back here and check your work against the following listing.

Listing 10.6   Simplifying a shared interface

```
import re


def _remove_spaces(query):
    query = query.strip()
    query = re.sub(r'\s+', ' ', query)
    return query
```

Transforms are made private because they're underlying details of cleaning.

```
def _normalize(query):
    query = query.casefold()
    return query


def _remove_quotes(query):
    query = re.sub(r'"', '', query)
    return query


def clean_query(query):
    query = _remove_spaces(query)
    query = _remove_quotes(query)
    query = _normalize(query)
    return query


if __name__ == '__main__':
    search_query = input('Enter your search query: ')
    search_query = clean_query(search_query)
    print(f'Running a search for "{search_query}"')
```

A single entry point receives the original query, cleans it, and returns it.

The consuming code needs to call only a single function now, reducing coupling.

Now when you think of another technique to clean your queries, you'll be able to do the following (shown in figure 10.3):

1 Create a function to perform the new transform on a query.

2 Call the new function inside clean_query.

3 Call it a day, confident that consumers are all cleaning queries properly.

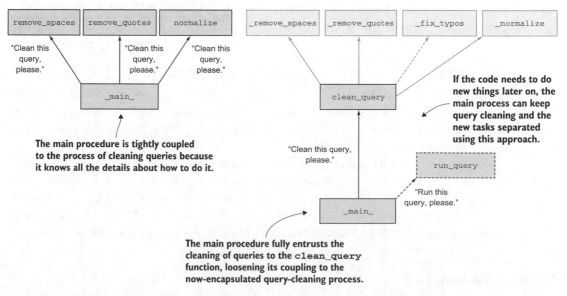

Figure 10.3 Using encapsulation and separation of concerns to maintain loose coupling

You can see that loose coupling, separation of concerns, and encapsulation all work together. The separation and encapsulation of behavior with a carefully thought out interface to the outside world helps achieve the loose coupling you desire.

10.2 Recognizing coupling

You've seen examples of tight and loose coupling now, but coupling can take on a few specific forms in practice. Giving a name to these forms, and recognizing the signs of each form, will help you mitigate tight coupling early on, keeping you more productive in the long term.

10.2.1 Feature envy

In the early version of your query-cleaning code, the consumer needed to call several functions from the search module. When code performs several tasks using mainly features from another area, that code is said to have *feature envy*. Your main procedure feels like it wants to *be* the search module because it uses all of its features explicitly. This is also common in classes, as shown in figure 10.4.

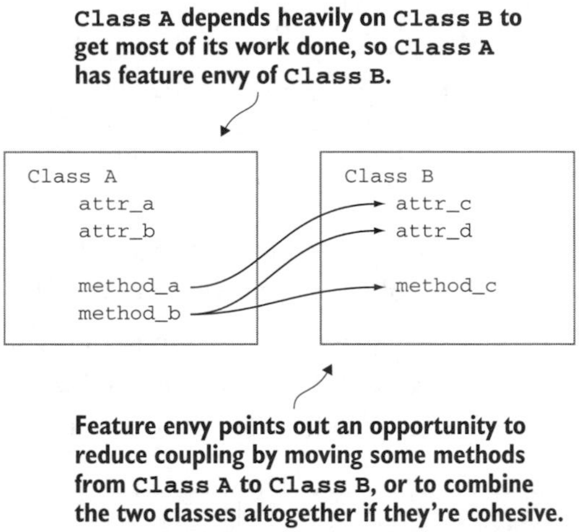
Class A depends heavily on Class B to get most of its work done, so Class A has feature envy of Class B.
Class A
attr_a
attr_b
method_a
method_b
Class B
attr_c
attr_d
method_c
Feature envy points out an opportunity to reduce coupling by moving some methods from Class A to Class B, or to combine the two classes altogether if they're cohesive.

Figure 10.4 Feature envy from one class to another

Feature envy can be solved the same way you fixed your query-cleaning logic: roll it up into a single entry point back at the source. In the previous example, you created a `clean_query` function in the search module. The search module is where query-cleaning logic goes, so a `clean_query` function is perfectly at home there. Other code can continue using `clean_query`, blissfully unaware of what happens underneath and trusting that it will receive a properly cleaned query in return. That code no longer has feature envy; it's happy letting the search module be in charge of search-related things.

As you refactor to remove feature envy, it will feel like you're giving up a certain amount of control. Before refactoring, you can see exactly how the information flows through the code, but afterward, that flow is often hidden under a layer of abstraction. This requires putting a certain amount of trust in the code you interact with to do what it says. It will feel uncomfortable occasionally, but a thorough test suite can help you remain confident in the functionality.

10.2.2 Shotgun surgery

You learned about shotgun surgery in chapter 7, and it often happens as a result of tight coupling. You make one change to a class or module, and you need to make changes far and wide to keep other code working. Peppering changes throughout your code each time you need to update behavior is tiresome!

By addressing feature envy, separating concerns, and practicing good encapsulation and abstraction, you'll minimize the amount of shotgun surgery you'll have to do. Anytime you find yourself jumping around to different functions, methods, or modules to realize the change you're trying to make, ask yourself if you're experiencing tight coupling between those areas of code. Then see what opportunities there are to move a method to a better-suited class, a function to a better-suited module, and so on—a place for everything, and everything in its place.

10.2.3 *Leaky abstractions*

The goal of abstraction, as you've learned, is to hide the details of a particular task from the consumer. The consumer triggers the behavior and receives the result but doesn't care about what happens under the hood. If you start to notice feature envy, it might be because of a *leaky abstraction*.

A leaky abstraction is one that doesn't sufficiently hide its details. The abstraction claims to provide a simple way to get something done, but it ultimately requires you to have some knowledge about what lies beneath when using it. This sometimes manifests as feature envy, but it can also be subtle, as you'll see in a moment.

Picture a Python package for making HTTP requests (`requests`, maybe). If your goal is purely to make a GET request to some URL and get the response back, you'd be best served by an abstraction on the GET behavior, such as `requests.get('https://www.google.com')`.

This abstraction works well *most* of the time, but what happens when you lose your internet connection? When Google is unavailable? When things are "just weird" for a moment and your GET request doesn't make it anywhere? In these cases, `requests` generally raises an exception indicating the problem (figure 10.5). This is useful for error handling, but it requires the calling code to know a bit about the *possible* errors so it knows which are likely to occur and how to handle them. Once you start handling errors from `requests` in many places, you're coupled to it, because your code expects a certain set of possible outcomes, which are specific to the requests package.

Leaks happen because there's a trade-off to consider with abstractions—generally speaking, the further you abstract a concept in code, the less customization you can provide. This is because abstraction is inherently meant to remove access to detail; the fewer details you can access, the fewer ways you have to change the details. As developers, we often want to tweak things to better suit our needs, though, so we sometimes provide lower-level access to the very details we tried to hide.

When you find yourself providing access to a low-level detail from a high-level layer of abstraction, you're likely introducing coupling. Remember that loose coupling relies on *interfaces*—shared abstractions—rather than specific low-level details. Read on to see some of the specific strategies you can use to achieve loose coupling in your code.

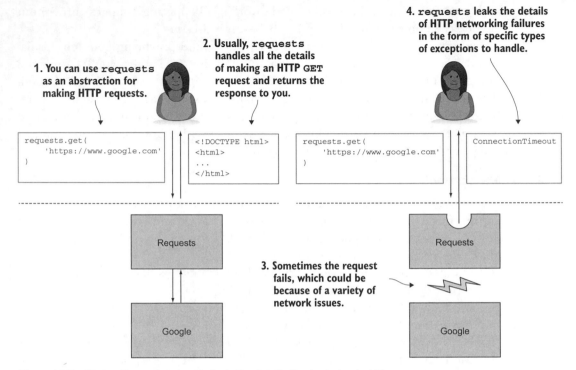

Figure 10.5 Abstractions occasionally leak the details they're trying to hide.

10.3 *Coupling in Bark*

You can separate concerns and encapsulate behaviors all you like, but those concerns inevitably need to interact with each other. Coupling is a necessary part of software development, but it doesn't have to be *tight* coupling. Now that you're familiar with some of the signs of tight coupling, it's time to look at techniques for reducing it while keeping your code in working order. Some of these will be familiar to you, and you'll see how they can be further applied to the Bark application.

Remember the multitier architecture you used for Bark, shown again in figure 10.6. Each tier has a distinct set of concerns:

- The presentation layer shows information to, and gets information from, the user.
- The business logic layer contains the "smarts" of the application—the logic related to the task at hand.
- The persistence layer stores data for the application, to be reused later on.

You hooked the presentation layer to the business logic layer using the command pattern. Each option in the menu triggers a corresponding command in the business logic, through that command's `execute` method. The set of commands with their shared `execute` abstraction are a great example of loose coupling.

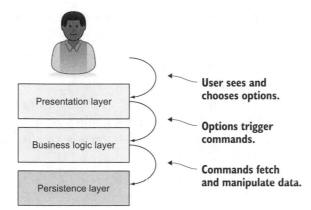

User sees and
chooses options.

Options trigger
commands.

Commands fetch
and manipulate data.

Figure 10.6   Separating concerns
into a multitier architecture

The presentation layer knows very little about the commands it's hooked up to, and the commands don't care why they were triggered, as long as they receive the data they expect. This allows each layer to change independently to adapt to new requirements.

Now think about how the business logic layer interacts with the persistence layer. Remember the `AddBookmarkCommand` you created, shown in listing 10.7. This command does the following:

1 Receives the data for a bookmark along with an optional timestamp
2 Generates a timestamp if needed
3 Tells the persistence layer to store the bookmark
4 Returns a message stating that the addition was a success

Listing 10.7   Command for adding a new bookmark

```
class AddBookmarkCommand(Command):          │ Receives bookmark data
    def execute(self, data, timestamp=None):  ◁─┘
        data['date_added'] = timestamp or datetime.utcnow().isoformat()  ◁─
        db.add('bookmarks', data)
        return 'Bookmark added!'  ◁─
```

Persists the bookmark data

Returns a success message

Generates a timestamp if needed

What if I told you there's some tight coupling in here? The whole class is five lines long—you might ask yourself, "How much coupling can there be in five lines?" As it turns out, the last two lines of the `execute` method show signs of tight coupling.

The first offending line, which calls `db.add`, demonstrates a tight coupling with not just the persistence layer, but the database itself. Put another way, if you decide in the future that you'd like to store your bookmarks in something other than a database—like a JSON file, for example—`db.add` doesn't fit well any longer. There's also some feature envy going on; most of the commands make direct use of one of the operations from `DatabaseManager`.

The second line that presents coupling is the `return` statement. What is its current purpose? It returns a message stating the addition was a success. Who is the message intended for? The user. You're handling a piece of presentation-level information in the business logic layer, which is an example of a leaky abstraction. The presentation layer should be in charge of what's shown to users. Some of the other commands you wrote have this same structure, which you'll fix shortly.

Another command, the `CreateBookmarksTableCommand`, introduces even tighter coupling. The `Table` in its name implies the presence of a database, a persistence layer feature, and then the command is referenced when the application starts, in the presentation layer. This command spans all the layers of abstraction you so carefully built! Don't worry, you'll be able to clean that up soon as well.

Read on to see how this coupling can cause problems in a real-life situation and how you should think about tackling it.

10.4   *Addressing coupling*

Imagine now that you're tasked with taking Bark mobile. (Also imagine phones that run Python!) You'd like to reuse as much of Bark's code as possible to optimize the experience for users on their phones while maintaining the existing command-line interface, as shown in figure 10.7.

Addressing new requirements often exposes tightly coupled areas of code. New use cases require you to swap out behavior and inevitably uncover the points in your code without flexibility. What will you find in Bark?

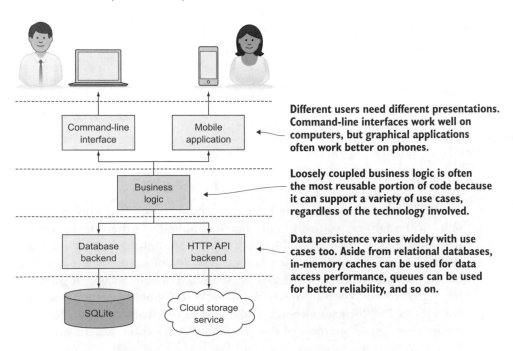

Different users need different presentations. Command-line interfaces work well on computers, but graphical applications often work better on phones.

Loosely coupled business logic is often the most reusable portion of code because it can support a variety of use cases, regardless of the technology involved.

Data persistence varies widely with use cases too. Aside from relational databases, in-memory caches can be used for data access performance, queues can be used for better reliability, and so on.

Figure 10.7   How core business logic supports a variety of use cases

10.4.1 User messaging

Because mobile apps tend to focus on visual and tactile elements, you'll want to use icons in addition to your messages to indicate success. A moment ago, you saw that the messaging in Bark is coupled to the business logic layer. To fix this limitation, you need to release control of the messaging fully to the presentation layer. How can you keep the interaction between commands and the presentation layer without each command having explicit knowledge of the message it shows?

Note that the outcome of some commands is a success message, whereas for others it's a result of some kind (a list of bookmarks, for example). You can handle this in the presentation layer by splitting up the concept of "success" and "result," with each command returning a tuple representing *both* the status and the result.

The commands you've built should all execute successfully, so for the moment the status for each command can be `True`. Eventually, you could have commands return `False` if they can fail. The commands that currently return a result can continue using the same result as before, and commands without a result can use `None`.

Update each of your commands to return a `status, result` tuple. You'll also need to update the `Option` class in the presentation layer to account for the new return behavior. What approach fits with how you've built the presentation layer so far?

1 Make `Option` print different success messages depending on the command executed.
2 Configure each `Option` instance with a specific message to use when a command succeeds.
3 Subclass `Option` for each kind of message you want to display.

Option 1 could work, but each new command would add to the conditional logic that determines which message to show. Option 3 might also work, but remember that inheritance should be used sparingly; it's unclear that there's enough specialized behavior present to justify creating all those subclasses. Option 2 gives you just the right amount of customization without a lot of extra effort. Remember that Bark should continue to function identically as you refactor the messaging—you're refactoring only to make development easier on yourself.

Try it yourself, and come back to the following two listings for help, or look at the full source code for this chapter (see https://github.com/daneah/practices-of-the-python-pro).

Listing 10.8 Decoupling layers of abstraction with interfaces

```
class AddBookmarkCommand(Command):          ◁──┐  The AddBookmarkCommand
    def execute(self, data, timestamp=None):    │  succeeds but doesn't return
        data['date_added'] = timestamp or datetime.utcnow().isoformat()  a result.
        db.add('bookmarks', data)
        return True, None       ◁──┐  The return value is a True
                                    │  status and a None result.
```

```
class ListBookmarksCommand(Command):
    def __init__(self, order_by='date_added'):
        self.order_by = order_by

    def execute(self, data=None):
        return True, db.select('bookmarks', order_by=self.order_by).fetchall()
```

> **The ListBookmarksCommand succeeds and returns a list of bookmarks.**

> **The return value is a True status and the bookmark list.**

Listing 10.9   Using statuses and results in the presentation layer

```
def format_bookmark(bookmark):
    return '\t'.join(
        str(field) if field else ''
        for field in bookmark
    )


class Option:
    def __init__(self, name, command, prep_call=None,
⮕ success_message='{result}'):
        self.name = name
        self.command = command
        self.prep_call = prep_call
        self.success_message = success_message

    def choose(self):
        data = self.prep_call() if self.prep_call else None
        success, result = self.command.execute(data)

        formatted_result = ''

        if isinstance(result, list):
            for bookmark in result:
                formatted_result += '\n' + format_bookmark(bookmark)
        else:
            formatted_result = result

        if success:
            print(self.success_message.format(result=formatted_result))

    def __str__(self):
        return self.name

def loop():
    ...

    options = OrderedDict({
        'A': Option(
            'Add a bookmark',
            commands.AddBookmarkCommand(),
            prep_call=get_new_bookmark_data,
            success_message='Bookmark added!',
```

> **The default message for commands that return a result is the result itself.**

> **Stores the configured success message for this option for later use**

> **Receives the status and result from the executed command**

> **Formats the result for display if needed**

> **Prints the success message, inserting the formatted result if needed**

> **Options without a result can specify a static success message.**

```
        ),
        'B': Option(
            'List bookmarks by date',
            commands.ListBookmarksCommand(),
        ),
        'T': Option(
            'List bookmarks by title',
            commands.ListBookmarksCommand(order_by='title'),
        ),
        'E': Option(
            'Edit a bookmark',
            commands.EditBookmarkCommand(),
            prep_call=get_new_bookmark_info,
            success_message='Bookmark updated!'
        ),
        'D': Option(
            'Delete a bookmark',
            commands.DeleteBookmarkCommand(),
            prep_call=get_bookmark_id_for_deletion,
            success_message='Bookmark deleted!',
        ),
        'G': Option(
            'Import GitHub stars',
            commands.ImportGitHubStarsCommand(),
            prep_call=get_github_import_options,
            success_message='Imported {result} bookmarks from starred repos!',
        ),
        'Q': Option(
            'Quit',
            commands.QuitCommand()
        ),
    })
```

> Options that should print only the result don't need to specify a message.

> Options that have a result and a custom message can put both together.

Congratulations! You've decoupled the business logic and presentation layer. They now interact using the idea of a status and a result instead of a specific hardcoded message. In the future, when you've built a new mobile frontend for Bark, it can use the statuses and results to determine the icons and messaging to show on phones.

10.4.2 *Bookmark persistence*

Your mobile users are always on the go, so you want them to have access to their bookmarks from anywhere. The database has to live in the cloud behind an API so they can see bookmarks on any of their devices.

As you saw, some areas of your command code are specific to local database operations. You need to swap out the database module for a new persistence layer that interacts with the new API. By this point, you should remember that shared abstractions are a good way to reduce coupling. Although it may sound like a big task, thinking about how the local database and the API are similar and different will help you conceptualize the abstraction to handle both (figure 10.8).

Both the database and API persistence layers need to deal with a similar set of concerns, despite the differences in some of the details. This is where abstraction

Database	API
Data represented as record objects	Data represented as record objects
CRUD operations with SQL (INSERT, SELECT, UPDATE, DELETE)	CRUD operations with HTTP (POST, GET, PUT, DELETE)
Configuration needed for the database's files and tables	Configuration needed for the API's domain and URLs

Figure 10.8   A database and an API share several commonalities.

shines. Just as you reduced each of your commands to an `execute` interface that returns a status and result to decouple them from the presentation layer, you can reduce your persistence layer to a more general set of CRUD operations to decouple it from the commands. Then, any new persistence layer you want to build can use the same abstraction.

10.4.3 *Try it out*

You've got the tools and knowledge you need to decouple your commands from `Data-baseManager`.

   Using an abstract base class, `PersistenceLayer`, to define the interface, create a `BookmarkDatabase` persistence layer that will sit between your commands and the `DatabaseManager` class, as shown in figure 10.9.

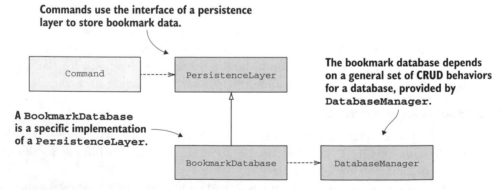

Commands use the interface of a persistence layer to store bookmark data.

The bookmark database depends on a general set of CRUD behaviors for a database, provided by `DatabaseManager`.

A `BookmarkDatabase` is a specific implementation of a `PersistenceLayer`.

Figure 10.9   Decoupling commands from database specifics with an interface and specific implementation

Create these classes in a new persistence module; you'll refactor your commands to use this instead of `DatabaseManager` directly. Instead of database- or API-specific method names, the interface should provide methods that would apply to most any persistence layer:

- __init__ for initial configuration
- create(data) to create a new bookmark
- list(order_by) to list all bookmarks
- edit(bookmark_id, data) to update a bookmark
- delete(bookmark_id) to remove a bookmark

The logic in CreateBookmarksTableCommand is really the initial configuration for a bookmark database persistence layer, so you can move it into BookmarksData-base.__init__. The instantiation of the DatabaseManager fits well there too. You can then write the implementation for each method of the PersistenceLayer abstraction in BookmarksDatabase. Each database-centric method call (db.add, for example) from your original commands can be moved into the appropriate method, freeing up the commands to call the methods from BookmarksDatabase. Give this a go, referencing the following listing and the full source code for this chapter as you go along.

Listing 10.10   A persistence interface and implementation

```python
from abc import ABC, abstractmethod

from database import DatabaseManager


class PersistenceLayer(ABC):
    @abstractmethod
    def create(self, data):
        raise NotImplementedError('Persistence layers must implement a
➥ create method')

    @abstractmethod
    def list(self, order_by=None):
        raise NotImplementedError('Persistence layers must implement a
➥ list method')

    @abstractmethod
    def edit(self, bookmark_id, bookmark_data):
        raise NotImplementedError('Persistence layers must implement an
➥ edit method')

    @abstractmethod
    def delete(self, bookmark_id):
        raise NotImplementedError('Persistence layers must implement a
➥ delete method')


class BookmarkDatabase(PersistenceLayer):
    def __init__(self):
        self.table_name = 'bookmarks'
        self.db = DatabaseManager('bookmarks.db')

        self.db.create_table(self.table_name, {
            'id': 'integer primary key autoincrement',
```

The abstract base class that defines the persistence layer interface

Each method corresponds to a CRUD-like operation for persistence.

A specific persistence layer implementation that uses a database

Handles database creation with DatabaseManager

```
                'title': 'text not null',
                'url': 'text not null',
                'notes': 'text',
                'date_added': 'text not null',     Database-specific
            })                                      implementation for
                                                    each of the behaviors
    def create(self, bookmark_data):          ←──┘ of the interface
        self.db.add(self.table_name, bookmark_data)

    def list(self, order_by=None):
        return self.db.select(self.table_name, order_by=order_by).fetchall()

    def edit(self, bookmark_id, bookmark_data):
        self.db.update(self.table_name, {'id': bookmark_id}, bookmark_data)

    def delete(self, bookmark_id):
        self.db.delete(self.table_name, {'id': bookmark_id})
```

Now that you have the interface for a persistence layer and a specific implementation of that interface that knows how to use DatabaseManager to persist bookmarks, you're ready to update your commands to depend on the PersistenceLayer interface instead of DatabaseManager. In the commands module, replace the db instance of DatabaseManager with persistence, an instance of BookmarkDatabase. Then go through the rest of the module, replacing calls to DatabaseManager methods (like db.select) with those from PersistenceLayer (like persistence.list). Refer to the following listing to check your work.

Listing 10.11   Updating business logic to use abstraction

```
from persistence import BookmarkDatabase        ←──  Imports BookmarksDatabase in
                                                     place of DatabaseManager
persistence = BookmarkDatabase()           ←──

                                                Sets up the persistence layer (This
                                                can be swapped in the future.)
class AddBookmarkCommand(Command):
    def execute(self, data, timestamp=None):
        data['date_added'] = timestamp or datetime.utcnow().isoformat()
        persistence.create(data)        ←──┐
        return True, None                   persistence.create takes
                                            the place of db.add.


class ListBookmarksCommand(Command):
    def __init__(self, order_by='date_added'):
        self.order_by = order_by
                                                      persistence.list takes
    def execute(self, data=None):                     the place of db.select.
        return True, persistence.list(order_by=self.order_by)    ←──


class DeleteBookmarkCommand(Command):
    def execute(self, data):             persistence.delete takes
        persistence.delete(data)     ←── the place of db.delete.
        return True, None
```

```
class EditBookmarkCommand(Command):
    def execute(self, data):
        persistence.edit(data['id'], data['update'])
        return True, None
```

persistence.edit takes the place of db.update.

Bark is now extensible to new use cases like importing stars from GitHub. Its concerns are well-separated so that you can reason about the presentation, business logic, and persistence in isolation. It's now feasible to swap any of those layers out to realize distinct new use cases.

You could swap `BookmarksDatabase` for, say, a `BookmarksStorageService` that sends bookmark data via an HTTP API to the cloud. You could also swap in a `DummyBookmarksDatabase` for testing that only persists bookmarks in memory for the duration of the tests. Loose coupling is rife with opportunities! I strongly encourage you to explore a few of these on your own.

The principles you've applied to Bark carry over readily to many real-world projects. By applying what you've learned here to your own projects, you'll be able to increase maintainability as well as help others pick up your code and make sense of it. I can't express just how much value this holds as you continue building software.

In the last part of this book, we'll recap the breadth of what you've learned and look at some recommendations for what to explore next. See you there!

Summary

- Separate concerns, encapsulate data and behaviors, and then create shared abstractions to loosen coupling.
- Classes that know and use many details of another class may need to be subsumed by that class.
- Tight coupling can be addressed by re-encapsulation with stronger cohesion, but it can often be well-served by the introduction of a new abstraction shared by both parties. (For example, a menu and a command may rely on the command returning a status and a result instead of specific messaging.)

Part 4

What's next?

Although it's been great teaching you, an author can cover only so much in a finite number of pages. This part of the book provides a strategy for tracking what you want to learn next. You'll also get a light introduction to several more concepts that may help you further your path to writing top-notch software. These learning suggestions are organized by topic, so you can learn about each topic at a high level or jump into one and explore it in depth.

Onward and upward

This chapter covers

- Choosing which avenues to explore next in your software development career
- Developing a plan of action for continued learning

Believe it or not, you've reached the last chapter of this book. Wasn't that fun? You've learned many of the facets of thoughtful software design in this book, but there's a whole world out there still to discover. It can be difficult to figure out what comes next. If you're feeling unsure about which trajectories to explore, read this chapter for some strategies and topic ideas.

11.1 What now?

As you gain experience, you'll continue learning a great deal. You'll also encounter things you *want* to learn but don't have the time or experience to cover just yet. There will also be an ever-present and near-infinite set of things you aren't aware of at all. These are concepts that either haven't occurred to you yet or you don't have the words to express.

Donald Rumsfeld succinctly (and humorously) put it like this:

There are known knowns—there are things we know we know. We also know there are known unknowns—that is to say, we know there are some things we do not know. But there are also unknown unknowns—the ones we don't know we don't know.

—Donald Rumsfeld

Being an effective engineer rarely amounts to being exhaustively knowledgeable on a subject. More often, you can work effectively by knowing the right thing to look up and which resources are available to you. In short, resourcefulness is more valuable than experience.

As you grow, you'll probably amass a list of blog posts, tools, and topics you're interested in. You'll also learn new things out of necessity as you build software. Eventually, when you decide it's time to dig into some of these new topics, it can help to set yourself up for success with a learning plan.

11.1.1 Develop a plan

Have you ever gone down the Wikipedia rabbit hole? You start reading about a topic, and suddenly it's 2:37 A.M., and you have 37 tabs open in your browser. You click through to links of interest, sometimes going several layers deep down a particular path. Although you might feel like you've wasted your evening, this turns out to be an effective strategy for uncovering information.

The philosophy game

You can also go the opposite direction—up—in Wikipedia. Starting with almost any article, clicking the first (or, occasionally, second) link in the first full paragraph on each subsequent article is likely to lead you to the "Philosophy" page. This is due to the fact that the first link is usually one of the most broad or general links. Give it a try:

- Beige > French > Romance language > Vulgar Latin > non-standard > language variety > sociolinguistics > society > group > social sciences > academic disciplines > knowledge > facts > reality > imaginary > object > philosophy
- Python (programming language) > interpreted > programming language > formal language > mathematics > quantity > multitude > number > mathematical object > abstract object > philosophy

---

A *mind map* organizes information in a hierarchical structure you can explore visually. A mind map starts from a central *node*—an overall concept you're interested in learning. It then branches out, with each node representing subtopics or related concepts to explore—like when you couldn't help but click the link to "Cosmic latte" from the page about "Beige." By using a mind map to enumerate things you want to learn about, you can build up a pretty good picture of different areas you'll need to cover.

If you want to learn about natural language processing, you might draw a mind map like the one shown in figure 11.1. A few high-level categories of activities eventually

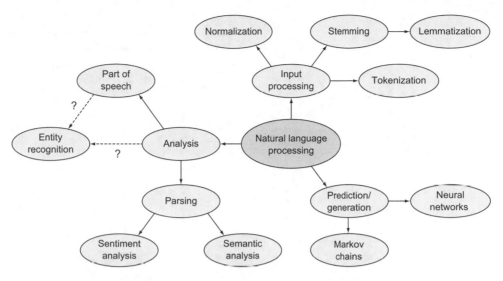

Figure 11.1 A mind map for learning about natural language processing

branch into specific and involved topics like lemmatization and Markov chains. Some of these may be things you've heard of but know little about, but you should still write them down. Even if you don't know what branch a topic falls under, you'll eventually figure out a path to it as you learn more about the topics around it.

This visual representation helps emphasize relationships between topics, which can help you retain the information you learn. It also acts as a kind of map in the traditional sense; concepts become regions of the map, and you can see which areas are charted well or remain unexplored. This comes in handy as you work on learning more.

If you don't have enough experience with a topic to draw a full map, don't worry. Writing down a short list of things can still be effective. The key is to have something you can refer to that reminds you what you've already done and what's left.

Once you've got your next steps mapped out, you're ready to do some learning.

11.1.2 Execute the plan

With your learning topics mapped out (or listed), you can start exploring the resources available to you. These may be books, online courses, or a friend or colleague with experience in the topic. Figure out your learning style too. Some people can learn just by reading, whereas others need to write some real code and see some real output for things to click. Be creative.

A mind map can work well because you can explore it nonlinearly. If you're still familiarizing yourself with the terminology and concepts, you might first explore the things one level out from the center, as shown in figure 11.2. This can help you get the lay of the land, which will help you build some footing as you choose what to learn next.

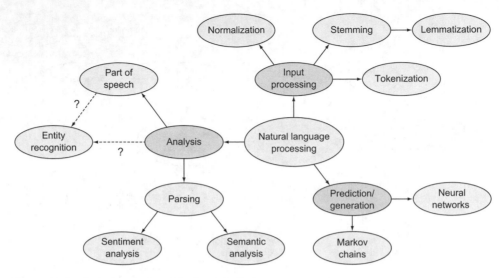

Figure 11.2   Exploring the breadth of a topic first

After you've got your bearings, you can choose a topic you find particularly riveting to explore more deeply, as shown in figure 11.3. The influx of new information about something that excites you is invigorating.

> **TIP**   A common pitfall is to do a deep dive into one topic without enough context about the rest of the bigger picture, so make sure you maintain a balance. Too much focus in one spot too soon can lead you to solidify an inaccurate or incomplete understanding that can inhibit future learning.

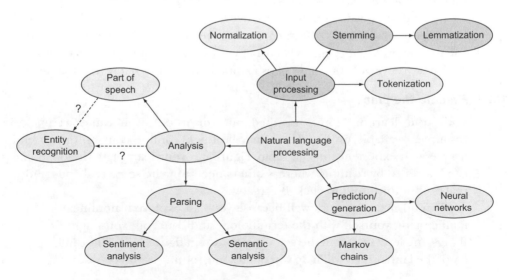

Figure 11.3   Exploring a single topic in depth

Successful learning requires an iterative approach—as you gain more experience with a topic, you'll naturally find more things to add to your mind map (or list). Adding things as you go along is perfectly fine, but make sure you feel comfortable with the topics you're already learning before expanding into new ones. It's easy to spread yourself too thin!

Keep it all sorted by tracking your progress.

11.1.3 *Track your progress*

Learning is subjective, so don't expect that you'll be able to say you're "done" with most things. There are a few distinct states in learning about a particular topic:

1 *Want or need to learn*—It's on your list of topics to cover, but you haven't started on it yet.
2 *Actively learning*—You've explored and read some resources on the topic, and you're looking for more.
3 *Familiar*—You understand the topic generally, and you have some idea how you might apply it.
4 *Comfortable*—You've applied the concepts from this topic a few times and have a handle on it.
5 *Proficient*—You've applied the concepts enough to know some of the nuances, and you know which resources to reach for when you encounter new kinds of problems.

Many expertise categorizations break these states down further, but each of these levels represents an observable shift in your behavior. It's good to recognize which level you're at so you can better understand which topics you want to invest your time in. You might not even *want* to reach "proficient" for topics you encounter only rarely or that don't align with the tasks you want to accomplish. Explicitly writing this down will help you keep your plan up to date, as shown in figure 11.4.

You'll probably learn several pertinent points about a topic at each level of your learning. They may not be large enough to justify adding more nodes to your mind map (although mind-mapping software makes this a low-cost activity), but it helps to write them down. You can use these notes to gauge what level of learning you're at on a topic, and they may prompt you to revisit ideas that need more work.

> **Mind-mapping software**
>
> Mind-mapping software helps you create visual representations of your thoughts and the relationships between them. The simplest mind maps are nodes with some text connected by lines. There are several commercial tools, like Lucidchart (www.lucidchart .com) and MindMup (www.mindmup.com), that have more advanced features, but any diagramming software, like draw.io (https://draw.io), can provide what you need to get started. Try something simple and free until you get comfortable with mapping.

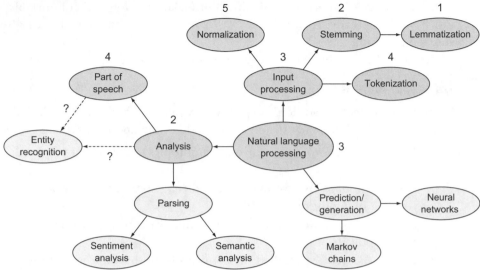

Keep track of which learning level you've reached for each topic
so you can see which areas need more of your time.

Figure 11.4   Keeping track of your learning progress for each topic

I struggled for a long time in school and my career, retaining information only after significant repetition. Mapping things out and tracking my progress proved to be an effective aid in learning many of the ideas expressed in this book and beyond. If you haven't tracked your learning like this before, give it a try.

With a framework for exploring and learning new ideas fresh in your mind, read on for some suggestions about where to go after you're finished with this book.

11.2   *Design patterns*

Over the last several decades, developers have solved the same problems many times over. Looking across all these solutions, certain patterns have emerged. Some of these patterns provide loose coupling and extensibility, but others don't.

These software *design patterns* are tried-and-true solutions, and naming them allows us to talk about them more concretely. A *ubiquitous language*, or shared vocabulary for the concepts a team needs to understand, goes a long way toward achieving the outcomes a team seeks.

You used a design pattern when you created the commands for Bark. The *command pattern*, as it's known, is used frequently in applications like Bark to decouple the code that requests an action from the action itself. The command pattern always has a few common pieces, regardless of the situation in which it's used:

1 *Receiver*—The entity that takes an action, like persisting data in a database or making an API call

2 *Command*—The entity that contains the info needed for the receiver to take its action

3 *Invoker*—The entity that triggers the command to alert the receiver
4 *Client*—The entity that assembles the invokers, commands, and receivers to achieve a task

In Bark, these pieces are as follows:

1 *The* PersistenceLayer *classes are the receivers.* They receive enough information to store or retrieve data (from a database, in the case of the BookmarkDatabase).
2 *The* Command *classes are the commands.* They store the information needed to communicate with the persistence layer.
3 *The* Option *instances are the invokers.* They trigger a command to take place when a user chooses an option in the menu.
4 *The client module is the client.* It hooks up options to commands properly so that users' menu choices ultimately result in the desired action.

A *unified modeling language* (UML) diagram of these classes is shown in figure 11.5.[1] UML diagrams are a common way of depicting the relationships between entities in a program. This book has been intentionally light on UML because it can add to the learning curve for the untrained eye. As you learn about design patterns, though, you'll see UML diagrams come up frequently. Remember that the patterns themselves are what's important to understand—if UML diagrams don't work well for you, read about them instead.

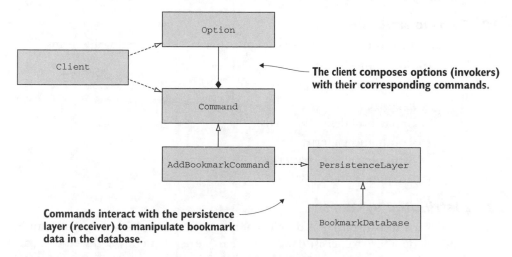

Figure 11.5 The command pattern as used in the Bark application

---

[1]For more on UML, see Wikipedia's "Unified Modeling Language" article: https://en.wikipedia.org/wiki/Unified_Modeling_Language.

11.2.1 *Ups and downs of design patterns in Python*

You've seen some of the benefits of using a specific design pattern in Python. The command pattern helped you decouple layers of abstraction in Bark, leading to flexible persistence, business logic, and presentation. Many of the other patterns you will learn may provide value as well.

To understand which design patterns you should learn and apply in Python, it's important to understand the context in which many design patterns were developed and used. One significant driver for some design patterns is the language or languages from which they emerged. A number of design patterns come from Java, a statically typed language. Because of static typing, languages like Java are intentionally limited in how they can create instances of classes and so on. As a result, a number of design patterns are *creational* ones. Python's dynamic typing frees it from many of these limitations, so many creational patterns simply aren't necessary in Python.

Ultimately, as with many topics in this book, design patterns are a tool to help you get your work done. If you're trying to use a design pattern to approach a problem, and it feels forced, it's okay to move ahead without a specific pattern. A better pattern might jump out at you in the meantime.

The canonical reference for learning more about design patterns is *Design Patterns: Elements of Reusable Object-Oriented Software*.[2] The online software development community also has many discussions on the topic, often with useful case studies that can help you further understand if and when to use a particular pattern.

11.2.2 *Terms to start with*

You can start your research into design patterns with the following terms:

- Design patterns
  - Creational design patterns
  - Factories
  - Behavioral design patterns
  - Command pattern
  - Structural design patterns
  - Adapter pattern

11.3 *Distributed systems*

In modern web-application development, you may need a server that handles HTTP traffic, a database to persist data, a cache to store frequently accessed data, and so on. These elements form a *system*—a group of interconnected pieces that make up a whole. The pieces of this system are frequently located on distinct machines, in separate data centers, and sometimes even on different continents, as shown in figure 11.6. These *distributed* systems add layers of value, complexity, and risk for developers to understand and address.

---

[2]Erich Gamma, Richard Helm, Ralph Johnson, and John Vlissides, *Design Patterns: Elements of Reusable Object-Oriented Software* (Addison-Wesley Professional, 1995).

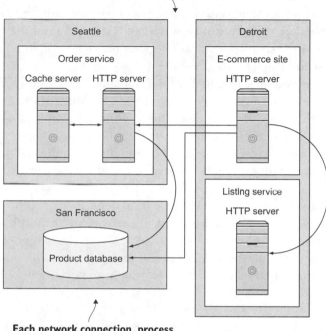

Distributed systems span many machines and even many geographies because of not only intentional design but also team history, budget decisions, and infrastructure provider offerings.

Each network connection, process communication, and so on, presents a potential point of failure.

Figure 11.6 A system distributed across several locations

Some of the more interesting complexities that distributed systems exhibit are the ways in which they fail.

11.3.1 *Modes of failure in distributed systems*

Even on a single machine, a program may crash unexpectedly. Other programs that expect that program to be running may also crash if they haven't accounted for the situation.

Chipping off pieces of an application to put them in new locations introduces new, exotic modes of failure. All applications may be running properly, but the network connection between them may fail. Most applications may be able to access a database, but one may not. Distributed systems techniques seek to withstand and recover from these modes of failure.

I've found that thinking about the ways a distributed system can fail is similar to thinking about functional testing. In chapter 5, you learned about creative exploratory testing as a way to enumerate as many facets of vulnerability as possible. Distributed systems require this same mindset on a larger scale because there are more moving parts.

11.3.2 *Addressing application state*

A big question in distributed systems is how to handle a part of the system crashing. You may be able to live without some pieces of the system, carrying on without the data they provide. Other pieces of the system may be necessary but not time-sensitive, so requests to them while they're down can be stored and deferred until they're back up. Remaining pieces of the system are critical to operations—the system comes to a halt without them. These are *single points of failure.*

Distributed systems are designed to minimize the single points of failure, favoring *graceful degradation*—carrying on without a particular action or information. Tools like Kubernetes (https://kubernetes.io/) augment the approach to processing failure through *eventual consistency,* which enables you to define the state you want for your system, providing a guarantee that the system will eventually reach the defined state. Pairing graceful degradation with eventual consistency leads to malleable systems that go down less often.

Although distributed systems aren't new, there have been many recent developments in tooling and philosophy. Kubernetes and the ecosystem around it can certainly be applied to small systems as you learn, but it shines on larger, complex systems. You may want to start with the principles and techniques and then get some practice building a few distributed systems before moving into specialized tools.

11.3.3 *Terms to start with*

You can begin your research into distributed systems with the following terms:

- Distributed systems
  - Fault tolerance
  - Eventual consistency
  - Desired state
  - Concurrency
  - Message queueing

11.4 *Take a Python deep dive*

This may seem obvious, but another area you can keep growing in is Python. Although this book used Python in its examples to convey ideas about software design, there's much to learn about the features, syntax, and power of the Python language.

11.4.1 *Python code style*

As you work more in Python, you'll eventually get a sense for the code formatting you like. You'll write your code in that style because it will be easier for you to read later on. But when someone else who's been following their own style reads your code, they might have a hard time understanding it. PEP 8, the Python Enhancement Proposal for a Python style guide, suggests a standard style for Python code formatting so that you don't have to spend time agonizing over it.[3] Tools like Black (https://github.com/psf/black) take these suggestions a step further, imposing a deterministic, opinionated formatting to all your code. This frees you up to think about bigger problems, like the larger design of the software and the business needs you're trying to address.

11.4.2 *Language features are patterns*

Design patterns are traditionally discussed in terms of objects and the interactions between them. But there are also common patterns in the way certain ideas are expressed in Python syntax. Things that are frequently done a certain way in Python because they're elegant, short, clear, or readable are called "Pythonic." These patterns can be just as important as design patterns to someone trying to understand your code.

Some patterns in Python involve using data types inherent to the situation, like using a `dict` to map keys to values. Some patterns involve using list comprehensions or ternary operators to reduce multiline statements when something is short and clear enough to do so. Knowing what's available to you and when to reach for each pattern is important. Knowing when *not* to reach for them is important too.

The Zen of Python provides a good set of general principles for writing Python code.

```
>>> import this
The Zen of Python, by Tim Peters

Beautiful is better than ugly.
Explicit is better than implicit.
Simple is better than complex.
Complex is better than complicated.
Flat is better than nested.
Sparse is better than dense.
Readability counts.
Special cases aren't special enough to break the rules.
Although practicality beats purity.
Errors should never pass silently.
Unless explicitly silenced.
In the face of ambiguity, refuse the temptation to guess.
There should be one--and preferably only one--obvious way to do it.
Although that way may not be obvious at first unless you're Dutch.
Now is better than never.
Although never is often better than *right* now.
If the implementation is hard to explain, it's a bad idea.
If the implementation is easy to explain, it may be a good idea.
Namespaces are one honking great idea--let's do more of those!
```

If you view these guidelines as a light rubric, you can turn a critical eye to areas of your code that rub you the wrong way or feel funny. Seeing a bit of ugly syntax, understanding what it's trying to do, and searching the web for "best way to do X in Python" can

---

[3]You can find "PEP 8—Style Guide for Python Code" on the Python website: www.python.org/dev/peps/pep-0008/.

generate some alternative ideas. Another tactic I've used to learn tips and tricks is following prominent users of Python—such as Python core developers—on Twitter. You can often find information this way that you didn't know you needed.

For a comprehensive guide to the language, books like *The Quick Python Book,* by Daryl Harms and Kenneth McDonald (Manning, 1999); *The Hitchhiker's Guide to Python,* by Kenneth Reitz and Tanya Schlusser (O'Reilly, 2016; https://docs.python-guide .org/); and *Python Cookbook,* by David Ascher and Alex Martelli (O'Reilly, 2002), can help immerse you in the language.

11.4.3 Terms to start with

You can start with the following terms as you begin your research into examples, patterns, and guidelines for Pythonic code:

- Pythonic code
  - Pythonic way to do X
- Idiomatic Python
- Python anti-patterns
- Python linters

11.5   Where you've been

As an author, I can't predict what motivated you to pick up this book or how much experience you had when you did. If you're still reading this, though, I do have a better picture of where you are now. You're your own worst critic, so here at the end, it's important to recapitulate everything you've learned. As you see it all laid out before you, keep a couple of things in mind:

- Software development isn't any one thing, but a myriad of practices that coalesce into software in the end.
- Balancing all these practices will be an ongoing challenge, and some practices will ebb and flow as you focus on improving others.
- None of this is an exact science. Take statements claiming that something is "the one true way" with a big grain of salt.
- You can apply the principles you've learned in this book to most any language, framework, or problem. Python is great, but don't box yourself in.

11.5.1 There and back again: A developer's tale

You jumped right into the idea of software design in chapter 1. Understanding that software can be an intentional, thoughtful process laid the foundation for all the following chapters. You will occasionally be hard-pressed to find time for up-front design because of deadlines and the like, but try to find your center as often as possible so that you can be deliberate about the software you build. The outcomes remain the most important goal, but design will help you continue achieving outcomes as smoothly as possible.

Chapter 2 introduced the foundational practice of separating concerns. Most modern programming languages encourage the use of functions, methods, classes, and modules, and for good reason. Breaking your software down into its constituent parts helps reduce cognitive load as well as improve the maintainability of code. Concerns can be separated at the lowest levels of code, all the way up to the broader architecture of the software.

Building on Python's structures for separation of concerns, you learned to use them for abstraction and encapsulation in chapter 3. Freeing yourself and other developers from the minutiae of a particular task unless they're interested in knowing more provides welcome relief. Exposing only critical details to other areas of software also reduces integration points and the likelihood of breaking code for your consumers.

Moving into more concrete territory, you learned about designing for performance in chapter 4. You saw some of the data structures Python provides and in what situations they're useful. You also learned about some of the tools for quantitatively measuring the performance of your software. Metrics measured trump speculation about what's fastest.

Where chapter 4 showed you how to test whether programs are efficient, chapter 5 focused on testing whether programs are *correct*. Functional testing helps you verify that you're building what you mean to build. You learned how functional tests are structured and how to write tests using Python tools. Functional testing patterns are quite similar across languages and frameworks, so you can take this information with you most anywhere.

Armed with some of the underpinnings of design, the next part of the book took you on a practical journey by building the Bark application. Through the course of this journey, you reached a number of milestones:

- You built a multitier architecture to support separate presentation, business logic, and persistence layers.
- You opened Bark up to extension to more easily add new functionality, and then added a new feature to import stars from GitHub as bookmarks.
- You used interfaces and the command pattern to further reduce the work needed to add or change features.
- You loosened the coupling between different areas of Bark, opening it up to new possibilities, like making a mobile or web app.

A bookmarking tool isn't flashy, but you learned some flashy techniques in building it. Applying the body of knowledge you've gained to your future projects for real tasks is bound to give you similarly effective results. You can get practice with any new concepts you learn by applying them to Bark as well. You may choose to add features, improve the existing code, or write tests for it. The sky's the limit!

11.5.2 *Signing off*

You've graduated from this book. It's been a pleasure teaching you, and I hope to hear tales of your journey as you go on to bigger and better things with software. Celebrate the wins, learn from the hurdles, and develop with heart.

Happy coding!

Summary

- Learning is not a passive process. Make a plan that works for you, write it down or map it out, and track your progress. This can generate more ideas or next steps to help keep you motivated and curious.

- Try to identify common patterns and approaches to problems. As you encounter those same problems, try a few different approaches early on to see which work most smoothly. Patterns are tools, and they should enhance your work rather than hinder it.

- Feel at home in your language. You don't need to pick it up all at once, but keep a curious mindset and ask often if there's a more idiomatic way to express a thought in code.

- You've come a long way from the start of this book, so use this time to reflect and take a break.

appendix
Installing Python

This appendix covers

- Which versions of Python are available, and which to use
- Installing Python on your computer

Python is fairly portable software that can be compiled from source on most systems. Fortunately for you, Python is probably also available prebuilt for your system. This appendix will help you get set up with Python so you can run any of the code in this book from the command line.

> **TIP** If you've already installed a version of Python 3 on your computer, you're in luck. There's not much more to do here. Feel free to get back to reading, and follow along with the code in this book.

> **NOTE** If you install a version of Python 3, you will almost certainly need to use the `python3` command when running code. `python` is reserved for a different Python installation on many operating systems (see section A.2).

A.1   *What version of Python should I use?*

The first version of Python 2.7 came out in 2010, and at the time of writing, macOS ships with Python 2.7.10, which is a few versions behind the latest Python 2.7 release. Python 2.7 will no longer be officially supported as of January 1, 2020.

If you're already familiar with Python 2 and worry about upgrading to Python 3, know that most code changes you'll need to make are small. When starting new projects, I recommend you use Python 3. This will set you up to write code that can last longer into the future.

> **TIP** There are tools to help you with a Python 2 to Python 3 upgrade. Python provides the __future__ module, which allows you to use newer Python 3 features that have been backported to Python 2. This way, when you upgrade, your syntax is already correct, and you can just remove the *future* import. The Six package (two times three, get it?) (https://six.readthedocs.io/) also helps straddle the two versions.

A.2   *The "system" Python*

On many operating systems, Python may already be installed because the system needs it for some of its own tasks. This Python installation is often referred to as the "system" Python. On macOS, for example, Python 2.7 is installed and available for you to use.

Using the system Python gets tricky when you need to install packages, because they will all get installed under this global version of Python. If you install a package that overrides something the operating system needs, or you have multiple projects that need different versions of a package, bad things can start to happen. I strongly recommend avoiding the system Python.

A.3   *Installing other versions of Python*

If you haven't installed your own Python version before, there are a couple of options available. Each one should be functionally equivalent, so which one you choose should depend on what fits your workflow best or makes sense to you.

The only important thing is making sure you have a relatively recent version of Python. I recommend Python 3.6+ for strong compatibility with most libraries out there, but as of this writing, Python 3.8 is already available. If you don't have any specific requirements, aim to install the latest version.

A.3.1   *Download the official Python*

You can download Python directly from Python's official website (www.python.org/downloads). The website should detect your operating system type and show you a big Download Python button, as shown in figure A.1. If it can't detect your operating system, or it gets it wrong, there are direct links underneath for various operating systems.

This download should act like most other applications you would install on your system. On macOS, opening the downloaded file will take you through an installation wizard, as shown in figure A.2. Which options you choose in the wizard are up to you, but the defaults are usually sane.

Figure A.1 The big yellow button gets you the latest Python, and you can find older versions or versions for other operating systems in the links below it.

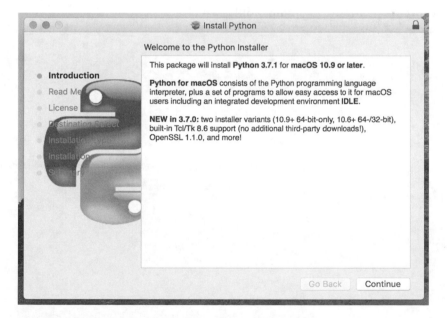

Figure A.2 I usually just click Continue with reckless abandon.

A.3.2 Download using Anaconda

If you're in the scientific computing community, you may be familiar with Anaconda (www.anaconda.com). Anaconda is a suite of tools that includes Python. As of this writing, Anaconda can be installed with either Python 2 or Python 3. Check which you have, and make sure you've got the Python 3 version.

Using Anaconda's `conda` command, you can install most versions of Python using `conda install python=3.7.3`, as an example. Read the official documentation to understand the installation process for your system.

A.4 *Verifying the installation*

Once you've gone through the installation process, open a terminal (the Terminal app on macOS). From anywhere, try running the `python` command (or `python3`, potentially). If Python is installed successfully, you should be greeted with the Python REPL prompt, which should say `Python 3` somewhere:

```
$ python3
Python 3.7.3 (default, Jun 17 2019, 14:09:05)
[Clang 10.0.1 (clang-1001.0.46.4)] on darwin
Type "help", "copyright", "credits" or "license" for more information.
>>>
```

Try typing your favorite code snippet and see what happens:

```
>>> print('Hello, world!')
Hello, world!
```

Now you're ready for world domination!

index